John Locke, S. H. Emmens

Selections from Locke's Essay on the Human Understanding

John Locke, S. H. Emmens

Selections from Locke's Essay on the Human Understanding

ISBN/EAN: 9783337277970

Printed in Europe, USA, Canada, Australia, Japan

Cover: Foto ©Thomas Meinert / pixelio.de

More available books at **www.hansebooks.com**

SELECTIONS FROM LOCKE'S ESSAY ON THE HUMAN UNDERSTANDING

WITH INTRODUCTION AND NOTES

By S. H. EMMENS

AUTHOR OF "A TREATISE ON LOGIC, PURE AND APPLIED," ETC.

Third Edition

LONDON
CROSBY LOCKWOOD AND SON
7, STATIONERS' HALL COURT, LUDGATE HILL
1890

CONTENTS.

	PAGE
INTRODUCTION	1
NO INNATE PRINCIPLES IN THE MIND	6
Note on the Laws of Thought	25
OTHER CONSIDERATIONS CONCERNING INNATE PRINCIPLES, BOTH SPECULATIVE AND PRACTICAL	26
Note on the Cartesian Doctrine of Innate Ideas . . .	46
OF IDEAS IN GENERAL AND THEIR ORIGINAL	47
Notes:—A. Locke's Metaphysical System considered historically and critically	63
B. Is the Mind always in a state of conscious activity?	68
OF IDENTITY AND DIVERSITY	69
Note on Personal Identity	92
OF THE IMPERFECTION OF WORDS	95
OF THE ABUSE OF WORDS	111
Notes:—A. The Schoolmen	131
B. Locke's Notion of Logic	132
OF THE REMEDIES OF THE FOREGOING IMPERFECTIONS AND ABUSES	134
Note—Are Disputes really verbal?	150

CONTENTS.

	PAGE
Of the Degrees of our Knowledge	151
Note on Sensitive Knowledge	157
Of the Extent of Human Knowledge	158
Notes:—A. Of Intuition	182
B. Of Locke's Theory concerning Knowledge	183
Of Reason	187
Note on the Syllogism	209
Of Faith and Reason, and their distinct Provinces	210

EDITOR'S PREFACE.

The design of the accompanying volume is to give, in small compass, a general view of Locke's philosophical system as exhibited in his celebrated Essay, and, at the same time, to present the reader with some of the most striking and brilliant passages that are to be found in that work.

As, however, a series of "selections" must in some measure produce but a fragmentary and imperfect idea of any system, it has been deemed advisable to add such critical notes as might serve to point out the unity of thought which pervades the following extracts, and elucidate those topics which would otherwise remain obscure. By this means the present work will, it is hoped, possess a completeness that may not only render it a mirror, as it were, of Locke's Essay, but may also enable it to be used as an introduction to the study of metaphysics. At the same time, it must not be supposed that there is, in these notes, any attempt whatsoever at a formal discussion of philosophical questions—all that they contain being merely a sketch of the more salient points connected with Locke's system, and a few outlines of the relations which obtain betwixt its precursors, itself, and its successors.

S. H. E.

LONDON, *October*, 1865

SELECTIONS FROM

LOCKE'S ESSAY ON THE HUMAN UNDERSTANDING.

―――•―――

INTRODUCTION.

In the bright annals of philosophy few names occupy a more conspicuous position than that of John Locke. Distinguished for his acute and penetrating intellect, for his proficiency in physical studies, and for the great learning which he brought to bear upon every subject, he has exercised a remarkable influence upon the progress of thought; and if at times the objections of his opponents have prevailed against some portions of the theories which he adopted, we must yet consider how much we owe to the illustrious philosopher whose exertions in the dawn of modern science were attended with such eminent success.

Foremost among Locke's works stands his "Essay on the Human Understanding," a book which early attained to European celebrity; and as the following pages are devoted to a series of Selections from this noble treatise, it is evident that they will be most fitly introduced by a short account of its general design and execution.

The purpose, then, with which the Essay was written was "to inquire into the original, certainty, and extent of human knowledge, together with the grounds and degrees of belief, opinion, and assent." This is sought to be accomplished by a discussion of the subject under four distinct heads, to each of which a book of the Essay is devoted. The first book treats upon the question of Innate Notions; and after a consideration of the arguments which tend to support this doctrine, it is finally concluded that all knowledge is the result of experience, and that none of our ideas are native to the mind. The second book then proceeds to discuss these ideas in detail, showing both the precise manner in which they are severally acquired, and the classes into which they may be most conveniently grouped. This gives occasion for an inquiry into the nature of some ideas which are more remarkable than the rest, such as those of Solidity, Space, Infinity, &c. The book concludes with a subtle disquisition on the various Relations which obtain betwixt our notions, that of Identity being most fully noticed, and with an admirable chapter upon the Association of Ideas. The third book is allotted to a consideration of that great instrument of thought—language; and this portion of the Essay is inferior to none, whether in force of reasoning, in fertility of illustration, or in permanency of value. It investigates the manner in which the meaning of words is acquired; the history and method of their application; the various imperfections and abuses to which they are liable; and, finally, discloses the most suitable remedies for the numerous defects of which language is susceptible. The fourth and concluding book is composed of a series of chapters which treat upon the degrees, extent, and reality of human knowledge; the means whereby we attain to a knowledge of existence in general, and of ourselves and the Deity in particular; the nature of judgment and probability; the degrees of assent, and how far this should be guided by faith or reason; the operations of enthusiasm and error; and the proper method of classifying the sciences.

Such is, in briefest outline, the general scope of the "Essay concerning Human Understanding," as it was termed by its author: and it must be confessed that the manner in which he has treated this great subject affords a striking proof of that practical sagacity and those varied abilities for which Locke was so renowned. The *style*, however, of the Essay has not been so fortunate as to escape all adverse criticism: indeed, it has at times been censured in terms of severe rebuke. Thus, to give but one instance, we find Sir William Hamilton speaking as follows:*—"In his *language*, Locke is, of all philosophers, the most figurative, ambiguous, vacillating, various, and even contradictory"—an opinion, which, coming from so distinguished a quarter, is not to be lightly esteemed. At the same time, it should be borne in mind that while from a strictly philosophical point of view many exceptions may be taken to Locke's style, yet there are few writers who are better calculated to please when we regard the ease and dexterity with which he handles the most complicated arguments, the force and aptness of his illustrations, and the singular beauty of his metaphors.

As regards the general character of Locke's philosophical system, it may be mentioned that it was, for the most part, taken from that propounded by Gassendi, a celebrated French metaphysician, who flourished in the first half of the seventeenth century. The latter, although a professed opponent of the Aristotelian philosophy, yet adopted many of his doctrines from the Schoolmen; and it is a matter of no little admiration to find that Locke, whose allusions to the schools are in the highest degree acrimonious, should, whilst following Gassendi, have become deeply indebted to those very philosophers whom he was treating with such asperity. The doctrines, however, which he thus acquired were (in general), greatly improved and amplified; and, interweaving these with the principles which he had himself developed, he succeeded in producing a system of great completeness and harmony. It was intended as a refutation of the celebrated Cartesian philosophy, and after a sharp struggle for existence against the attacks of Serjeant and others, it at length succeeded in

* "Discussions," p. 78.

firmly establishing itself as the basis of English speculation In France, also, under the auspices of Voltaire and Condillac, it speedily met with almost universal favour; but in Germany the case was different. In that country, Locke's doctrine of Sensualism, as it is generally termed, was opposed with great vigour and ability by Leibnitz, the celebrated rival of Newton; the result being that it was finally rejected in favour of the Rationalistic system, established by the joint efforts of Leibnitz and Wolf.

Between these two systems, then, of Sensualism, or the relegation of all knowledge to sensible experience, and Rationalism, or the assumption of a native source of knowledge (speaking broadly) in the mind itself, was the empire of European thought divided; and this state of things continued to obtain until it was brought to an end by the writings of David Hume, who showed that both the Lockian and Leibnitian philosophies, if pushed to their logical consequences, must result in the establishment of Nihilism or Scepticism. Such a deduction roused all the dormant energies of speculation by exposing to the broad light of day the glaring defects of those doctrines, which, whilst immured in the dark temples of custom and inactivity, philosophers had for so long a period been content to worship as perfect. In Britain, the Scottish metaphysicians were the first to take the alarm; and under the guidance of Dr. Thomas Reid, they replaced the Sensualist doctrine of Locke by a system which is generally known as the Common-Sense Philosophy, and of which the main positions are, first, an intuitive knowledge of material existence; and, secondly, a recognition of some notions as native to the mind. In Germany, the revolution of opinion induced by Hume was consummated by Immanuel Kant and his followers; the Leibnitian system being superseded by New Rationalism or Transcendentalism, a doctrine which, commencing with the principle that the mind can know nothing beyond itself, has by Fichte and Schelling been raised to the summit of absolute idealism; thus identifying Reason (as distinct from Understanding) with absolute Being, that is, with the Deity. This system has, however, for the most part, given place to the Scottish philosophy, which, owing to the exertions of Cousin, Royer-Collard, and Jouffroy, is also very generally accepted in France and Italy; so that it may fairly be considered as the prevalent doctrine of the present day.*

I have thus attempted to point out the position which Locke's Essay occupies in the progress of philosophy; and I trust that I have succeeded in conveying some idea of the relations which exist between it and the most prominent doctrines of modern speculation. Nor is this, I venture to think, of little consequence as regards the nature of the present volume; for while each selection is complete in itself, yet a general knowledge of the system to which it belongs, and of that system's distinguishing features, must evidently be indispensable to a correct appreciation of its value.

* Of late years the Scottish philosophy has undergone some modifications, but these it is unnecessary to notice.

NO INNATE PRINCIPLES IN THE MIND.

1. *The way shown how we come by any knowledge, sufficient to prove it not innate.*—It is an established opinion among some men, that there are in the understanding certain innate principles; some primary notions, κοιναὶ ἔννοιαι,* characters, as it were, stamped upon the mind of man, which the soul receives in its very first being, and brings into the world with it. It would be sufficient to convince unprejudiced readers of the falseness of this supposition, if I should only show (as I hope I shall in the following parts of this discourse) how men, barely by the use of their natural faculties, may attain to all the knowledge they have, without the help of any innate impressions, and may arrive at certainty without any such original notions or principles. For I imagine, any one will easily grant, that it would be impertinent to suppose the ideas of colours innate in a creature to whom God hath given sight, and a power to receive them by the eyes from external objects: and no less unreasonable would it be to attribute several truths to the impressions of nature and innate characters, when we may observe in ourselves faculties fit to attain as easy and certain knowledge of them as if they were originally imprinted on the mind.

But because a man is not permitted without censure to follow his own thoughts in the search of truth, when they lead him ever so little out of the common road, I shall set down the reasons that made me doubt of the truth of that opinion, as an excuse for my mistake, if I be in one; which I leave to be considered by those who, with me, dispose themselves to embrace truth wherever they find it.

2. *General assent the great argument.*—There is nothing more commonly taken for granted, than that there are certain

* *Common thoughts, i.e. thoughts shared in by all the world.*—Ed.

principles, both speculative and practical (for they speak of both), universally agreed upon by all mankind; which therefore, they argue, must needs be constant impressions which the souls of men receive in their first beings, and which they bring into the world with them, as necessarily and really as they do any of their inherent faculties.

3. *Universal consent proves nothing innate.*—This argument, drawn from universal consent, has this misfortune in it, that if it were true in matter of fact, that there were certain truths wherein all mankind agreed, it would not prove them innate, if there can be any other way shown, how men may come to that universal agreement in the things they do consent in; which I presume may be done.

4. *" What is, is;" and, "It is impossible for the same thing to be, and not to be," not universally assented to.*—But, which is worse, this argument of universal consent, which is made use of to prove innate principles, seems to me a demonstration that there are none such; because there are none to which all mankind give an universal assent. I shall begin with the speculative, and instance in those magnified principles of demonstration: "Whatsoever is, is;" and "It is impossible for the same thing to be, and not to be," which, of all others, I think, have the most allowed title to innate. These have so settled a reputation of maxims universally received, that it will, no doubt, be thought strange if any one should seem to question it. But yet I take liberty to say, that these propositions are so far from having an universal assent, that there are a great part of mankind to whom they are not so much as known.

5. *Not on the mind naturally imprinted, because not known to children, idiots, &c.*—For, first, it is evident, that all children and idiots have not the least apprehension or thought of them; and the want of that is enough to destroy that universal assent, which must needs be the necessary concomitant of all innate truths: it seeming to me near a contradiction to say, that there are truths imprinted on the soul which it perceives or understands not; imprinting, if it

signify anything, being nothing else but the making certain truths to be perceived. For to imprint anything on the mind, without the mind's perceiving it, seems to me hardly intelligible. If, therefore, children and idiots have souls, have minds, with those impressions upon them, they must unavoidably perceive them, and necessarily know and assent to these truths; which, since they do not, it is evident that there are no such impressions. For if they are not notions naturally imprinted, how can they be innate? And if they are notions imprinted, how can they be unknown? To say, a notion is imprinted on the mind, and yet at the same time to say that the mind is ignorant of it, and never yet took notice of it, is to make this impression nothing. No proposition can be said to be in the mind which it never yet knew, which it was never yet conscious of. For if any one may, then, by the same reason, all propositions that are true, and the mind is capable ever of assenting to, may be said to be in the mind, and to be imprinted; since if any one can be said to be in the mind, which it never yet knew, it must be only because it is capable of knowing it; and so the mind is of all truths it ever shall know. Nay, thus truths may be imprinted on the mind which it never did, nor ever shall, know: for a man may live long, and die at last in ignorance of many truths which his mind was capable of knowing, and that with certainty. So that if the capacity of knowing be the natural impression contended for, all the truths a man ever comes to know will, by this account, be every one of them innate: and this great point will amount to no more, but only to a very improper way of speaking; which, whilst it pretends to assert the contrary, says nothing different from those who deny innate principles. For nobody, I think, ever denied that the mind was capable of knowing several truths. The capacity, they say, is innate; the knowledge acquired. But then, to what end such contest for certain innate maxims? If truths can be imprinted on the understanding without being perceived, I can see no difference there can be between any truths the mind is capable of knowing in respect of their original: they must all be innate, or all adventitious; in vain shall a man go about to distinguish them. He therefore that talks of innate notions in the understanding, cannot (if he intend thereby any distinct sort of truths) mean such truths to be in the understanding as it never perceived, and is yet wholly ignorant of. For if these words ("to be in the understanding") have any propriety, they signify to be understood. So that, to be in the understanding, and not to be understood; to be in the mind, and never to be perceived; is all one as to say, any thing is, and is not, in the mind or understanding. If therefore these two propositions: "Whatsoever is, is," and "It is impossible for the same thing to be, and not to be," are by nature imprinted, children cannot be ignorant of them; infants, and all that have souls, must necessarily have them in their understandings, know the truth of them, and assent to it.

6. *That men know them when they come to the use of reason, answered.*—To avoid this, it is usually answered, that all men know and assent to them, when they come to the use of reason; and this is enough to prove them innate. I answer.

7. Doubtful expressions, that have scarce any signification, go for clear reasons to those who, being prepossessed, take not the pains to examine even what they themselves say. For, to apply this answer with any tolerable sense to our present purpose, it must signify one of these two things; either, that, as soon as men come to the use of reason, these supposed native inscriptions come to be known and observed by them; or else, that the use and exercise of men's reasons assist them in the discovery of these principles, and certainly makes them known to them.

8. *If reason discovered them, that would not prove them innate.*—If they mean that by the use of reason men may discover these principles, and that this is sufficient to prove them innate, their way of arguing will stand thus: viz. That, whatever truths reason can certainly discover to us, and make us firmly assent to, those are all naturally imprinted on the mind; since that universal assent which is made the mark of

them, amounts to no more but this—that by the use of reason we are capable to come to a certain knowledge of, and assent to, them; and by this means there will be no difference between the maxims of the mathematicians and theorems they deduce from them: all must be equally allowed innate, they being all discoveries made by the use of reason, and truths that a rational creature may certainly come to know, if he apply his thoughts rightly that way.

9. *It is false that reason discovers them.*—But how can these men think the use of reason necessary to discover principles that are supposed innate, when reason (if we may believe them) is nothing else but the faculty of deducing unknown truths from principles or propositions that are already known? That certainly can never be thought innate which we have need of reason to discover, unless, as I have said, we will have all the certain truths that reason ever teaches us to be innate. We may as well think the use of reason necessary to make our eyes discover visible objects, as that there should be need of reason, or the exercise thereof, to make the understanding see what is originally engraven in it, and cannot be in the understanding before it be perceived by it. So that to make reason discover those truths thus imprinted, is to say, that the use of reason discovers to a man what he knew before; and if men have those innate impressed truths originally, and before the use of reason, and yet are always ignorant of them till they come to the use of reason, it is in effect to say that men know, and know them not, at the same time.

10. It will here perhaps be said, that mathematical demonstrations, and other truths that are not innate, are not assented to, as soon as proposed, wherein they are distinguished from these maxims and other innate truths. I shall have occasion to speak of assent upon the first proposing more particularly by-and-by. I shall here only, and that very readily, allow, that these maxims and mathematical demonstrations are in this different—that the one has need of reason, using of proofs, to make them out and to gain our assent; but the other, as soon as understood, are, without any the least

reasoning, embraced and assented to. But I withal beg leave to observe, that it lays open the weakness of this subterfuge which requires the use of reason for the discovery of these general truths, since it must be confessed that in their discovery there is no use made of reasoning at all. And I think those who give this answer will not be forward to affirm, that the knowledge of this maxim, "That it is impossible for the same thing to be, and not to be," is a deduction of our reason. For this would be to destroy that bounty of nature they seem so fond of, whilst they make the knowledge of those principles to depend on the labour of our thoughts; for all reasoning is search and casting about, and requires pains and application. And how can it with any tolerable sense be supposed that what was imprinted by nature, as the foundation and guide of our reason, should need the use of reason to discover it?

11. Those who will take the pains to reflect with a little attention on the operations of the understanding, will find that this ready assent of the mind to some truths depends not either on native inscription or the use of reason; but on a faculty of the mind quite distinct from both of them, as we shall see hereafter. Reason, therefore, having nothing to do in procuring our assent to these maxims, if by saying that "men know and assent to them when they come to the use of reason," be meant that the use of reason assists us in the knowledge of these maxims, it is utterly false; and, were it true, would prove them not to be innate.

12. *The coming to the use of reason, not the time we come to know these maxims.*—If by knowing and assenting to them "when we come to the use of reason," be meant, that this is the time when they come to be taken notice of by the mind; and that as soon as children come to the use of reason, they come also to know and assent to these maxims; this also is false and frivolous. First, it is *false;* because it is evident these maxims are not in the mind so early as the use of reason, and therefore the coming to the use of reason is falsely assigned as the time of their discovery. How many instances of the use of reason may we observe in children, a

long time before they have any knowledge of this maxim, "That it is impossible for the same thing to be and not to be!" And a great part of illiterate people and savages pass many years, even of their rational age, without ever thinking on this and the like general propositions. I grant, men come not to the knowledge of these general and more abstract truths, which are thought innate, till they come to the use of reason; and I add, nor then neither. Which is so, because, till after they come to the use of reason, those general abstract ideas are not framed in the mind, about which those general maxims are, which are mistaken for innate principles, but are indeed discoveries made, and verities introduced, and brought into the mind by the same way, and discovered by the same steps, as several other propositions which nobody was ever so extravagant as to suppose innate. This I hope to make plain in the sequel of this discourse. I allow, therefore, a necessity that men should come to the use of reason before they get the knowledge of those general truths; but deny that men's coming to the use of reason is the time of their discovery.

13. *By this they are not distinguished from other knowable truths.*—In the mean time it is observable, that this saying, "That men know and assent to these maxims when they come to the use of reason," amounts, in reality of fact, to no more but this: That they are never known nor taken notice of before the use of reason, but may possibly be assented to some time after during a man's life; but when, is uncertain: and so may all other knowable truths as well as these; which therefore have no advantage nor distinction from others, by this note of being known when we come to the use of reason, nor are thereby proved to be innate, but quite the contrary.

14. *If coming to the use of reason were the time of their discovery, it would not prove them innate.*—But, secondly, were it true that the precise time of their being known and assented to were when men come to the use of reason, neither would that prove them innate. This way of arguing is as *frivolous*, as the supposition of itself is false. For by what kind of

logic will it appear that any notion is originally by nature imprinted in the mind in its first constitution, because it comes first to be observed and assented to when a faculty of the mind, which has quite a distinct province, begins to exert itself? And therefore the coming to the use of speech, if it were supposed the time that these maxims are first assented to (which it may be with as much truth as the time when men come to the use of reason), would be as good a proof that they were innate, as to say they are innate because men assent to them when they come to the use of reason. I agree, then, with these men of innate principles, that there is no knowledge of these general and self-evident maxims in the mind till it comes to the exercise of reason; but I deny that the coming to the use of reason is the precise time when they are first taken notice of; and if that were the precise time, I deny that it would prove them innate. All that can, with any truth, be meant by this proposition, "That men assent to them when they come to the use of reason," is no more but this,—That the making of general abstract ideas, and the understanding of general names, being a concomitant of the rational faculty, and growing up with it, children commonly get not those general ideas, nor learn the names that stand for them, till, having for a good while exercised their reason about familiar and more particular ideas, they are, by their ordinary discourse and actions with others, acknowledged to be capable of rational conversation. If assenting to these maxims, when men come to the use of reason, can be true in any other sense, I desire it may be shown; or, at least, how in this, or any other sense, it proves them innate.

15. *The steps by which the mind attains several truths.*—The senses at first let in particular ideas, and furnish the yet empty cabinet; and the mind by degrees growing familiar with some of them, they are lodged in the memory, and names got to them. Afterwards the mind, proceeding further, abstracts them, and by degrees learns the use of general names. In this manner the mind comes to be furnished with ideas and language, the materials about which to exercise its

discursive faculty; and the use of reason becomes daily more visible, as these materials, that give it employment, increase. But though the having of general ideas, and the use of general words and reason, usually grow together, yet I see not how this any way proves them innate. The knowledge of some truths, I confess, is very early in the mind; but in a way that shows them not to be innate. For, if we will observe, we shall find it still to be about ideas not innate, but acquired; it being about those first, which are imprinted by external things, with which infants have earliest to do, which make the most frequent impressions on their senses. In ideas thus got, the mind discovers that some agree, and others differ, probably as soon as it has any use of memory, as soon as it is able to retain and receive distinct ideas. But whether it be then or no, this is certain, it does so long before it has the use of words, or comes to that which we commonly call "the use of reason." For a child knows as certainly, before it can speak, the difference between the ideas of sweet and bitter (that is, that sweet is not bitter), as it knows afterwards, when it comes to speak, that wormwood and sugarplums are not the same thing.

16. A child knows not that three and four are equal to seven till he comes to be able to count to seven, and has got the name and idea of equality; and then, upon explaining those words, he presently assents to, or rather perceives the truth of that proposition. But neither does he then readily assent because it is an innate truth, nor was his assent wanting till then because he wanted the use of reason; but the truth of it appears to him as soon as he has settled in his mind the clear and distinct ideas that these names stand for; and then he knows the truth of that proposition upon the same grounds, and by the same means, that he knew before, that a rod and cherry are not the same thing; and upon the same grounds also, that he may come to know afterwards, "that it is impossible for the same thing to be, and not to be," as shall be more fully shown hereafter: so that the later it is before any one comes to have those general ideas

about which those maxims are, or to know the signification of those general terms that stand for them, or to put together in his mind the ideas they stand for; the later also will it be before he comes to assent to those maxims, whose terms, with the ideas they stand for, being no more innate than those of a cat or weasel, he must stay till time and observation have acquainted him with them; and then he will be in a capacity to know the truth of these maxims, upon the first occasion that shall make him put together those ideas in his mind, and observe whether they agree or disagree, according as is expressed in those propositions. And therefore it is that a man knows that eighteen and nineteen are equal to thirty-seven, by the same self-evidence that he knows one and two to be equal to three; yet a child knows this not so soon as the other; not for the want of the use of reason, but because the ideas the words eighteen, nineteen, and thirty-seven stand for, are not so soon got as those which are signified by one, two, and three.

17. *Assenting as soon as proposed and understood, proves them not innate.*—This evasion, therefore, of general assent when men come to the use of reason, failing as it does, and leaving no difference between those supposed innate and other truths that are afterwards acquired and learnt, men have endeavoured to secure an universal assent to those they call maxims, by saying, they are generally assented to as soon as proposed and the terms they are proposed in understood: seeing all men, even children, as soon as they hear and understand the terms, assent to these propositions, they think it is sufficient to prove them innate. For, since men never fail, after they have once understood the words, to acknowledge them for undoubted truths, they would infer that certainly these propositions were first lodged in the understanding, which without any teaching, the mind, at the very first proposal, immediately closes with, and assents to, and after that never doubts again.

18. *If such an assent be a mark of innate, then that one and two are equal to three, that sweetness is not bitterness, and a*

thousand the like, must be innate.—In answer to this, I demand whether ready assent, given to a proposition upon first hearing and understanding the terms, be a certain mark of an innate principle? If it be not, such a general assent is in vain urged as a proof of them: if it be said, that it is a mark of innate, they must then allow all such propositions to be innate which are generally assented to as soon as heard; whereby they will find themselves plentifully stored with innate principles. For upon the same ground, viz. of assent at first hearing and understanding the terms, that men would have those maxims pass for innate, they must also admit several propositions about numbers to be innate, and thus, that "one and two are equal to three," that "two and two are equal to four," and a multitude of other the like propositions in numbers, that everybody assents to at first hearing and understanding the terms, must have a place amongst these innate axioms. Nor is this the prerogative of numbers alone, and propositions made about several of them; but even natural philosophy, and all the other sciences, afford propositions which are sure to meet with assent as soon as they are understood. That "two bodies cannot be in the same place," is a truth that nobody any more sticks at than at this maxim, that "it is impossible for the same thing to be and not to be," that "white is not black," that "a square is not a circle," that "yellowness is not sweetness:" these, and a million of other such propositions, as many at least as we have distinct ideas, every man in his wits at first hearing, and knowing what the names stand for, must necessarily assent to. If these men will be true to their own rule, and have "assent at first hearing and understanding the terms" to be a mark of innate, they must allow not only as many innate propositions as men have distinct ideas, but as many as men can make propositions wherein different ideas are denied one of another; since every proposition, wherein one different idea is denied of another, will as certainly find assent at first hearing and understanding the terms, as this general one, "It is impossible for the same to be and not to be;" or that which is the foundation of it, and is the easier understood of the two, "The same is not different;" by which account they will have legions of innate propositions of this one sort, without mentioning any other. But since no proposition can be innate, unless the ideas about which it is be innate, this will be to suppose all our ideas of colours, sounds, tastes, figure, &c., innate; than which there cannot be anything more opposite to reason and experience. Universal and ready assent upon hearing and understanding the terms is, I grant, a mark of self-evidence; but self-evidence, depending not on innate impressions, but on something else (as we shall show hereafter), belongs to several propositions, which nobody was yet so extravagant as to pretend to be innate.

19. *Such less general propositions known before these universal maxims.*—Nor let it be said that those more particular self-evident propositions which are assented to at first hearing, as, that "one and two are equal to three," that "green is not red," &c., are received as the consequences of those more universal propositions, which are looked on as innate principles; since any one who will but take the pains to observe what passes in the understanding will certainly find that these and the like less general propositions are certainly known and firmly assented to by those who are utterly ignorant of those more general maxims; and so, being earlier in the mind than those (as they are called) first principles, cannot owe to them the assent wherewith they are received at first hearing.

20. *One and one equal to two, &c., not general nor useful, answered.*—If it be said that these propositions, viz. "Two and two are equal to four," "Red is not blue," &c., are not general maxims, nor of any great use; I answer, That makes nothing to the argument of universal assent, upon hearing and understanding. For, if that be the certain mark of innate, whatever proposition can be found that receives general assent, as soon as heard and understood, that must be admitted for an innate proposition, as well as this maxim, that "it is impossible for the same thing to be and not to be," they being upon this ground equal. And as to the difference

of being more general, that makes this maxim more remote from being innate; those general and abstract ideas being more strangers to our first apprehensions, than those of more particular self-evident propositions; and therefore it is longer before they are admitted and assented to by the growing understanding. And as to the usefulness of these magnified maxims, that perhaps will not be found so great as is generally conceived, when it comes in its due place to be more fully considered.

21. *These maxims not being known sometimes till proposed, proves them not innate.*—But we have not yet done with "assenting to propositions at first hearing and understanding their terms:" it is fit we first take notice, that this, instead of being a mark that they are innate, is a proof of the contrary; since it supposes that several who understand and know other things, are ignorant of these principles till they are proposed to them, and that one may be unacquainted with these truths till he hears them from others. For if they were innate, what need they be proposed in order to gaining assent; when, by being in the understanding, by a natural and original impression (if there were any such), they could not but be known before? Or doth the proposing them print them clearer in the mind than nature did? If so, then the consequence will be, that a man knows them better after he has been thus taught them than he did before. Whence it will follow, that these principles may be made more evident to us by others' teaching than nature has made them by impression; which will ill agree with the opinion of innate principles, and give but little authority to them; but, on the contrary, make them unfit to be the foundations of all our other knowledge, as they are pretended to be. This cannot be denied, that men grow first acquainted with many of these self-evident truths, upon their being proposed; but it is clear that whosoever does so, finds in himself that he then begins to know a proposition which he knew not before; and which, from thenceforth, he never questions; not because it was innate, but because the consideration of the nature of the

things contained in those words would not suffer him to think otherwise, how or whensoever he is brought to reflect on them. And if whatever is assented to at first hearing and understanding the terms, must pass for an innate principle, every well-grounded observation drawn from particulars into a general rule must be innate; when yet it is certain, that not all but only sagacious heads light at first on these observations, and reduce them into general propositions; not innate, but collected from a preceding acquaintance and reflection on particular instances. These, when observing men have made them, unobserving men, when they are proposed to them, cannot refuse their assent to.

22. *Implicitly known before proposing, signifies that the mind is capable of understanding them, or else signifies nothing.*—If it be said, "The understanding hath an implicit knowledge of these principles, but not an explicit, before the first hearing" (as they must who will say that they are in the understanding before they are known), it will be hard to conceive what is meant by a principle imprinted on the understanding implicitly; unless it be this, that the mind is capable of understanding and assenting firmly to such propositions. And thus all mathematical demonstrations, as well as first principles, must be received as native impressions on the mind: which I fear they will scarce allow them to be, who find it harder to demonstrate a proposition than assent to it when demonstrated. And few mathematicians will be forward to believe, that all the diagrams they have drawn were but copies of those innate characters which nature had engraven upon their minds.

23. *The argument of assenting on first hearing, is upon a false supposition of no precedent teaching.*—There is, I fear, this farther weakness in the foregoing argument, which would persuade us that therefore those maxims are to be thought innate which men admit at first hearing, because they assent to propositions which they are not taught nor do receive from the force of any argument or demonstration, but a bare explication or understanding of the terms. Under which there

seems to me to lie this fallacy : that men are supposed not to be taught, nor to learn anything *de novo;* when in truth they are taught and do learn something they were ignorant of before. For, first, it is evident they have learned the terms and their signification; neither of which was born with them. But this is not all the acquired knowledge in the case; the ideas themselves, about which the proposition is, are not born with them no more than their names, but got afterwards. So that in all propositions that are assented to at first hearing, the terms of the proposition, their standing for such ideas, and the ideas themselves that they stand for, being neither of them innate, I would fain know what there is remaining in such propositions that is innate. For I would gladly have any one name that proposition whose terms or ideas were either of them innate. We by degrees get ideas and names, and learn their appropriated connection one with another; and then to propositions, made in such terms whose signification we have learnt, and wherein the agreement or disagreement we can perceive in our ideas when put together is expressed, we at first hearing assent; though to other propositions, in themselves as certain and evident, but which are concerning *ideas* not so soon or so easily got, we are at the same time no way capable of assenting. For though a child quickly assents to this proposition, that "an apple is not fire," when, by familiar acquaintance, he has got the ideas of those two different things distinctly imprinted on his mind, and has learnt that the names "apple" and "fire" stand for them; yet it will be some years after, perhaps, before the same child will assent to this proposition, that "it is impossible for the same thing to be and not to be," because that, though perhaps the words are as easy to be learnt, yet the signification of them being more large, comprehensive, and abstract than of the names annexed to those sensible things the child hath to do with, it is longer before he learns their precise meaning, and it requires more time plainly to form in his mind those general ideas they stand for. Till that be done, you will in vain endeavour to make any child assent to a proposition made up of such general terms; but as soon as ever he has got those ideas, and learned their names, he forwardly closes with the one as well as the other of the fore-mentioned propositions, and with both for the same reason, viz. because he finds the ideas he has in his mind to agree or disagree, according as the words standing for them are affirmed or denied one of another in the proposition. But if propositions be brought to him in words which stand for ideas he has not yet in his mind; to such propositions, however evidently true or false in themselves, he affords neither assent nor dissent, but is ignorant. For words being but empty sounds, any farther than they are signs of our ideas, we cannot but assent to them as they correspond to those ideas we have, but no farther than that. But the showing by what steps and ways knowledge comes into our minds, and the grounds of several degrees of assent being the business of the following discourse, it may suffice to have only touched on it here, as one reason that made me doubt of those innate principles.

24. *Not innate, because not universally assented to.*—To conclude this argument of universal consent, I agree with these defenders of innate principles, that if they are innate, they must needs have universal assent. For, that a truth should be innate and yet not assented to, is to me as unintelligible as for a man to know a truth and be ignorant of it at the same time. But then, by these men's own confession, they cannot be innate; since they are not assented to by those who understand not the terms, nor by a great part of those who do understand them, but have yet never heard nor thought of those propositions; which, I think, is at least one-half of mankind. But were the number far less, it would be enough to destroy universal assent, and thereby show these propositions not to be innate, if children alone were ignorant of them.

25. *These maxims not the first known.*—But that I may not be accused to argue from the thoughts of infants, which are unknown to us, and to conclude from what passes in their

understandings, before they express it, I say next, that these two general propositions are not the truths that first possess the minds of children, nor are antecedent to all acquired and adventitious notions; which, if they were innate, they must needs be. Whether we can determine it or no, it matters not; there is certainly a time when children begin to think, and their words and actions do assure us that they do so. When therefore they are capable of thought, of knowledge, of assent, can it rationally be supposed they can be ignorant of those notions that nature has imprinted, were there any such? Can it be imagined, with any appearance of reason, that they perceive the impressions from things without, and are at the same time ignorant of those characters which nature itself has taken care to stamp within? Can they receive and assent to adventitious notions, and be ignorant of those which are supposed woven into the very principles of their being, and imprinted there in indelible characters, to be the foundation and guide of all their acquired knowledge and future reasonings? This would be to make nature take pains to no purpose, or, at least, to write very ill; since its characters could not be read by those eyes which saw other things very well: and those are very ill supposed the clearest parts of truth and the foundations of all our knowledge, which are not first known, and without which the undoubted knowledge of several other things may be had. The child certainly knows that the nurse that feeds it is neither the cat it plays with, nor the Blackmoor it is afraid of; that the worm seed or mustard it refuses is not the apple or sugar it cries for; this it is certainly and undoubtedly assured of: but will any one say it is by virtue of this principle that "it is impossible for the same thing to be and not to be," that it so firmly assents to these and other parts of its knowledge? or that the child has any notion or apprehension of that proposition at an age wherein yet, it is plain, it knows a great many other truths? He that will say, "Children join these general abstract speculations with their sucking-bottles and their rattles," may perhaps, with justice, be thought to have more passion and zeal for his opinion, but less sincerity and truth, than one of that age.

26. *And so not innate.*—Though therefore there be several general propositions that meet with constant and ready assent as soon as proposed to men grown up, who have attained the use of more general and abstract ideas, and names standing for them; yet they not being to be found in those of tender years, who nevertheless know other things, they cannot pretend to universal assent of intelligent persons, and so by no means can be supposed innate; it being impossible that any truth which is innate (if there were any such) should be unknown, at least to any one who knows anything else: since, if they are innate truths, they must be innate thoughts; there being nothing a truth in the mind that it has never thought on. Whereby it is evident if there be any innate truths [in the mind], they must necessarily be the first of any thought on, the first that appear there.

27. *Not innate, because they appear least where what is innate shows itself clearest.*—That the general maxims we are discoursing of are not known to children, idiots, and a great part of mankind, we have already sufficiently proved; whereby it is evident, they have not an universal assent, nor are general impressions. But there is this farther argument in it against their being innate: that these characters, if they were native and original impressions, should appear fairest and clearest in those persons in whom yet we find no footsteps of them; and it is, in my opinion, a strong presumption that they are not innate, since they are least known to those in whom, if they were innate, they must needs exert themselves with most force and vigour. For children, idiots, savages, and illiterate people, being of all others the least corrupted by custom or borrowed opinions—learning and education having not cast their native thoughts into new moulds, nor by superinducing foreign and studied doctrines confounded those fair characters nature had written there—one might reasonably imagine, that in their minds these innate notions should lie open fairly to every one's view, as it is certain

the thoughts of children do. It might very well be expected that these principles should be perfectly known to naturals; which, being stamped immediately on the soul (as these men suppose), can have no dependence on the constitutions or organs of the body, the only confessed difference between them and others. One would think, according to these men's principles, that all these native beams of light (were there any such) should in those who have no reserves, no arts of concealment, shine out in their full lustre, and leave us in no more doubt of their being there than we are of their love of pleasure and abhorrence of pain. But, alas! amongst children, idiots, savages, and the grossly illiterate, what general maxims are to be found? what universal principles of knowledge? Their notions are few and narrow, borrowed only from those objects they have had most to do with, and which have made upon their senses the frequentest and strongest impressions. A child knows his nurse and his cradle, and, by degrees, the playthings of a little more advanced age; and a young savage has perhaps his head filled with love and hunting, according to the fashion of his tribe. But he that from a child untaught, or a wild inhabitant of the woods, will expect these abstract maxims and reputed principles of sciences, will, I fear, find himself mistaken. Such kind of general propositions are seldom mentioned in the huts of Indians; much less are they to be found in the thoughts of children, or any impressions of them on the minds of naturals. They are the language and business of the schools and academies of learned nations, accustomed to that sort of conversation or learning where disputes are frequent: these maxims being suited to artificial argumentation and useful for conviction; but not much conducing to the discovery of truth or advancement of knowledge.

28. *Recapitulation.*—I know not how absurd this may seem to the masters of demonstration: and probably it will hardly down with anybody at first hearing. I must, therefore, beg a little truce with prejudice and the forbearance of censure till I have been heard out in the sequel of this dis-

course, being very willing to submit to better judgments. And since I impartially search after truth, I shall not be sorry to be convinced that I have been too fond of my own notions; which, I confess, we are all apt to be when application and study have warmed our heads with them.

Upon the whole matter, I cannot see any ground to think these two famed speculative maxims innate, since they are not universally assented to; and the assent they so generally find is no other than what several propositions, not allowed to be innate, equally partake in with them; and since the assent that is given them is produced another way, and comes not from natural inscription, as I doubt not but to make appear in the following discourse. And if these first principles of knowledge and science are found not to be innate, no other speculative maxims can, I suppose, with better right pretend to be so.

NOTE ON THE LAWS OF THOUGHT.

Page 7, Section IV.

The "speculative principles" here alluded to are the famous "laws of thought," which have obtained a place in all systems of philosophy, from Plato downwards. They are three in number, and may be thus expressed:—

1°. Whatever is, is. This, known as the law of Identity, was not thoroughly discriminated from the two following laws, and enunciated as a co-ordinate principle, until the time of the Schoolmen.

2°. It is impossible for the same thing at the same time both to be and not to be. The name appropriated to this principle is the law of Contradiction.

3°. A thing either is or is not. This axiom is denominated the law of Excluded Middle.

The second of these laws is that which has most excited discussion, and is that to which, it will be observed, Locke most frequently alludes. The point which he endeavours to prove is that the law, considered as an explicit statement, or fact of knowledge, does not exist in the mind until it has been acquired by a generalisation or inference from experience. Leibnitz, however, succeeded in re-establishing the *à priori* characters of these laws, which for a time had been apparently deposed by Locke; but, as is usual in discussions of this nature, the opposing parties were far more nearly allied in opinion than their words would seem to show. The fact is, that the whole of the disputes which the "laws of thought" have occasioned may be traced to a confusion of the two points of view from which these principles may be examined. Thus, they may be considered as articulate enunciations of certain conditions or forms of thinking—that is, as laws, a compliance with which is necessary to all valid thought; or they may be looked upon as certain truths, a knowledge of which is acquired by due reflection. The former of these views is that which in the main (though obscurely) is held by Leibnitz, while the latter has received the support of Locke's able pen; and as the two opinions are by no means incompatible, it will be seen that, as was, indeed, the case, these philosophers might very readily play at cross purposes; for, each of them in a great measure mistaking the point which the other was discussing, it resulted that that was attacked which was never defended, and that was defended which was never attacked.

There is a fourth law of thought, termed the law of Sufficient Reason, which, although recognised by Plato, Aristotle, and Cicero, had fallen into neglect for ages previous to the time of Leibnitz, who first, among modern philosophers, gave this principle a prominent position in the science of mind. It has been thus expressed —"Whatever exists or is true must have a sufficient reason why the thing or proposition should be as it is, and not otherwise." Latterly, however, this principle has been relegated to the class of derivative, instead of fundamental laws.

All further particulars with reference to Locke's remarks upon innate notions will be found in the notes at the end of the two following selections.

OTHER CONSIDERATIONS CONCERNING INNATE PRINCIPLES, BOTH SPECULATIVE AND PRACTICAL.

1. *Principles not innate, unless their ideas be innate.*—Had those who would persuade us that there are innate principles, not taken them together in gross, but considered separately the parts out of which those propositions are made, they would not, perhaps, have been so forward to believe they were innate; since, if the ideas which made up those truths were not, it was impossible that the propositions made up of them should be,

innate, or our knowledge of them be born with us. For if the ideas be not innate, there was a time when the mind was without those principles; and then they will not be innate, but be derived from some other original: for where the ideas themselves are not, there can be no knowledge, no assent, no mental or verbal propositions about them.

2. *Ideas, especially those belonging to principles, not born with children.*—If we will attentively consider new-born children, we shall have little reason to think that they bring many ideas into the world with them: for, bating, perhaps, some faint ideas of hunger, and thirst, and warmth, and some pains which they may have felt in the womb, there is not the least appearance of any settled ideas at all in them; especially of ideas answering the terms which make up those universal propositions that are esteemed innate principles. One may perceive how, by degrees, afterwards, ideas come into their minds; and that they get no more, nor no other, than what experience, and the observation of things that come in their way, furnish them with; which might be enough to satisfy us that they are not original characters stamped on the mind.

3. " It is impossible for the same thing to be, and not to be," is certainly (if there be any such) an innate principle. But can any one think, or will any one say, that impossibility and identity are two innate ideas? Are they such as all mankind have, and bring into the world with them? And are they those that are the first in children, and antecedent to all acquired ones? If they are innate, they must needs be so. Hath a child an idea of impossibility and identity before it has of white or black, sweet or bitter? And is it from the knowledge of this principle that it concludes that wormwood rubbed on the nipple hath not the same taste that it used to receive from thence? Is it the actual knowledge of *Impossibile est idem esse, et non esse,** that makes a child distinguish between its mother and a stranger; or that makes it fond of the one and fly the other? Or does the mind regulate itself, and its assent, by ideas that it never yet had? or the understanding draw conclusions from principles which

* *It is impossible for the same thing to be and not to be.*—Ed.

it never yet knew or understood? The names "impossibility" and "identity" stand for two ideas so far from being innate, or born with us, that, I think, it requires great care and attention to form them right in our understandings: they are so far from being brought into the world with us, so remote from the thoughts of infancy and childhood, that, I believe, upon examination, it will be found that many grown men want them.

4. *Identity, an idea not innate.*—If identity (to instance in that alone) be a native impression, and, consequently, so clear and obvious to us that we must needs know it even from our cradles, I would gladly be resolved, by one of seven or seventy years old, whether a man being a creature consisting of soul and body, be the same man when his body is changed; whether Euphorbus and Pythagoras,* having had the same soul, were the same man, though they lived several ages asunder; nay, whether the cock,† too, which had the same soul, were not the same with both of them? Whereby, perhaps, it will appear, that our idea of sameness is not so settled and clear as to deserve to be thought innate in us. For if those innate ideas are not clear and distinct, so as to be universally known and naturally agreed on, they cannot be subjects of universal and undoubted truths, but will be the unavoidable occasion of perpetual uncertainty. For, I suppose, every one's idea of identity will not be the same that Pythagoras and thousands others of his followers have; and which, then, shall be the true? which innate? or are there two different ideas of identity, both innate?

5. Nor let any one think that the questions I have here proposed, about the identity of man, are bare, empty speculations; which if they were, would be enough to show that there was in the understandings of men no innate idea of identity. He that shall, with a little attention, reflect on the resurrection, and consider that Divine Justice shall bring to judgment, at the last day, the very same persons, to be happy or miserable in

---

* An allusion to the Pythagorean doctrine of transmigration as manifested in the existence of Pythagoras himself. A detailed account of the changes which he underwent may be found in *Diogenes Laertius,* viii.—ED.

† See Lucian's *Dream of Micyllus.*—ED.

the other, who did well or ill in this, life, will find it, perhaps, not easy to resolve with himself what makes the same man, or wherein identity consists; and will not be forward to think he and every one, even children themselves, have naturally a clear idea of it.

6. *Whole and part, not innate ideas.*—Let us examine that principle of mathematics, viz. that the "whole is bigger than a part." This, I take it, is reckoned amongst innate principles. I am sure it has as good a title as any to be thought so; which yet nobody can think it to be, when he considers the ideas it comprehends in it, whole and part, are perfectly relative; but the positive ideas to which they properly and immediately belong are extension and number, of which alone whole and part are relations. So that if whole and part are innate ideas, extension and number must be so too; it being impossible to have an idea of a relation, without having any at all of the thing to which it belongs, and in which it is founded. Now, whether the minds of men have naturally imprinted on them the ideas of extension and number, I leave to be considered by those who are the patrons of innate principles.

7. *Idea of worship not innate.*—That "God is to be worshipped," is, without doubt, as great a truth as any can enter into the mind of man, and deserves the first place amongst all practical principles; but yet it can by no means be thought innate, unless the ideas of God and worship are innate. That the idea the term "worship" stands for is not in the understanding of children, and a character stamped on the mind in its first original, I think, will be easily granted by any one that considers how few there be, amongst grown men, who have a clear and distinct notion of it. And, I suppose, there cannot be anything more ridiculous than to say that children have this practical principle innate—that "God is to be worshipped;" and yet that they know not what that worship of God is, which is their duty. But, to pass by this.

8. *Idea of God not innate.*—If any idea can be imagined innate, the idea of God may, of all others, for many reasons, be thought so; since it is hard to conceive how there should

be innate moral principles without an innate idea of a Deity: without a notion of a law-maker, it is impossible to have a notion of a law, and an obligation to observe it. Besides the atheists taken notice of amongst the ancients, and left branded upon the records of history, hath not navigation discovered, in these later ages, whole nations, at the Bay of Soldania,* in Brazil,† in Boranday,‡ and the Carribee Islands, &c., amongst whom there was to be found no notion of a God, no religion? Nicholaus del Techo *in Literis, ex Paraquariá de Caaiguarum Conversione*, has these words: *Reperi eam gentem nullum nomen habere, quod Deum et hominis animam significet: nulla sacra habet, nulla idola.*§ These are instances of nations where uncultivated nature has been left to itself, without the help of letters and discipline, and the improvements of arts and sciences. But there are others to be found, who have enjoyed these in a very great measure, who yet for want of a due application of their thoughts this way, want the idea and knowledge of God. It will, I doubt not, be a surprise to others, as it was to me, to find the Siamites of this number; but for this let them consult the king of France's late envoy thither,‖ who gives no better account of the Chinese themselves.¶ And if we will not believe La Loubere, the missionaries of China, even the Jesuits themselves, the great encomiasts of the Chinese, do all to a man agree, and will convince us, that the sect of the *Literati*, or "Learned," keeping to the old religion of China, and the ruling party there, are all of them atheists. (*Vid.* Navarette, in the Collection of Voyages, vol. i.; and *Historia Cultûs Sinensium*). And, perhaps, if we should with attention mind

* Roe *apud* Thevenot, p. 2.
† Jo. de Lery, cap. xvi.
‡ Martiniere, $\frac{3}{5}\frac{2}{1}\frac{1}{2}$; Terry, $\frac{1}{5}\frac{7}{4}\frac{7}{5}$, and $\frac{2}{6}\frac{3}{4}\frac{3}{5}$; Ovington, $\frac{1}{8}\frac{8}{0}\frac{8}{8}$.
§ *Relatio triplex de Rebus Indicis Caaiguarum*, $\frac{4}{7}\frac{3}{0}$. [The translation of the passage quoted may be thus given:—"I found that this nation has no name which signifies either God or the soul of man: neither has it any holy rites or idols." *Soldania* is another name for *Saldanha*.—Ed.]
‖ La Loubere, *Du Royaume de Siam*, tom. i. cap. ix. sect. xv. &c.; cap. xx. sect. xxii. &c.; cap. xxii. sect. vi.
¶ *Ibid.*, tom. i. cap. xx. sect. iv. &c.; cap. xxiii.

the lives and discourses of people not so far off, we should have too much reason to fear that many, in more civilised countries, have no very strong and clear impressions of a Deity upon their minds; and the complaints of atheism made from the pulpit are not without reason. And though only some profligate wretches own it too barefacedly now, yet, perhaps, we should hear more than we do of it from others, did not the fear of the magistrate's sword, or their neighbour's censure, tie up people's tongues; which, were the apprehensions of punishment or shame taken away, would as openly proclaim their atheism as their lives do.

9. But had all mankind everywhere a notion of a God (whereof yet history tells us the contrary), it would not from thence follow that the idea of him was innate. For though no nation were to be found without a name and some few dark notions of him, yet that would not prove them to be natural impressions on the mind, no more than the names of "fire," or the "sun," "heat," or number," do prove the ideas they stand for to be innate, because the names of those things, and the ideas of them, are so universally received and known amongst mankind. Nor, on the contrary, is the want of such a name, or the absence of such a notion out of men's minds, any argument against the being of a God, any more than it would be a proof that there was no loadstone in the world, because a great part of mankind had neither a notion of any such thing, nor a name for it; or be any show of argument to prove that there are no distinct and various species of angels or intelligent beings above us, because we have no ideas of such distinct species or names for them. For men, being furnished with words by the common language of their own countries, can scarce avoid having some kind of ideas of those things whose names those they converse with have occasion frequently to mention to them: and if it carry with it the notion of excellency, greatness, or something extraordinary; if apprehension and concernment accompany it: if the fear of absolute and irresistible power set it upon the mind; the idea is likely to sink the deeper and spread the

farther, especially if it be such an idea as is agreeable to the common light of reason, and naturally deducible from every part of our knowledge, as that of a God is. For the visible marks of extraordinary wisdom and power appear so plainly in all the works of the creation, that a rational creature who will but seriously reflect on them, cannot miss the discovery of a Deity; and the influence that the discovery of such a Being must necessarily have on the minds of all that have but once heard of it is so great, and carries such a weight of thought and communication with it, that it seems stranger to me that a whole nation of men should be anywhere found so brutish as to want the notion of a God, than that they should be without any notion of numbers or fire.

10. The name of God being once mentioned in any part of the world to express a superior, powerful, wise, invisible Being, the suitableness of such a notion to the principles of common reason, and the interest men will always have to mention it often, must necessarily spread it far and wide, and continue it down to all generations; though yet the general reception of this name, and some imperfect and unsteady notions conveyed thereby to the unthinking part of mankind, prove not the idea to be innate; but only that they who made the discovery had made a right use of their reason, thought maturely of the causes of things, and traced them to their original; from whom other less considering people having once received so important a notion, it could not easily be lost again.

11. This is all could be inferred from the notion of a God, were it to be found universally in all the tribes of mankind, and generally acknowledged by men grown to maturity in all countries. For the generality of the acknowledging of a God, as I imagine, is extended no farther than that; which, if it be sufficient to prove the idea of God innate, will as well prove the idea of fire innate; since, I think, it may truly be said, that there is not a person in the world who has a notion of a God who has not also the idea of fire. I doubt not but if a colony of young children should be placed in an island

where no fire was, they would certainly neither have any notion of such a thing nor name for it, how generally soever it were received and known in all the world besides; and perhaps, too, their apprehensions would be as far removed from any name or notion of a God, till some one amongst them had employed his thoughts to inquire into the constitution and causes of things, which would easily lead him to the notion of a God; which having once taught to others, reason and the natural propensity of their own thoughts would afterwards propagate and continue amongst them.

12. "*Suitable to God's goodness, that all men should have an idea of him, therefore naturally imprinted by him,*" *answered.*— Indeed it is urged that it is suitable to the goodness of God to imprint upon the minds of men characters and notions of himself, and not to leave them in the dark and doubt in so grand a concernment; and also by that means to secure to himself the homage and veneration due from so intelligent a creature as man; and therefore he has done it.

This argument, if it be of any force, will prove much more than those who use it in this case expect from it. For if we may conclude that God hath done for men all that men shall judge is best for them, because it is suitable to his goodness so to do, it will prove not only that God has imprinted on the minds of men an idea of himself, but that he hath plainly stamped there, in fair characters, all that men ought to know or believe of him—all that they ought to do in obedience to his will; and that he hath given them a will and affections conformable to it. This, no doubt, every one will think it better for men, than that they should, in the dark, grope after knowledge, as St. Paul tells us, all nations did after God (Acts xvii. 27); than that their wills should clash with their understandings, and their appetites cross their duty. The Romanists say, it is best for men, and so suitable to the goodness of God, that there should be an infallible judge of controversies on earth; and therefore there is one. And I, by the same reason, say, it is better for men that every man himself should be infallible. I leave them to consider whether, by the force of this argument, they shall think that every man is so. I think it a very good argument to say, "The infinitely wise God hath made it so, and therefore it is best." But it seems to me a little too much confidence of our own wisdom to say, "I think it best, and therefore God hath made it so;" and in the matter in hand, it will be in vain to argue from such a topic that God hath done so, when certain experience shows us that he hath not. But the goodness of God hath not been wanting to men without such original impressions of knowledge or ideas stamped on the mind; since he hath furnished man with those faculties which will serve for the sufficient discovery of all things requisite to the end of such a being; and I doubt not but to show that a man, by the right use of his natural abilities, may, without any innate principles, attain the knowledge of a God, and other things that concern him. God, having endued man with those faculties of knowing which he hath, was no more obliged by his goodness to implant those innate notions in his mind, than that, having given him reason, hands, and materials, he should build him bridges or houses; which some people in the world, however of good parts, do either totally want, or are but ill provided of, as well as others are wholly without ideas of God and principles of morality, or at least have but very ill ones: the reason in both cases being that they never employed their parts, faculties, and powers industriously that way, but contented themselves with the opinions, fashions, and things of their country as they found them, without looking any farther. Had you or I been born at the Bay of Soldania, possibly our thoughts and notions had not exceeded those brutish ones of the Hottentots that inhabit there: and had the Virginian king Apochancana been educated in England, he had, perhaps, been as knowing a divine, and as good a mathematician, as any in it; the difference between him and a more improved Englishman lying barely in this, that the exercise of his faculties was bounded within the ways, modes, and notions of his own country, and never directed to any other or farther inquiries; and if he had not any idea of a God, it was only because he pursued not those thoughts that would have led him to it.

13. *Ideas of God various in different men.*—I grant that if there were any ideas to be found imprinted on the minds of men, we have reason to expect it should be the notion of his Maker, as a mark God set on his own workmanship, to mind man of his dependence and duty; and that herein should appear the first instances of human knowledge. But how late is it before any such notion is discoverable in children! and when we find it there, how much more does it resemble the opinion and notion of the teacher than represent the true God! He that shall observe in children the progress whereby their minds attain the knowledge they have, will think that the objects they do first and most familiarly converse with are those that make the first impressions on their understandings; nor will he find the least footsteps of any other. It is easy to take notice how their thoughts enlarge themselves only as they come to be acquainted with a greater variety of sensible objects, to retain the ideas of them in their memories, and to get the skill to compound and enlarge them, and several ways put them together. How by these means they come to frame in their minds an idea men have of a Deity, I shall hereafter show.

14. Can it be thought that the ideas men have of God are the characters and marks of himself, engraven in their minds by his own finger, when we see that in the same country, under one and the same name, men have far different, nay, often contrary and inconsistent ideas and conceptions of him? Their agreeing in a name or sound will scarce prove an innate notion of him.

15. What true or tolerable notion of a Deity could they have who acknowledged and worshipped hundreds? Every deity that they owned above one was an infallible evidence of their ignorance of him, and a proof that they had no true notion of God, where unity, infinity, and eternity were excluded. To which, if we add their gross conceptions of corporeity, expressed in their images and representations of their deities,

the amours, marriages, copulations, lusts, quarrels, and other mean qualities attributed by them to their gods, we shall have little reason to think that the heathen world, *i.e.*, the greatest part of mankind, had such ideas of God in their minds as he himself, out of care that they should not be mistaken about him, was author of. And this universality of consent, so much argued, if it prove any native impressions, it will be only this: That God imprinted on the minds of all men, speaking the same language, a name for himself, but not any idea; since those people who agreed in the name had, at the same time, far different apprehensions about the thing signified. If they say that the variety of deities worshipped by the heathen world were but figurative ways of expressing the several attributes of that incomprehensible Being, or several parts of his providence; I answer, What they might be in their original, I will not here inquire, but that they were so in the thoughts of the vulgar I think nobody will affirm; and he that will consult the voyage of the Bishop of Beryte, cap. xiii. (not to mention other testimonies), will find that the theology of the Siamites professedly owns a plurality of gods; or, as the Abbé de Choisy more judiciously remarks, in his Journal *du Voyage de Siam*, $\frac{1}{2}\frac{9}{7}$, it consists properly in acknowledging no God at all.

If it be said that wise men of all nations came to have true conceptions of the unity and infinity of the Deity, I grant it. But then this,

First, excludes universality of consent in anything but the name; for those wise men being very few—perhaps one of a thousand—this universality is very narrow.

Secondly, it seems to me plainly to prove that the truest and best notions men had of God were not imprinted, but acquired by thought and meditation and a right use of their faculties; since the wise and considerate men of the world, by a right and careful employment of their thoughts and reason, attained true notions in this as well as other things; whilst the lazy and inconsiderate part of men, making the far greater number, took up their notions, by chance, from common tradition and vulgar conceptions, without much beating their heads about them. And if it be a reason to think the notion of God innate because all wise men had it, virtue, too, must be thought innate; for that also wise men have always had.

16. This was evidently the case of all Gentilism : nor hath, even amongst Jews, Christians, and Mahometans, who acknowledge but one God, this doctrine, and the care taken in those nations to teach men to have true notions of a God, prevailed so far as to make men to have the same and true ideas of him. How many, even amongst us, will be found, upon inquiry, to fancy him in the shape of a man, sitting in heaven; and to have many other absurd and unfit conceptions of him! Christians, as well as Turks, have had whole sects owning and contending earnestly for it, that the Deity was corporeal and of human shape; and though we find few amongst us who profess themselves anthropomorphites (though some I have met with that own it), yet, I believe, he that will make it his business may find, amongst the ignorant and uninstructed Christians, many of that opinion. Talk but with country-people almost of any age, or young people almost of any condition, and you shall find, that though the name of God be frequently in their mouths, yet the notions they apply this name to are so odd, low, and pitiful, that nobody can imagine they were taught by a rational man, much less that they were characters writ by the finger of God himself. Nor do I see how it derogates more from the goodness of God that he has given us minds unfurnished with these ideas of himself, than that he hath sent us into the world with bodies unclothed, and that there is no art or skill born with us. For being fitted with faculties to attain these, it is want of industry and consideration in us, and not of bounty in him, if we have them not. It is as certain that there is a God, as that the opposite angles made by the intersection of two straight lines are equal. There was never any rational creature, that set himself sincerely to examine the truth of these propositions, that could fail to assent to them; though yet it be past doubt that there are many men who, having not applied their

thoughts that way, are ignorant both of the one and the other. If any one think fit to call this (which is the utmost of its extent) universal consent, such an one I easily allow; but such an universal consent as this proves not the idea of God, no more than it does the idea of such angles, innate.

17. *If the idea of God be not innate, no other can be supposed innate.*—Since, then, though the knowledge of a God be the most natural discovery of human reason, yet the idea of him is not innate, as, I think, is evident from what has been said; I imagine there will be scarce any other idea found that can pretend to it; since, if God had set any impression, any character, on the understanding of men, it is most reasonable to expect it should have been some clear and uniform idea of himself, as far as our weak capacities were capable to receive so incomprehensible and infinite an object. But our minds being at first void of that idea which we are most concerned to have, it is a strong presumption against all other innate characters. I must own, as far as I can observe, I can find none, and would be glad to be informed by any other.

18. *Ideas of substance not innate.*—I confess there is another idea which would be of general use for mankind to have, as it is of general talk as if they had it; and that is the idea of substance, which we neither have nor can have by sensation or reflection. If nature took care to provide us any idea, we might well expect it should be such as by our own faculties we cannot procure to ourselves: but we see, on the contrary, that, since by those ways whereby other ideas are brought into our minds this is not, we have no such clear idea at all, and therefore signify nothing by the word "substance," but only an uncertain supposition of we know not what (*i.e.*, of something whereof we have no particular, distinct, positive idea), which we take to be the *substratum*, or support of those ideas we do know.

19. *No propositions can be innate since no ideas are innate.*—Whatever, then, we talk of innate, either speculative or practical, principles, it may with as much probability be said, that a man hath £100 sterling in his pocket, and yet denied that

he hath either penny, shilling, crown, or any other coin out of which the sum is to be made up; as to think, that certain propositions are innate, when the ideas about which they are can by no means be supposed to be so. The general reception and assent that is given doth not at all prove that the ideas expressed in them are innate; for in many cases, however the ideas came there, the assent to words expressing the agreement or disagreement of such ideas will necessarily follow. Every one that hath a true idea of God and worship, will assent to this proposition, that "God is to be worshipped," when expressed in a language he understands; and every rational man that hath not thought on it to-day, may be ready to assent to this proposition to-morrow; and yet millions of men may be well supposed to want one or both of those ideas to-day. For if we will allow savages and most country-people to have ideas of God and worship (which conversation with them will not make one forward to believe), yet, I think, few children can be supposed to have those ideas, which therefore they must begin to have some time or other; and then they will also begin to assent to that proposition, and make very little question of it ever after. But such an assent upon hearing, no more proves the ideas to be innate, than it does that one born blind (with cataracts which will be couched to-morrow) had the innate ideas of the sun or light, or saffron or yellow, because, when his sight is cleared, he will certainly assent to this proposition, that "the sun is lucid," or that "saffron is yellow;" and therefore if such an assent upon hearing cannot prove the ideas innate, it can much less the propositions made up of those ideas. If they have any innate ideas, I would be glad to be told what and how many they are.

20. *No innate ideas in the memory.*—To which let me add: If there be any innate ideas, any ideas in the mind which the mind does not actually think on, they must be lodged in the memory, and from thence must be brought into view by remembrance; *i. e.*, must be known, when they are remembered, to have been perceptions in the mind before, unless remembrance can be without remembrance. For to remember is to per-

ceive anything with memory, or with a consciousness that it was known or perceived before; without this, whatever idea comes into the mind is new and not remembered; this consciousness of its having been in the mind before, being that which distinguishes remembering from all other ways of thinking. Whatever idea was never perceived by the mind, was never in the mind. Whatever idea is in the mind, is either an actual perception, or else, having been an actual perception, is so in the mind, that by the memory it can be made an actual perception again. Whenever there is the actual perception of an idea without memory, the idea appears perfectly new and unknown before to the understanding. Whenever the memory brings any idea into actual view, it is with a consciousness that it had been there before, and was not wholly a stranger to the mind. Whether this be not so, I appeal to every one's observation: and then I desire an instance of an idea, pretended to be innate, which (before any impression of it by ways hereafter to be mentioned) any one could revive and remember as an idea he had formerly known; without which consciousness of a former perception there is no remembrance; and whatever idea comes into the mind without that consciousness, is not remembered, or comes not out of the memory, nor can be said to be in the mind before that appearance. For what is not either actually in view or in the memory, is in the mind no way at all, and is all one as if it never had been there. Suppose a child had the use of his eyes till he knows and distinguishes colours; but then cataracts shut the windows, and he is forty or fifty years perfectly in the dark, and in that time perfectly loses all memory of the ideas of colours he once had. This was the case of a blind man I once talked with, who lost his sight by the small-pox when he was a child, and had no more notion of colours than one born blind. I ask whether any one can say this man had then any ideas of colours in his mind any more than one born blind? And I think nobody will say, that either of them had in his mind any ideas of colours at all. His cataracts are couched, and then he has the ideas (which he remembers not) of colours, *de novo*, by his restored sight conveyed to his mind, and that without any consciousness of a former acquaintance. And these now he can revive, and call to mind in the dark. In this case all these ideas of colours which, when out of view can be revived, with a consciousness of a former acquaintance, being thus in the memory, are said to be in the mind. The use I make of this is, that whatever idea, being not actually in view, is in the mind, is there only by being in the memory; and if it be not in the memory, it is not in the mind; and if it be in the memory it cannot by the memory be brought into actual view, without a perception that it comes out of the memory; which is this, that it had been known before, and is now remembered. If, therefore, there be any innate ideas, they must be in the memory, or else nowhere in the mind; and if they be in the memory, they can be revived without any impression from without; and whenever they are brought into the mind, they are remembered, *i. e.* they bring with them a perception of their not being wholly new to it; this being a constant and distinguishing difference between what is, and what is not in the memory or in the mind—that what is not in the memory, whenever it appears there, appears perfectly new and unknown before; and what is in the memory or in the mind, whenever it is suggested by the memory, appears not to be new, but the mind finds it in itself, and knows it was there before. By this it may be tried, whether there be any innate ideas in the mind before impression from sensation or reflection. I would fain meet with the man who, when he came to use of reason, or at any other time remembered any of them; and to whom, after he was born, they were never new. If any one will say, there are ideas in the mind that are not in the memory, I desire him to explain himself, and make what he says intelligible.

21. *Principles not innate, because of little use or little certainty.*—Besides what I have already said, there is another reason why I doubt that neither these nor any other principles are innate. I that am fully persuaded that the infinitely wise God made all things in perfect wisdom, cannot

satisfy myself why he should be supposed to print upon the minds of men some universal principles, whereof those that are pretended innate and concern speculation are of no great use, and those that concern practice not self-evident, and neither of them distinguishable from some other truths not allowed to be innate. For to what purpose should characters be graven on the mind by the finger of God, which are not clearer there than those which are afterwards introduced, or cannot be distinguished from them? If any one thinks there are such innate ideas and propositions, which by their clearness and usefulness are distinguishable from all that is adventitious in the mind and acquired, it will not be a hard matter for him to tell us which they are, and then every one will be a fit judge whether they be so or no: since, if there be such innate ideas and impressions, plainly different from all other perceptions and knowledge, every one will find it true in himself. Of the evidence of these supposed innate maxims I have spoken already; of their usefulness I shall have occasion to speak more hereafter.

22. *Difference of men's discoveries depends upon the different application of their faculties.*—To conclude: some ideas forwardly offer themselves to all men's understandings; some sorts of truths result from any ideas as soon as the mind puts them into propositions; other truths require a train of ideas placed in order, a due comparing of them, and deductions made with attention, before they can be discovered and assented to. Some of the first sort, because of their general and easy reception, have been mistaken for innate; but the truth is, ideas and notions are no more born with us than arts and sciences; though some of them, indeed, offer themselves to our faculties more readily than others, and therefore are more generally received; though that, too, be according as the organs of our bodies and powers of our minds happen to be employed; God having fitted men with faculties and means to discover, receive, and retain truths accordingly as they are employed. The great difference that is to be found in the notions of mankind is, from the different use they put

their faculties to: whilst some (and those the most), taking things upon trust, misemploy their power of assent, by lazily enslaving their minds to the dictates and dominion of others, in doctrines which it is their duty carefully to examine, and not blindly, with an implicit faith, to swallow; others, employing their thoughts only about some few things, grow acquainted sufficiently with them, attain great degrees of knowledge in them, and are ignorant of all other, having never let their thoughts loose in the search of other inquiries. Thus, that the three angles of a triangle are equal to two right ones, is a truth as certain as anything can be, and I think more evident than many of those propositions that go for principles; and yet there are millions, however expert in other things, who know not this at all, because they never set their thoughts on work about such angles; and he that certainly knows this proposition may yet be utterly ignorant of the truth of other propositions in mathematics itself, which are as clear and evident as this, because, in his search of those mathematical truths, he stopped his thoughts short, and went not so far. The same may happen concerning the notions we have of the being of a Deity; for though there be no truth which a man may more evidently make out to himself than the existence of a God, yet he that shall content himself with things as he finds them in this world, as they minister to his pleasures and passions, and not make inquiry a little farther into their causes, ends, and admirable contrivances, and pursue the thoughts thereof with diligence and attention, may live long without any notion of such a Being: and if any person hath, by talk, put such a notion into his head, he may, perhaps, believe it; but if he hath never examined it, his knowledge of it will be no perfecter than his who, having been told that the three angles of a triangle are equal to two right ones, takes it upon trust, without examining the demonstration, and may yield his assent as a probable opinion, but hath no knowledge of the truth of it; which yet his faculties, if carefully employed, were able to make clear and evident to him. But this only by-the-bye, to show how much our knowledge depends upon the right use of those powers nature hath bestowed upon us, and how little upon such innate principles as are in vain supposed to be in all mankind for their direction; which all men could not but know, if they were there, or else they would be there to no purpose; and which since all men do not know, nor can distinguish from other adventitious truths, we may well conclude there are no such.

23. *Men must think and know for themselves.*—What censure doubting thus of innate principles may deserve from men who will be apt to call it "pulling up the old foundations of knowledge and certainty," I cannot tell: I persuade myself, at least, that the way I have pursued, being conformable to truth, lays those foundations surer. This I am certain, I have not made it my business either to quit or follow any authority in the ensuing discourse: truth has been my only aim; and wherever that has appeared to lead, my thoughts have impartially followed, without minding whether the footsteps of any other lay that way or no. Not that I want a due respect to other men's opinions; but, after all, the greatest reverence is due to truth; and I hope it will not be thought arrogance to say, that perhaps we should make greater progress in the discovery of rational and contemplative knowledge, if we sought it in the fountain, in the consideration of things themselves, and made use rather of our own thoughts than other men's to find it: for, I think, we may as rationally hope to see with other men's eyes as to know by other men's understandings. So much as we ourselves consider and comprehend of truth and reason, so much we possess of real and true knowledge. The floating of other men's opinions in our brains makes us not one jot the more knowing, though they happen to be true. What in them was science is in us but opiniatrety, whilst we give up our assent only to reverend names, and do not, as they did, employ our own reason to understand those truths which gave them reputation. Aristotle was certainly a knowing man; but nobody ever thought him so because he blindly embraced and confidently vented the opinions of another. And if the taking

up of another's principles without examining them made not him a philosopher, I suppose it will hardly make any one else so. In the sciences, every one has so much as he really knows and comprehends; what he believes only, and takes upon trust, are but shreds; which, however well in the whole piece, make no considerable addition to his stock who gathers them. Such borrowed wealth, like fairy money, though it were gold in the hand from which he received it, will be but leaves and dust when it comes to use.

24. *Whence the opinion of innate principles.*—When men have found some general propositions that could not be doubted of as soon as understood, it was, I know, a short and easy way to conclude them innate. This being once received, it eased the lazy from the pains of search, and stopped the inquiry of the doubtful, concerning all that was once styled innate; and it was of no small advantage to those who affected to be masters and teachers, to make this the principle of principles,—that principles must not be questioned; for, having once established this tenet,—that there are innate principles, it put their followers upon a necessity of receiving some doctrines as such; which was to take them off from the use of their own reason and judgment, and put them upon believing and taking them upon trust, without farther examination; in which posture of blind credulity, they might be more easily governed by, and made useful to, some sort of men who had the skill and office to principle and guide them. Nor is it a small power it gives one man over another, to have the authority to be the dictator of principles, and teacher of unquestionable truths; and to make a man swallow that for an innate principle which may serve to his purpose who teacheth them. Whereas had they examined the ways whereby men came to the knowledge of many universal truths, they would have found them to result in the minds of men from the being of things themselves, when duly considered; and that they were discovered by the application of those faculties that were fitted by nature to receive and judge of them, when duly employed about them.

NOTE ON THE CARTESIAN DOCTRINE OF INNATE IDEAS.

The philosophers to whom Locke alludes in the two preceding selections, and against whom the Essay was directed, were the famous Descartes and his followers. These writers were supposed by Locke to maintain that the mind is possessed of certain principles (*i. e.* has a knowledge of certain truths) antecedently to all sensible experience; and it is this view which he essayed to refute. His argument, it will be noticed, is divided into two divisions—first, where he denies the *a priori* character of various axioms or *propositions;* and secondly, where the *ideas* about which these propositions are conversant are declared to be adventitious, and not innate. In each of these divisions the principal heads of his reasoning are—the non-universality of such principles or ideas; the necessity for everything in the mind to be either in actual consciousness, or in the memory, and so at some previous time to have been actually perceived; the fact that such principles and ideas are neither the first of which we become conscious, nor those perceived by persons of the fewest notions and faculties; and, finally, the superfluous nature of innate principles and ideas, since we have powers sufficient for the acquirement of every truth that it may be necessary for us to know.

Now, the garrison of this stronghold which Locke so successfully stormed, had, in reality, no existence apart from his own imagination; for neither Descartes nor his followers had ever attempted to maintain an opinion so erroneous as that which is imputed to them by the English philosopher. That this is so may be proved by the following passage from the reply which Descartes made to the Programme of Regius:—"I have never either said or thought that the mind has need of innate ideas which are in any way diverse from its faculty of thinking; but when I remarked that there were within me certain thoughts which did not proceed from external objects, ... I called them *innate* in the same sense in which we say that generosity is innate in certain families, and in others certain diseases, as gout or gravel; not that, therefore, the infants of those families labour under those diseases in the womb of the mother, but because they are born with a certain *disposition or faculty of contracting them:*" that is to say, the nature of our mind is such, that when a suitable occasion is presented to us by our senses, we cannot refrain from forming certain ideas, and entertaining certain beliefs. "Hence it is, that our knowledge has its *commencement* in sense, external or internal, but its *origin* in intellect."

Here, then, we see that the Cartesian doctrine of innate ideas had nothing in common with that which Locke combated; for the former merely asserts that *dispositions* exist in the mind to conceive certain ideas immediately that (but not *until*) the senses afford a suitable occasion; whereas the latter holds that actual facts of knowledge dwell in the mind previously to all sensible experience. And this leads us to notice a somewhat curious fact, which is, that Locke implicitly held the Cartesian doctrine of innate ideas, the same, indeed, which he nominally opposed. Thus, in one part of his essay (Book I., c. 3, § 4), he says—"He would be thought void of common sense, who, asked on the one side or the other, went to give a reason why it is impossible for the same thing to be and not to be ;" and "in admitting, as he here virtually does, that experience must ultimately ground its procedure on the laws of intellect, he admits that intellect contains principles of judgment, on which experience being dependent cannot possibly be their precursor or their cause." (Hamilton's "Reid," Diss. I.) This affords a further illustration of the remarks contained in the note at the end of the first selection.

But, although Locke's misconception of the Cartesian doctrine renders his argument altogether inept as regards its professed object, it is still of great value as presenting a noble example of philosophical reasoning, and as throwing much light upon the general character of human knowledge. It is for this reason, doubtless, that the Essay succeeded in obtaining such a widespread dominion both in England and in France; its evident beauty and utility being a golden apple to charm its readers into a deviation from the only path which could lead to speculative truth.

The object of the preceding remarks has been merely to point out the precise aim with which Locke discussed the question of innate ideas, and the real bearing of his argument as regards the Cartesian doctrines. With reference to the validity of his reasoning, either in whole or in part, or to the general character of the reception with which it has met, I have said nothing; this more properly falling to be considered after a perusal of the next selection, where Locke discloses his theory of the exact manner in which all our ideas are obtained. Accordingly, I must refer to the note which is appended thereto for a historical and critical notice of Locke's metaphysical system.

OF IDEAS IN GENERAL, AND THEIR ORIGINAL.

1. *Idea is the object of thinking.*—Every man being conscious to himself, that he thinks, and that which his mind is applied about, whilst thinking, being the ideas that are there, it is past doubt that men have in their minds several ideas,

such as are those expressed by the words, "whiteness, hardness, sweetness, thinking, motion, man, elephant, army, drunkenness," and others. It is in the first place then to be inquired, How he comes by them? I know it is a received doctrine, that men have native ideas and original characters stamped upon their minds in their very first being. This opinion I have at large examined already; and, I suppose, what I have said in the foregoing book will be much more easily admitted, when I have shown whence the understanding may get all the ideas it has, and by what ways and degrees they may come into the mind; for which I shall appeal to every one's own observation and experience.

2. *All ideas come from sensation or reflection.*—Let us then suppose the mind to be, as we say, white paper, void of all characters, without any ideas; how comes it to be furnished? Whence comes it by that vast store, which the busy and boundless fancy of man has painted on it with an almost endless variety? Whence has it all the materials of reason and knowledge? To this I answer, in one word, From experience: in that all our knowledge is founded, and from that it ultimately derives itself. Our observation, employed either about external sensible objects, or about the internal operations of our minds, perceived and reflected on by ourselves, is that which supplies our understandings with all the materials of thinking. These two are the fountains of knowledge, from whence all the ideas we have, or can naturally have, do spring.

3. *The object of sensation one source of ideas.*—First. Our senses, conversant about particular sensible objects, do convey into the mind several distinct perceptions of things, according to those various ways wherein those objects do affect them; and thus we come by those ideas we have of yellow, white, heat, cold, soft, hard, bitter, sweet, and all those which we call sensible qualities; which when I say the senses convey into the mind, I mean, they from external objects convey into the mind what produces there those perceptions. This great source of most of the ideas we have, depending wholly upon

our senses, and derived by them to the understanding, I call, "sensation."

4. *The operations of our minds the other source of them.*—Secondly. The other fountain, from which experience furnisheth the understanding with ideas, is the perception of the operations of our own minds within us, as it is employed about the ideas it has got; which operations, when the soul comes to reflect on and consider, do furnish the understanding with another set of ideas which could not be had from things without; and such are perception, thinking, doubting, believing, reasoning, knowing, willing, and all the different actings of our own minds; which we, being conscious of, and observing in ourselves, do from these receive into our understandings as distinct ideas, as we do from bodies affecting our senses. This source of ideas every man has wholly in himself; and though it be not sense as having nothing to do with external objects, yet it is very like it, and might properly enough be called "internal sense." But as I call the other "sensation," so I call this "reflection," the ideas it affords being such only as the mind gets by reflecting on its own operations within itself. By reflection, then, in the following part of this discourse, I would be understood to mean that notice which the mind takes of its own operations, and the manner of them, by reason whereof there come to be ideas of these operations in the understanding. These two, I say, viz., external material things as the objects of sensation, and the operations of our own minds within as the objects of reflection, are, to me, the only originals from whence all our ideas take their beginnings. The term "operations" here, I use in a large sense, as comprehending not barely the actions of the mind about its ideas, but some sort of passions arising sometimes from them, such as is the satisfaction or uneasiness arising from any thought.

5. *All our ideas are of the one or the other of these.*—The understanding seems to me not to have the least glimmering of any ideas which it doth not receive from one of these two. External objects furnish the mind with the ideas of sensible

qualities, which are all those different perceptions they produce in us; and the mind furnishes the understanding with ideas of its own operations.

These, when we have taken a full survey of them, and their several modes, combinations, and relations, we shall find to contain all our whole stock of ideas; and that we have nothing in our minds which did not come in one of these two ways. Let any one examine his own thoughts, and thoroughly search into his understanding, and then let him tell me, whether all the original ideas he has there, are any other than of the objects of his senses, or of the operations of his mind considered as objects of his reflection; and how great a mass of knowledge soever he imagines to be lodged there, he will, upon taking a strict view, see that he has not any idea in his mind but what one of these two have imprinted, though perhaps with infinite variety compounded and enlarged by the understanding, as we shall see hereafter.

6. *Observable in children.*—He that attentively considers the state of a child at his first coming into the world, will have little reason to think him stored with plenty of ideas that are to be the matter of his future knowledge. It is by degrees he comes to be furnished with them; and though the ideas of obvious and familiar qualities imprint themselves before the memory begins to keep a register of time and order, yet it is often so late before some unusual qualities come in the way, that there are few men that cannot recollect the beginning of their acquaintance with them: and, if it were worth while, no doubt a child might be so ordered as to have but a very few even of the ordinary ideas till he were grown up to a man. But all that are born into the world being surrounded with bodies that perpetually and diversely affect them, variety of ideas, whether care be taken about it, or no, are imprinted on the minds of children. Light and colours are busy at hand everywhere when the eye is but open; sounds and some tangible qualities fail not to solicit their proper senses, and force an entrance to the mind; but yet I think it will be granted easily, that if a child were

kept in a place where he never saw any other but black and white till he were a man, he would have no more ideas of scarlet or green, than he that from his childhood never tasted an oyster or a pine-apple has of those particular relishes.

7. *Men are differently furnished with these according to the different objects they converse with.*—Men then come to be furnished with fewer or more simple ideas from without, according as the objects they converse with afford greater or less variety; and from the operations of their minds within, according as they more or less reflect on them. For, though he that contemplates the operations of his mind cannot but have plain and clear ideas of them; yet, unless he turn his thoughts that way, and considers them attentively, he will no more have clear and distinct ideas of all the operations of his mind, and all that may be observed therein, than he will have all the particular ideas of any landscape, or of the parts and motions of a clock, who will not turn his eyes to it, and with attention heed all the parts of it. The picture or clock may be so placed, that they may come in his way every day; but yet he will have but a confused idea of all the parts they are made of, till he applies himself with attention to consider them each in particular.

8. *Ideas of reflection later, because they need attention.*—And hence we see the reason why it is pretty late before most children get ideas of the operations of their own minds; and some have not any very clear or perfect ideas of the greatest part of them all their lives :—because, though they pass there continually, yet like floating visions, they make not deep impressions enough to leave in the mind, clear, distinct, lasting ideas, till the understanding turns inwards upon itself, reflects on its own operations, and makes them the object of its own contemplation. Children, when they come first into it, are surrounded with a world of new things, which, by a constant solicitation of their senses, draw the mind constantly to them, forward to take notice of new, and apt to be delighted with the variety of changing objects. Thus the first years are usually employed and diverted in looking abroad. Men's

business in them is to acquaint themselves with what is to be found without; and so, growing up in a constant attention to outward sensations, seldom make any considerable reflection on what passes within them till they come to be of riper years; and some scarce ever at all.

9. *The soul begins to have ideas when it begins to perceive.*—To ask, at what time a man has first any ideas, is to ask when he begins to perceive; having ideas, and perception, being the same thing. I know it is an opinion that the soul always thinks; and that it has the actual perception of ideas within itself constantly, as long as it exists; and that actual thinking is as inseparable from the soul, as actual extension is from the body: which if true, to inquire after the beginning of a man's ideas is the same as to inquire after the beginning of his soul. For, by this account, soul and its ideas, as body and its extension, will begin to exist both at the same time.

10. *The soul thinks not always; for this wants proofs.*—But whether the soul be supposed to exist antecedent to, or coeval with, or some time after, the first rudiments or organization, or the beginnings of life in the body, I leave to be disputed by those who have better thought of that matter. I confess myself to have one of those dull souls that doth not perceive itself always to contemplate ideas; nor can conceive it any more necessary for the soul always to think, than for the body always to move; the perception of ideas being, as I conceive, to the soul, what motion is to the body: not its essence, but one of its operations; and, therefore, though thinking be supposed never so much the proper action of the soul, yet it is not necessary to suppose that it should be always thinking, always in action; that, perhaps, is the privilege of the infinite Author and Preserver of things, " who never slumbers nor sleeps;" but it is not competent to any finite being, at least not to the soul of man. We know certainly, by experience, that we sometimes think; and thence draw this infallible consequence—that there is something in us that has a power to think; but whether that substance perpetually thinks, or no, we can be no farther assured than experience informs us.

For to say, that actual thinking is essential to the soul and inseparable from it, is to beg what is in question, and not to prove it by reason; which is necessary to be done, if it be not a self-evident proposition. But whether this—that "the soul always thinks," be a self-evident proposition, that every body assents to on first hearing, I appeal to mankind. It is doubted whether I thought all last night, or no; the question being about a matter of fact, it is begging it to bring as a proof for it an hypothesis which is the very thing in dispute; by which way one may prove anything; and it is but supposing that all watches, whilst the balance beats, think, and it is sufficiently proved, and past doubt, that my watch thought all last night. But he that would not deceive himself ought to build his hypothesis on matter of fact, and make it out by sensible experience, and not presume on matter of fact because of his hypothesis; that is, because he supposes it to be so; which way of proving amounts to this —that I must necessarily think all last night because another supposes I always think, though I myself cannot perceive that I always do so.

But men in love with their opinions may not only suppose what is in question, but allege wrong matter of fact. How else could any one make it an inference of mine, that a thing is not because we are not sensible of it in our sleep? I do not say there is no soul in a man because he is not sensible of it in his sleep; but I do say, he cannot think at any time, waking, or sleeping, without being sensible of it. Our being sensible of it is not necessary to anything but to our thoughts; and to them it is, and to them it will always be, necessary, till we can think without being conscious of it.

11. *It is not always conscious of it.*—I grant that the soul in a waking man is never without thought, because it is the condition of being awake; but whether sleeping without dreaming be not an affection of the whole man, mind as well as body, may be worth a waking man's consideration; it being hard to conceive that anything should think and not be conscious of it. If the soul doth think in a sleeping man without being

conscious of it, I ask, whether, during such thinking, it has any pleasure or pain, or be capable of happiness or misery? I am sure the man is not, no more than the bed or earth he lies on. For to be happy or miserable without being conscious of it, seems to me utterly inconsistent and impossible. Or if it be possible that the soul can, whilst the body is sleeping, have its thinking, enjoyments, and concerns, its pleasure or pain, apart, which the man is not conscious of, nor partakes in, it is certain that Socrates asleep, and Socrates awake, is not the same person; but his soul when he sleeps, and Socrates the man, consisting of body and soul, when he is waking, are two persons; since waking Socrates has no knowledge of, or concernment for that happiness or misery of his soul which it enjoys alone by itself whilst he sleeps, without perceiving anything of it, no more than he has for the happiness or misery of a man in the Indies, whom he knows not. For if we take wholly away all consciousness of our actions and sensations, especially of pleasure and pain, and the concernment that accompanies it, it will be hard to know wherein to place personal identity.

12. *If a sleeping man thinks without knowing it, the sleeping and waking man are two persons.*—"The soul, during sound sleep, thinks," say these men. Whilst it thinks and perceives, it is capable, certainly, of those of delight or trouble, as well as any other perceptions; and it must necessarily be conscious of its own perceptions. But it has all this apart. The sleeping man, it is plain, is conscious of nothing of all this. Let us suppose, then, the soul of Castor, whilst he is sleeping, retired from his body; which is no impossible supposition for the men I have here to do with, who so liberally allow life without a thinking soul to all other animals. These men cannot, then, judge it impossible, or a contradiction, that the body should live without the soul; nor that the soul should subsist and think, or have perception, even perception of happiness or misery, without the body. Let us, then, as I say, suppose the soul of Castor separated, during his sleep, from his body, to think apart. Let us suppose, too, that it chooses for its

scene of thinking the body of another man, *v. g.* Pollux, who is sleeping without a soul: for if Castor's soul can think whilst Castor is asleep, what Castor is never conscious of, it is no matter what place it chooses to think in. We have here, then, the bodies of two men with only one soul between them, which we will suppose to sleep and wake by turns; and the soul still thinking in the waking man, whereof the sleeping man is never conscious, has never the least perception. I ask, then, whether Castor and Pollux, thus, with only one soul between them, which thinks and perceives in one what the other is never conscious of, nor is concerned for, are not two as distinct persons as Castor and Hercules, or as Socrates and Plato were? and whether one of them might not be very happy and the other very miserable? Just by the same reason they make the soul and the man two persons, who make the soul think apart what the man is not conscious of. For, I suppose, nobody will make identity of persons to consist in the soul's being united to the very same numerical particles of matter; for if that be necessary to identity, it will be impossible, in that constant flux of the particles of our bodies, that any man should be the same person two days or two moments together.

13. *Impossible to convince those that sleep without dreaming, that they think.*—Thus, methinks, every drowsy nod shakes their doctrine who teach that their soul is always thinking. Those, at least, who do at any time sleep without dreaming can never be convinced that their thoughts are sometimes for hours busy without their knowing of it; and if they are taken in the very act, waked in the middle of that sleeping contemplation, can give no manner of account of it.

14. *That men dream without remembering it, in vain urged.*— It will perhaps be said, that the soul thinks even in the soundest sleep, but the memory retains it not. That the soul in a sleeping man should be this moment busy a-thinking, and the next moment in a waking man not remember, nor be able to recollect one jot of all those thoughts, is very hard to be conceived, and would need some better proof than bare assertion to make it be believed. For who can, without any more

ado but being barely told so, imagine that the greatest part of men do, during all their lives, for several hours every day think of something which, if they were asked even in the middle of these thoughts, they could remember nothing at all of? Most men, I think, pass a great part of their sleep without dreaming. I once knew a man that was bred a scholar, and had no bad memory, who told me, he had never dreamed in his life till he had that fever he was then newly recovered of, which was about the five-or-six-and-twentieth year of his age. I suppose the world affords more such instances; at least, every one's acquaintance will furnish him with examples enough of such as pass most of their nights without dreaming.

15. *Upon this hypothesis, the thoughts of a sleeping man ought to be most rational.*—To think often and never to retain it so much as one moment, is a very useless sort of thinking; and the soul, in such a state of thinking, does very little if at all excel that of a looking-glass, which constantly receives a variety of images, or ideas, but retains none; they disappear and vanish, and there remain no footsteps of them; the looking-glass is never the better for such ideas, nor the soul for such thoughts. Perhaps it will be said, "that in a waking man the materials of the body are employed and made use of in thinking; and that the memory of thoughts is retained by the impressions that are made on the brain, and the traces there left after such thinking; but that in the thinking of the soul which is not perceived in the sleeping man, there the soul thinks apart, and, making no use of the organs of the body, leaves no impression on it, and consequently no memory of such thoughts." Not to mention again the absurdity of two distinct persons, which follows from this supposition, I answer farther, that whatever ideas the mind can receive and contemplate without the help of the body, it is reasonable to conclude it can retain without the help of the body too; or else the soul, or any separate spirit, will have but little advantage by thinking. If it has no memory of its own thoughts; if it cannot lay them up for its use, and be able to recall them upon occasion; if it cannot reflect upon what is past, and

make use of its former experiences, reasonings, and contemplations,—to what purpose does it think? They who make the soul a thinking thing, at this rate will not make it a much more noble being than those do whom they condemn for allowing it to be nothing but the subtilest parts of matter. Characters drawn on dust that the first breath of wind effaces, or impressions made on a heap of atoms or animal spirits, are altogether as useful, and render the subject as noble, as the thoughts of a soul that perish in thinking; that, once out of sight, are gone for ever, and leave no memory of themselves behind them. Nature never makes excellent things for mean or no uses; and it is hardly to be conceived that our infinitely wise Creator should make so admirable a faculty as the power of thinking, that faculty which comes nearest the excellency of his own incomprehensible being, to be so idly and uselessly employed, at least a fourth part of its time here, as to think constantly without remembering any of those thoughts, without doing any good to itself or others, or being any way useful to any other part of the creation. If we will examine it, we shall not find, I suppose, the motion of dull and senseless matter anywhere in the universe made so little use of, and so wholly thrown away.

16. *On this hypothesis, the soul must have ideas not derived from sensation or reflection, of which there is no appearance.*—It is true we have sometimes instances of perception whilst we are asleep, and retain the memory of those thoughts: but how extravagant and incoherent for the most part they are, how little conformable to the perfection and order of a rational being, those who are acquainted with dreams need not be told. This I would willingly be satisfied in: Whether the soul, when it thinks thus apart, and as it were separate from the body, acts less rationally than when conjointly with it, or no? If its separate thoughts be less rational, then these men must say that the soul owes the perfection of rational thinking to the body; if it does not, it is a wonder that our dreams should be for the most part so frivolous and irrational, and that the soul should retain none of 'its more rational soliloquies and meditations.

17. *If I think when I know it not, nobody else can know it.*—Those who so confidently tell us that the soul always actually thinks, I would they would also tell us what those ideas are that are in the soul of a child before or just at the union with the body, before it hath received any by sensation. The dreams of sleeping men are, as I take it, all made up of the waking man's ideas, though for the most part oddly put together. It is strange, if the soul has ideas of its own that it derived not from sensation or reflection (as it must have, if it thought before it received any impression from the body), that it should never in its private thinking (so private, that the man himself perceives it not) retain any of them the very moment it wakes out of them, and then make the man glad with new discoveries. Who can find it reasonable that the soul should in its retirement, during sleep, have so many hours' thoughts, and yet never light on any of those ideas it borrowed not from sensation or reflection, or at least preserve the memory of none but such which, being occasioned from the body, must needs be less natural to a spirit? It is strange that the soul should never once in a man's whole life recall over any of its pure, native thoughts, and those ideas it had before it borrowed anything from the body; never bring into the waking man's view any other ideas but what have a tang of the cask, and manifestly derive their original from that union. If it always thinks, and so had ideas before it was united, or before it received any from the body, it is not to be supposed but that during sleep it recollects its native ideas; and during that retirement from communicating with the body, whilst it thinks by itself, the ideas it is busied about should be, sometimes at least, those more natural and congenial ones which it had in itself, underived from the body, or its own operations about them; which since the waking man never remembers, we must from this hypothesis conclude, either that the soul remembers something that the man does not, or else that memory belongs only to such ideas as are derived from the body, or the mind's operations about them.

18. *How knows any one that the soul always thinks? For if it be not a self-evident proposition, it needs proof.*—I would be

glad also to learn from these men, who so confidently pronounce that the human soul, or, which is all one, that a man always thinks, how they come to know it; nay, how they come to know that they themselves think, when they themselves do not perceive it? This, I am afraid, is to be sure without proofs, and to know without perceiving. It is, I suspect, a confused notion taken up to serve an hypothesis; and none of those clear truths that either their own evidence forces us to admit, or common experience makes it impudence to deny. For the most that can be said of it is, that it is possible the soul may always think, but not always retain it in memory; and I say, it is as possible that the soul may not always think, and much more probable that it should sometimes not think, than that it should often think, and that a long while together, and not be conscious to itself, the next moment after, that it had thought.

19. *That a man should be busy in thinking, and yet not retain it the next moment, very improbable.*—To suppose the soul to think, and the man not to perceive it, is, as has been said, to make two persons in one man; and if one considers well these men's way of speaking, one should be led into a suspicion that they do so. For they who tell us that the soul always thinks, do never, that I remember, say, that a man always thinks. Can the soul think, and not the man? or a man think, and not be conscious of it? This perhaps would be suspected of jargon in others. If they say, "The man thinks always, but is not always conscious of it," they may as well say, his body is extended without having parts. For it is altogether as intelligible to say, that a body is extended without parts, as that anything thinks without being conscious of it, or perceiving that it does so. They who talk thus may, with as much reason, if it be necessary to their hypothesis, say, that a man is always hungry, but that he does not always feel it: whereas hunger consists in that very sensation, as thinking consists in being conscious that one thinks. If they say, that a man is always conscious to himself of thinking, I ask how they know it? Consciousness is the perception of what passes

in a man's own mind. Can another man perceive that I am conscious of anything, when I perceive it not myself? No man's knowledge here can go beyond his experience. Wake a man out of a sound sleep, and ask him what he was that moment thinking on. If he himself be conscious of nothing he then thought on, he must be a notable diviner of thoughts that can assure him that he was thinking: may he not with more reason assure him he was not asleep? This is something beyond philosophy; and it cannot be less than revelation that discovers to another thoughts in my mind when I can find none there myself: and they must needs have a penetrating sight who can certainly see that I think, when I cannot perceive it myself, and when I declare that I do not; and yet can see that dogs or elephants do not think, when they give all the demonstration of it imaginable, except only telling us that they do so. This some may suspect to be a step beyond the Rosicrucians; it seeming easier to make one's self invisible to others than to make another's thoughts visible to me, which are not visible to himself. But it is but defining the soul to be a substance that always thinks, and the business is done. If such definition be of any authority, I know not what it can serve for, but to make many men suspect that they have no souls at all, since they find a good part of their lives pass away without thinking. For no definitions that I know, no suppositions of any sect, are of force enough to destroy constant experience; and perhaps it is the affectation of knowing beyond what we perceive that makes so much useless dispute and noise in the world.

20. *No ideas but from sensation or reflection evident, if we observe children.*—I see no reason therefore to believe that the soul thinks before the senses have furnished it with ideas to think on; and as those are increased and retained, so it comes by exercise to improve its faculty of thinking in the several parts of it; as well as afterwards, by compounding those ideas and reflecting on its own operations, it increases its stock, as well as facility in remembering, imagining, reasoning, and other modes of thinking.

21. He that will suffer himself to be informed by observation and experience, and not make his own hypothesis the rule of nature, will find few signs of a soul accustomed to much thinking in a new-born child, and much fewer of any reasoning at all. And yet it is hard to imagine, that the rational soul should think so much and not reason at all. And he that will consider that infants newly come into the world spend the greatest part of their time in sleep, and are seldom awake, but when either hunger calls for the teat, or some pain (the most importunate of all sensations), or some other violent impression on the body, forces the mind to perceive and attend to it:—he, I say, who considers this will, perhaps, find reason to imagine, that a fœtus in the mother's womb differs not much from the state of a vegetable; but passes the greatest part of its time without perception or thought, doing very little but sleep in a place where it needs not seek for food, and is surrounded with liquor always equally soft, and near of the same temper; where the eyes have no light, and the ears so shut up are not very susceptible of sounds; and where there is little or no variety or change of objects to move the senses.

22. Follow a child from its birth, and observe the alterations that time makes, and you shall find, as the mind by the senses comes more and more to be furnished with ideas, it comes to be more and more awake, thinks more the more it has matter to think on. After some time it begins to know the objects which, being most familiar with it, have made lasting impressions. Thus it comes by degrees to know the persons it daily converses with, and distinguish them from strangers; which are instances and effects of its coming to retain and distinguish the ideas the senses convey to it: and so we may observe how the mind, by degrees, improves in these, and advances to the exercise of those other faculties of enlarging, compounding, and abstracting its ideas, and of reasoning about them, and reflecting upon all these; of which I shall have occasion to speak more hereafter.

23. If it shall be demanded, then, when a man begins to

have any ideas? I think the true answer is, When he first has any sensation. For since there appear not to be any ideas in the mind before the senses have conveyed any in, I conceive that ideas in the understanding are coeval with sensation; which is such an impression or motion made in some part of the body as produces some perception in the understanding. It is about these impressions made on our senses by outward objects that the mind seems first to employ itself in such operations as we call " perception, remembering, consideration, reasoning," &c.

24. *The original of all our knowledge.*—In time the mind comes to reflect on its own operations about the ideas got by sensation, and thereby stores itself with a new set of ideas, which I call "ideas of reflection." These are the impressions that are made on our senses by outward objects, that are extrinsical to the mind; and its own operations, proceeding from powers intrinsical and proper to itself, which, when reflected on by itself, become also objects of its contemplation, are, as I have said, the original of all knowledge. Thus the first capacity of human intellect is, that the mind is fitted to receive the impressions made on it, either through the senses by outward objects, or by its own operations when it reflects on them. This is the first step a man makes towards the discovery of anything, and the groundwork whereon to build all those notions which ever he shall have naturally in this world. All those sublime thoughts which tower above the clouds, and reach as high as heaven itself, take their rise and footing here: in all that great extent wherein the mind wanders in those remote speculations it may seem to be elevated with, it stirs not one jot beyond those ideas which sense or reflection have offered for its contemplation.

25. *In the reception of simple ideas, the understanding is for the most part passive.*—In this part the understanding is merely passive; and whether or no it will have these beginnings, and, as it were, materials of knowledge, is not in its own power. For the objects of our senses do many of them obtrude their particular ideas upon our minds, whether we

will or no; and the operations of our minds will not let us be without at least some obscure notions of them. No man can be wholly ignorant of what he does when he thinks. These simple ideas, when offered to the mind, the understanding can no more refuse to have, nor alter when they are imprinted, nor blot them out and make new ones itself, than a mirror can refuse, alter, or obliterate the images or ideas which the objects set before it do therein produce. As the bodies that surround us do diversely affect our organs, the mind is forced to receive the impressions, and cannot avoid the perception of those ideas that are annexed to them.

NOTES.

A. Locke's Metaphysical System considered Historically and Critically.

The course which I propose to adopt in this note is to divide the subject into three heads, viz.,—first, a precise statement of Locke's system; secondly, a chronological view of the different systems which mark the epochs of philosophical history; and lastly, a *résumé* of the arguments by which Locke's system has been assailed.

1°. *A Statement of Locke's System.*—"We have nothing in our minds which did not come in one of these two ways," viz., either by sensation or by reflection. Sensation is the state of being impressed by the qualities of objects exterior to ourselves, such impressions being followed by certain *ideas* in the mind; and the perception or consciousness of these ideas by the understanding constitutes a knowledge of them. Reflection is the act of directing our attention upon the operations of our minds about the ideas produced by sensation; and the result of thus reflecting is, that *ideas* of these operations (thinking, doubting, reasoning, willing, &c.) are formed in the mind. It is by our understanding perceiving these ideas, that we become conscious of, or know them. Since, therefore, the knowledge acquired by sensation depends entirely upon our experience of an outer world, and since that acquired by reflection depends upon previous sensation; it follows that we can have no knowledge or ideas whatever until they are provided by sensible experience of some sort.

Now, the fundamental and distinguishing features of every system of philosophy are the doctrines which it advocates relative to, first, the origin of our knowledge, and, secondly, the manner in which we perceive or become conscious of the existence of an outer world. These points, it will be seen, are, in Locke's system, resolved as follows :—1. Our knowledge is all adventitious and acquired ; 2. Our understanding perceives only *ideas*, and not the objects themselves which originate them.

Such is Locke's system, as explicitly stated in his essay; but he can be shown (*vide* note to preceding selection) to have implicitly surrendered that portion of it which refers to the origin of our knowledge. This apparent contradiction is owing to his misconception of the Cartesian doctrine of innate ideas.

2°. *A Chronological View of the principal Philosophical Systems which have existed.*—In stating these, I shall merely give such portions of the various doctrines as bear upon the two fundamental points which I have mentioned, viz., the origin of knowledge, and the perception of an outer world.

a. The Greek metaphysicians prior to Plato mainly directed their speculations to the question of existence, rather than of knowledge; and, consequently, for our present purpose, they may be passed over.

b. Plato :—*Origin of Knowledge.* There can be no fact of knowledge unless the mind or intellect contributes something to it in addition to what is provided by experience. *Mode of Perception.* His doctrine is doubtful; the most probable opinion being that he considered the objects of perception to be ideas consisting of a modification of the mind itself, and called into existence by the senses being impressed by an outer world.

c. Aristotle :—*Origin of Knowledge.* There is a faculty (Intellect) in the mind which contains various primary facts or principles, these being required by the thinking faculty (Reason) in order to arrive at valid and consequential results. *Mode of Perception.* The outer world is viewed immediately and directly by the understanding, there being no intervening *ideas.*

d. Epicurus and Democritus :—*Origin of Knowledge.* The soul is material; and when movements take place in it, either from within or from without, it thinks. *Mode of Perception.* Little images or pellicles are continually being thrown off from the surfaces of bodies, and, by striking the soul, cause themselves to be perceived.

e. The Peripatetics of the Middle Ages; the Schoolmen :— *Origin of Knowledge.* In addition to what we gain by experience, we have certain innate principles—*innate*, that is to say, in the sense of being latent in the intellect until sense affords an occasion of their manifestation. *Mode of Perception.* Certain existences, neither material nor immaterial, and termed *intentional* or *sensible species,* are continually emitted by objects of the outer world, and proceed to our senses. These species, when affecting any particular sense, are termed *species impressæ;* and when felt, as it were, by the sense, the ideas thus formed constitute *species expressæ.* When the operations of sense are thus completed, the active intellect steps in, and examining the *sensible species*, proceeds to construct from its own immaterial substance certain *intelligible* species, and transmits them as *species intelligibiles impressæ*, to the passive intellect. Arrived there, and being perceived, they become *species intelligibiles expressæ*, or, in other words, knowledge. This, of course, is but a faint shadowing of the mediæval philosophy, and can but ill portray its shifting phases. It will, however, serve as an illustrative sample of the doctrines then current.

f. Descartes:—*Origin of Knowledge.* The same doctrine as that held by the Schoolmen. (See, also, note to preceding selection.) *Mode of Perception.* Exterior objects produce, through the organs of sense, certain impressions in the brain. The mind, however, cannot perceive or be conscious of anything else but mind; and therefore, the Deity, whenever an impression is made upon the brain, excites a corresponding thought in the mind; and whenever a thought occurs to the mind, He produces an equivalent motion in the body. This is the famous doctrine of Divine Assistance, or of Occasional Causes, which Malebranche expanded into the Vision of all things in God; his theory holding that the perceptions which the Deity excites in us, as before explained, are directed upon the ideas of God himself.

g. Locke:—See above.

h. Leibnitz and Wolf:—*Origin of Knowledge.* Their doctrine is similar to that held by the Schoolmen and Descartes. *Mode of Perception.* God, before uniting souls and bodies, knew all the movements and modifications of which each body would be susceptible, and all thoughts which would occur to each soul. He then assorted the souls and bodies, uniting them so that every soul should have a body whose movements would correspond to its own thoughts. Accordingly, "the soul and body are like two clocks accurately regulated, which point to the same hour and minute, although the spring which gives motion to the one is not the spring which gives motion to the other." Such is the doctrine of Pre-established Harmony.

i. Berkeley:—*Origin of Knowledge.* It is derived partly from beliefs co-existent with the mind, and partly from occasional thoughts produced by the Deity. *Mode of Perception.* The common account of his doctrine is that he denied the existence of any outer, material world, and held that what we perceive is merely a succession of ideas implanted in our minds by God. There are, however, reasons for believing that he maintained the immediate object of perception to be the material universe, conjoined inseparably with some modification of the mind.

k. Hume:—*Origin of Knowledge.* It is all derived from experience, no portion being innate. *Mode of Perception.* We perceive nothing but ideas, corresponding to which no realities exist, whether of body or of mind.

l. Reid:—*Origin of Knowledge.* Our minds themselves supply some principles and facts, experience the rest. *Mode of Perception.* Nothing intervenes between the real outer world and our perception of it. *Ideas* are entirely discarded, even for the faculties of memory and imagination.

m. Kant:—*Origin of Knowledge.* Partly from the mind, and partly from experience. *Mode of Perception.* We perceive nothing but modifications of our own minds; of these alone can we be conscious; and of an outer, material world we are ignorant.

n. Schelling:—*Origin of Knowledge.* The mind is divided into intellect and reason; of these, the former knows by experience, the latter by native supplies. *Mode of Perception.* The intellect perceives merely the phenomena of mind; the reason its own self, this being identical with the Deity.

Such are the principal theories which have been held with reference to the fundamental points of philosophy; and before quitting this portion of the subject, it will be well to say a word respecting the nomenclature of such systems, this having frequently given rise to serious misconceptions, in consequence of the principles employed not being properly discriminated.

Names, then, are given to systems as considered from three points of view, viz., as regarding, first, their doctrines with reference to the source of our knowledge; secondly, their theories of perception; and thirdly, their opinions respecting the nature of ourselves and the universe. The principal classes under these three heads are—

A. Sensualists, who derive all knowledge from experience; and Rationalists, who admit that the mind furnishes some knowledge from its own stores.

B. Those (Realists) who hold an *immediate* perception of outer objects; and those holding a *mediate* perception, this class comprising what are known as Cosmothetic Idealists.

C. Materialists, who doubt the existence of a spiritual mind; Idealists, who recognise nothing but mind and its ideas; Nihilists, who deny that either mind or body exists; and Absolutists, who view mind as identical with the Deity.

3°. *A Résumé of the Arguments by which Locke's Essay has been assailed.*—In accordance with the principles already laid down, the arguments here recapitulated will be confined to the questions of native knowledge, and the manner of perception.

A. *Native Knowledge.*—Truths are of two kinds, necessary and contingent. Experience may, indeed, show us that winter always succeeds summer, and that two and two always make four; but yet the understanding recognises a difference between these truths over and above that which our senses declare. Thus, that two and two should make four is a truth necessary and inseparable from the very idea of things; whereas that winter should succeed summer is by no means an inevitable fact, as, under certain circumstances, a perpetual winter or summer might easily occur.

Whence, then, comes the knowledge that these truths are *necessary*, since experience cannot impart it? Obviously, from the intellect itself; and therefore such knowledge, at least, must be held to be innate.

This distinction between necessary and contingent knowledge, which underlies the whole fabric of modern philosophy, we owe to the genius of Leibnitz. That celebrated metaphysician, in his "Nouveaux Essais sur l'Entendement Humain," a work written in refutation of Locke's essay, first explicitly enounced the doctrine that *necessity* is the criterion of all truth which is native to the mind; and this is justly considered as the brightest discovery in philosophy since the days of Plato and Aristotle. The following passage from his "Nouveaux Essais" very clearly points out the distinction which I have mentioned:—"All the examples which confirm a general truth, how numerous soever, would not suffice to establish the universal necessity of this same truth; for it does not follow that what has hitherto occurred will always occur in future. If Locke had sufficiently considered the difference between truths which are necessary or demonstrative, and those which we infer from induction alone, he would have perceived that necessary truths could only be proved from principles which command our assent by their *intuitive evidence*, inasmuch as our senses can inform us only of what is, not of what must necessarily be."

B. *Mode of Perception.*—Locke, it will be remembered, was a cosmothetic idealist—that is to say, he maintained that the only objects of perception are *ideas* in the mind. On this point his principal opponents were Berkeley, Hume, and Reid; but their methods of procedure were very different, for the two former accepted his doctrine of ideas, while the latter rejected it. Accordingly, the statement that Berkeley and Hume were Locke's *opponents* may seem somewhat paradoxical; for, by accepting his principles, it is evident that they agreed with him: the fact is, however, that, while desirous of befriending him, they unwittingly made a shipwreck of his doctrine of perception. This was done by reasoning it out to its ultimate consequences; from whence it appears that cosmothetic idealism must lead to scepticism. The arguments are too extensive to be given here, but their general drift may be thus stated:—Our only objects of knowledge are ideas, these being neither matter nor mind. Accordingly, as we are conscious of nothing else, we certainly cannot be entitled to assume the existence of anything besides ideas; therefore we cannot *assume* either mind or body to exist. Neither can such an existence be *proved* from the mere fact of our perceiving *ideas;* and since neither assumption nor proof can take place, we are not able to believe that there is any such thing as body or soul. Here, virtually, we have a *reductio ad absurdum* of Locke's doctrine.

Reid and the Scottish school proceed upon higher grounds, thus:—Our mental consciousness is the grand criterion of philosophy; and all the facts which it presents must be assumed to be perfectly true, as, if consciousness itself were mendacious, we could be certain of nothing. But, as is agreed to by all philosophers, in every act of external perception we are conscious of ourselves as existing and perceiving, and of an outer material object as existing and perceived: we are conscious of a self and a not-self, of an *ego* and a *non-ego*. Therefore, we must believe in the existence of ourselves and a material world; and therefore the hypothesis of a representative perception (*i. e.*, a perception by means of *ideas*) is false, as subverting those facts of consciousness which in the outset were admitted to be true.

B. Is the mind always in a state of conscious activity?

This question Locke, it will be observed, answers in the negative; and the only fact upon which he grounds his reply is that of sleep. Furthermore, the only phenomenon connected with sleep to which he appeals for confirmation of his opinion is our frequent inability to remember that we have been dreaming; and, accordingly, his argument resolves itself into this:—"Since it has not been proved that we do dream without a remembrance of our visions; and since it is certain that we frequently awake without any memory of having dreamt; it follows that the assertion of our always dreaming during sleep is a mere arbitrary assumption, and, as such, is inadmissible."

But here Locke argued from an insufficient examination of the facts; for recent investigations have conclusively shown that his first premiss is unfounded—that is to say, the fact of our minds being consciously active during sleep, without any memory of such a state being retained upon awakening, has been established beyond the possibility of a doubt. Thus, a person, when sleeping, is often observed to be occupied with the ideas which possess his mind, this being shown by his talking about them, and in other ways; yet if he be awakened in the midst of such mental activity, or if he be suffered to wake of himself, it frequently happens that in either case no remembrance of any vision is retained. So much for ordinary sleep: but if we refer to the evidence of somnambulism, the fact of which we are speaking is still more unmistakeable. Indeed, the question in hand is decided by the very existence of somnambulism, the essential feature of this state being that the events of mental activity which occur are never remembered. And yet, during the somnambulic crisis, the mind is usually far more active than when the body is awake. For instance:—"The patient has recollections of what he has wholly forgotten. He speaks languages of which, when awake, he remembers not a word. If he use a vulgar dialect when out of this state, in it he employs only a correct and elegant phraseology. The imagination, the sense of propriety, and the faculty of reasoning, are all, in general, exalted."

It is certain, then, that during sleep and somnambulism the mind remains consciously active, without any necessity existing for a remembrance of its thoughts; this not merely refuting the argument of Locke regarding sleep, but, by analogy, leading us to infer that in cases of insensibility and trance the same conditions obtain; so that our most probable conclusion can only be that the mind thinks always.

Such is a sketch of the argument from induction with reference to this question; but it may also be treated in an *a priori* manner. This Locke has, in a measure, done, by founding on his denial of innate notions, and on his doctrine of personal identity. The former of these grounds has been already discussed; the latter will be found more explicitly set forth in the next selection. As regards the *a priori* reasons for maintaining the *affirmative* of the question, the principle upon which they are based is the impossibility of being conscious of mind without thought; and the conclusion to which the deduction leads is that mind cannot exist without thinking, that is, without being consciously active.*

OF IDENTITY AND DIVERSITY.

1. *Wherein identity consists.*—Another occasion the mind often takes of comparing is the very being of things, when, considering anything as existing at any determined time and place, we compare it with itself existing at another time, and thereon form the ideas of identity and diversity. When we see anything to be in any place in any instant of time, we are sure (be it what it will) that it is that very thing, and not another, which at that same time exists in another place, how like and undistinguishable soever it may be in all other respects: and in this consists identity, when the ideas it is attributed to vary not at all from what they were that moment wherein we consider their former existence, and to which we compare the present. For we never finding, nor conceiving it possible, that two things of the same kind should exist in the same place at the same time, we rightly conclude that whatever exists anywhere at any time excludes

* For a brilliant example of pure *a priori* reasoning as regards the science of Knowledge and Being, see the late Professor Ferrier's "Institutes of Metaphysic."—ED.

all of the same kind, and is there itself alone. When therefore we demand whether anything be the same or no? it refers always to something that existed such a time in such a place, which it was certain at that instant was the same with itself and no other: from whence it follows, that one thing cannot have two beginnings of existence, nor two things one beginning, it being impossible for two things of the same kind to be or exist in the same instant, in the very same place, or one and the same thing in different places. That therefore that had one beginning, is the same thing; and that which had a different beginning in time and place from that, is not the same, but diverse. That which has made the difficulty about this relation has been the little care and attention used in having precise notions of the things to which it is attributed.

2. *Identity of substances. Identity of modes.**—We have the ideas but of three sorts of substances: 1. God. 2. Finite intelligences. 3. Bodies. First. God is without beginning, eternal, unalterable, and everywhere; and therefore concerning his identity there can be no doubt. Secondly. Finite spirits having had each its determinate time and place of beginning to exist, the relation to that time and place will always determine to each of them its identity as long as it exists. Thirdly. The same will hold of every particle of matter, to which no addition or subtraction of matter being made, it is the same. For though these three sorts of substances, as we term them, do not exclude one another out of the same place, yet we cannot conceive but that they must necessarily each of them exclude any of the same kind out of the same place; or else the notions and names of "identity and diversity" would be in vain, and there could be no such distinction of substances, or anything else, one from another. For example: Could two bodies be in the same place at the same time, then those two parcels of matter must be one and the same, take them great or little; nay, all bodies must be

---

* *Modes* are complex ideas of properties and affections of substances; things which exist not by themselves, but as inhering in some other beings. Thus, "triangle," "gratitude," "murder," "a dozen," "beauty," &c., are *modes.*—ED.

one and the same. For by the same reason that two particles of matter may be in one place, all bodies may be in one place; which, when it can be supposed, takes away the distinction of identity and diversity, of one and more, and renders it ridiculous. But, it being a contradiction that two or more should be one, identity and diversity are relations and ways of comparing well-founded, and of use to the understanding. All other things being but modes or relations ultimately terminated in substances, the identity and diversity of each particular existence of them too will be by the same way determined: only as to things whose existence is in succession, such as are the actions of finite beings, *v. g.*, motion and thought, both which consist in a continued train of succession, concerning their diversity there can be no question; because, each perishing the moment it begins, they cannot exist in different times, or in different places, as permanent beings can at different times exist in distant places; and therefore no motion or thought, considered as at different times, can be the same, each part thereof having a different beginning of existence.

3. *Principium individuationis.**—From what has been said, it is easy to discover, what is so much inquired after, the *principium individuationis;* and that, it is plain, is existence itself, which determines a being of any sort to a particular time and place incommunicable to two beings of the same kind. This, though it seems easier to conceive in simple substances or modes, yet, when reflected on, is not more difficult in compounded ones, if care be taken to what it is applied; *v. g.*, let us suppose an atom—*i. e.*, a continued body under one immutable superficies, existing in a determined time and place; it is evident that, considered in any instant of its existence, it is in that instant the same with itself. For, being at that instant what it is and nothing else, it is the same, and so must continue as long as its existence is continued—for so long it will be the same and no other. In like

---

* The principle of individuation—*i. e.* that which confers individuality upon any object.—Ed.

manner, if two or more atoms be joined together into the same mass, every one of those atoms will be the same, by the foregoing rule: and whilst they exist united together, the mass, consisting of the same atoms, must be the same mass, or the same body, let the parts be ever so differently jumbled; but if one of these atoms be taken away, or one new one added, it is no longer the same mass, or the same body. In the state of living creatures, their identity depends not on a mass of the same particles, but on something else. For in them the variation of great parcels of matter alters not the identity; an oak, growing from a plant to a great tree, and then lopped, is still the same oak; and a colt, grown up to a horse, sometimes fat, sometimes lean, is all the while the same horse—though, in both these cases, there may be a manifest change of the parts; so that truly they are not either of them the same masses of matter, though there be truly one of them the same oak, and the other the same horse. The reason whereof is, that, in these two cases of a mass of matter and a living body, identity is not applied to the same thing.

4. *Identity of vegetables.* — We must therefore consider wherein an oak differs from a mass of matter; and that seems to me to be in this: That the one is only the cohesion of particles of matter anyhow united; the other such a disposition of them as constitutes the parts of an oak, and such an organisation of those parts as is fit to receive and distribute nourishment, so as to continue and frame the wood, bark, and leaves, &c., of an oak, in which consists the vegetable life. That being then one plant, which has such an organisation of parts in one coherent body, partaking of one common life, it continues to be the same plant as long as it partakes of the same life, though that life be communicated to new particles of matter vitally united to the living plant in a like continued organisation, conformable to that sort of plants. For this organisation being at any one instant in any one collection of matter, is in that particular concrete distinguished from all other, and is that individual life which, existing constantly from that moment both forwards and backwards, in the same

continuity of insensibly succeeding parts united to the living body of the plant, has that identity which makes the same plant, and all the parts of it, parts of the same plant, during all the time that they exist united in that continued organisation, which is fit to convey that common life to all the parts so united.

5. *Identity of animals.*—The case is not so much different in brutes, but that any one may hence see what makes an animal, and continues it the same. Something we have like this in machines, and may serve to illustrate it. For example: what is a watch? It is plain that it is nothing but a fit organisation or construction of parts to a certain end, which, when a sufficient force is added to it, it is capable to attain. If we would suppose this machine one continued body, all whose organised parts were repaired, increased, or diminished, by a constant addition or separation of insensible parts, with one common life, we should have something very much like the body of an animal, with this difference—that in an animal the fitness of the organisation, and the motion wherein life consists, begin together, the motion coming from within; but in machines, the force coming sensibly from without, is often away when the organ is in order, and well fitted to receive it.

6. *Identity of man.*—This also shows wherein the identity of the same man consists; viz., in nothing but a participation of the same continued life by constantly fleeting particles of matter, in succession vitally united to the same organised body. He that shall place the identity of man in anything else but, like that of other animals, in one fitly organised body, taken in any one instant, and from thence continued under one organisation of life in several successively fleeting particles of matter united to it, will find it hard to make an embryo, one of years, mad, and sober, the same man, by any supposition that will not make it possible for Seth, Ismael, Socrates, Pilate, St. Austin, and Cæsar Borgia, to be the same man. For if the identity of soul alone makes the same man, and there be nothing in the nature of matter why the

same individual spirit may not be united to different bodies, it will be possible that those men living in distant ages, and of different tempers, may have been the same man: which way of speaking must be from a very strange use of the word "man," applied to an idea out of which body and shape is excluded: and that way of speaking would agree yet worse with the notions of those philosophers who allow of transmigration, and are of opinion that the souls of men may, for their miscarriages, be detruded into the bodies of beasts, as fit habitations, with organs suited to the satisfaction of their brutal inclinations. But yet, I think, nobody, could he be sure that the soul of Heliogabalus were in one of his hogs, would yet say that hog were a man or Heliogabalus.

7. *Identity suited to the idea.*—It is not therefore unity of substance that comprehends all sorts of identity, or will determine it in every case; but, to conceive and judge of it aright, we must consider what idea the word it is applied to stands for; it being one thing to be the same substance, another the same man, and a third the same person, if "person, man, and substance," are three names standing for three different ideas; for such as is the idea belonging to that name, such must be the identity; which, if it had been a little more carefully attended to, would possibly have prevented a great deal of that confusion which often occurs about this matter, with no small seeming difficulties, especially concerning personal identity, which therefore we shall in the next place a little consider.

8. *Same man.*—An animal is a living organised body; and consequently the same animal, as we have observed, is the same continued life communicated to different particles of matter, as they happen successively to be united to that organised living body. And, whatever is talked of other definitions, ingenious observation puts it past doubt, that the idea in our minds, of which the sound "man" in our mouths is the sign, is nothing else but of an animal of such a certain form; since I think I may be confident, that whoever should see a creature of his own shape and make, though it had no

OF IDENTITY AND DIVERSITY.

more reason all its life than a cat or a parrot, would call him still a "man;" or whoever should hear a cat or a parrot discourse, reason, and philosophise, would call or think it nothing but a cat or a parrot; and say, the one was a dull irrational man, and the other a very intelligent rational parrot. A relation we have in an author of great note, is sufficient to countenance the supposition of a rational parrot. His words are :—

" I had a mind to know from Prince Maurice's own mouth the account of a common, but much credited story, that I had heard so often from many others of an old parrot he had in Brazil, during his government there, that spoke, and asked and answered common questions like a reasonable creature; so that those of his train there generally concluded it to be witchery or possession; and one of his chaplains who lived long afterwards in Holland, would never from that time endure a parrot, but said they all had a devil in them. I had heard many particulars of this story, and assevered by people hard to be discredited, which made me ask Prince Maurice what there was of it. He said, with his usual plainness and dryness in talk, there was something true, but a great deal false, of what had been reported. I desired to know of him what there was of the first? He told me short and coldly, that he had heard of such an old parrot when he came to Brazil; and though he believed nothing of it, and it was a good way off, yet he had so much curiosity as to send for it: that it was a very great and a very old one; and when it came first into the room where the prince was, with a great many Dutchmen about him, it said presently, 'What a company of white men are here?' They asked it what he thought that man was, pointing at the prince! It answered, 'Some general or other.' When they brought it close to him, he asked it, *D'où venez-vous?* It answered, *De Marinnan.* The prince,—*A qui estes vous?* The parrot,—*A un Portugais.* Prince,—*Que fais-tu là?* Parrot,—*Je garde les poules.* The prince laughed, and said, *Vous gardez les poules?* The parrot answered,—*Ouy, moy, et je sçay bien faire;* and made the chuck four or five times that people use to make to chickens when they call them.* I set down the words of this worthy dialogue in French, just as Prince Maurice said them to me. I asked him in what language the parrot spoke? and he said, In Brazilian. I asked whether he understood Brazilian? He said, No: but he had taken care to have two interpreters by him, the one a Dutchman that spoke Brazilian, and the other a Brazilian that spoke Dutch; that he asked them separately and privately, and both of them agreed in telling him just the same thing that the parrot said. I could not but tell this odd story, because it is so much out of the way, and from the first hand, and what may pass for a good one; for I dare say this prince, at least, believed himself in all he told me, having ever passed for a very honest and pious man. I leave it to naturalists to reason, and to other men to believe, as they please upon it; however, it is not perhaps amiss to relieve or enliven a busy scene sometimes with such digressions, whether to the purpose or no."†

I have taken care that the reader should have the story at large in the author's own words, because he seems to me not to have thought it incredible; for it cannot be imagined that so able a man as he, who had sufficiency enough to warrant all the testimonies he gives of himself, should take so much pains, in a place where it had nothing to do, to pin so close— not only on a man whom he mentions as his friend, but on a prince, in whom he acknowledges very great honesty and piety—a story which, if he himself thought incredible, he could not but also think ridiculous. The prince, it is plain, who vouches this story, and our author, who relates it from him, both of them call this talker "a parrot;" and I ask any one else, who thinks such a story fit to be told, whether if this parrot, and all of its kind, had always talked, as we have

---

* "'Whence come ye?' It answered, 'From Marinnan.' The PRINCE,— 'To whom do you belong?' The PARROT,—'To a Portuguese.' PRINCE,— 'What do you there?' PARROT,—'I look after the chickens.' The PRINCE laughed, and said, '*You* look after the chickens?' The PARROT answered, 'Yes, I, and I know well enough how to do it.'"

† "Memoirs of what passed in Christendom, from 1672 to 1679," p. $\frac{57}{562}$.

a prince's word for it, as this one did; whether, I say, they would not have passed for a race of rational animals; but yet whether for all that, that would have been allowed to be men, and not parrots? For I presume it is not the idea of a thinking or rational being alone that makes the idea of a man in most people's sense, but of a body, so and so shaped, joined to it; and if that be the idea of a man, the same successive body not shifted all at once must, as well as the same immaterial spirit, go to the making of the same man.

9. *Personal identity.*—This being premised, to find wherein personal identity consists, we must consider what " person " stands for; which, I think, is a thinking intelligent being, that has reason and reflection, and can consider itself as itself, the same thinking thing, in different times and places; which it does only by that consciousness which is inseparable from thinking, and it seems to me essential to it: it being impossible for any one to perceive, without perceiving that he does perceive. When we see, hear, smell, taste, feel, meditate, or will anything, we know that we do so. Thus it is always as to our present sensations and perceptions: and by this every one is to himself that which he calls " self; " it not being considered, in this case, whether the same self be considered in the same or diverse substances. For since consciousness always accompanies thinking, and it is that that makes every one to be what he calls " self," and thereby distinguishes himself from all other thinking things; in this alone consists personal identity, *i. e.* the sameness of a rational being: and as far as this consciousness can be extended backwards to any past action or thought, so far reaches the identity of that person; it is the same self now it was then; and it is by the same self with this present one that now reflects on it, that that action was done.

10. *Consciousness makes personal identity.*—But it is farther inquired, whether it be the same identical substance? This, few would think they had reason to doubt of, if these perceptions, with their consciousness, always remained present in the mind, whereby the same thinking thing would be always

consciously present, and, as would be thought, evidently the same to itself. But that which seems to make the difficulty is this, that this consciousness being interrupted always by forgetfulness, there being no moment of our lives wherein we have the whole train of all our past actions before our eyes in one view; but even the best memories losing the sight of one part whilst they are viewing another; and we sometimes, and that the greatest part of our lives, not reflecting on our past selves, being intent on our present thoughts, and, in sound sleep, having no thoughts at all, or, at least, none with that consciousness which remarks our waking thoughts: I say, in all these cases, our consciousness being interrupted, and we losing the sight of our past selves, doubts are raised whether we are the same thinking thing, *i.e.* the same substance, or no? which, however reasonable or unreasonable, concerns not personal identity at all: the question being, what makes the same person? and not, whether it be the same identical substance which always thinks in the same person? which in this case matters not at all; different substances, by the same consciousness (where they do partake in it), being united into one person, as well as different bodies by the same life are united into one animal, whose identity is preserved, in that change of substances, by the unity of one continued life. For it being the same consciousness that makes a man be himself to himself, personal identity depends on that only, whether it be annexed only to one individual substance, or can be continued in a succession of several substances. For as far as any intelligent being can repeat the idea of any past action with the same consciousness it had of it at first, and with the same consciousness it has of any present action; so far it is the same personal self. For it is by the consciousness it has of its present thoughts and actions that it is self to itself now, and so will be the same self, as far as the same consciousness can extend to actions past or to come; and would be by distance of time, or change of substance, no more two persons than a man be two men, by wearing other clothes to-day than he did yesterday, with a long or short sleep between: the same consciousness uniting those distant actions into the same person, whatever substances contributed to their production.

11. *Personal identity in change of substances.*—That this is so, we have some kind of evidence in our very bodies, all whose particles—whilst vitally united to this same thinking conscious self, so that we feel when they are touched, and are affected by and conscious of good or harm that happens to them—are a part of ourselves—*i. e.* of our thinking conscious self. Thus the limbs of his body is to every one a part of himself: he sympathises and is concerned for them. Cut off an hand and thereby separate it from that consciousness he had of its heat, cold, and other affections, and it is then no longer a part of that which is himself, any more than the remotest part of matter. Thus we see the substance, whereof personal self consisted at one time, may be varied at another, without the change of personal identity; there being no question about the same person, though the limbs, which but now were a part of it, be cut off.

12. *Whether in the change of thinking substances.*—But the question is, Whether, if the same substance which thinks be changed, it can be the same person, or remaining the same, it can be different persons?

And to this I answer, First, this can be no question at all to those who place thought in a purely material, animal constitution, void of an immaterial substance. For, whether their supposition be true or no, it is plain they conceive personal identity preserved in something else than identity of substance; as animal identity is preserved in identity of life, and not of substance. And, therefore, those who place thinking in an immaterial substance only, before they can come to deal with these men, must show why personal identity cannot be preserved in the change of immaterial substances, or variety of particular immaterial substances, as well as animal identity is preserved in the change of material substances, or variety of particular bodies: unless they will say, it is one immaterial spirit that makes the same life in brutes, as it is one immaterial spirit that makes the same person in men, which the

Cartesians at least will not admit, for fear of making brutes thinking things too.

13. But next, as to the first part of the question, Whether, if the same thinking substance (supposing immaterial substances only to think) be changed, it can be the same person? I answer, That cannot be resolved but by those who know what kind of substances they are that do think, and whether the consciousness of past actions can be transferred from one thinking substance to another. I grant, were the same consciousness the same individual action, it could not; but it being but a present representation of a past action, why it may not be possible that *that* may be represented to the mind to have been *which* really never was, will remain to be shown. And, therefore, how far the consciousness of past actions is annexed to any individual agent, so that another cannot possibly have it, will be hard for us to determine, till we know what kind of action it is that cannot be done without a reflex act of perception accompanying it, and how performed by thinking substances who cannot think without being conscious of it. But that which we call "the same consciousness" not being the same individual act, why one intellectual substance may not have represented to it as done by itself what it never did, and was perhaps done by some other agent; why, I say, such a representation may not possibly be without reality of matter of fact, as well as several representations in dreams are, which yet, whilst dreaming, we take for true, will be difficult to conclude from the nature of things. And that it never is so, will by us (till we have clearer views of the nature of thinking substances) be best resolved into the goodness of God, who, as far as the happiness or misery of any of his sensible creatures is concerned in it, will not by a fatal error of theirs transfer from one to another that consciousness which draws reward or punishment with it. How far this may be an argument against those who would place thinking in a system of fleeting animal spirits, I leave to be considered. But yet, to return to the question before us, it must be allowed, that if the same consciousness (which, as has been shown, is

quite a different thing from the same numerical figure or motion in body) can be transferred from one thinking substance to another, it will be possible that two thinking substances may make but one person. For the same consciousness being preserved, whether in the same or different substances, the personal identity is preserved.

14. As to the second part of the question, Whether, the same immaterial substance remaining, there may be two distinct persons? Which question seems to me to be built on this, Whether the same immaterial being, being conscious of the actions of its past duration, may be wholly stripped of all the consciousness of its past existence, and lose it beyond the power of ever retrieving again; and so, as it were, beginning a new account from a new period, have a consciousness that cannot reach beyond this new state? All those who hold pre-existence are evidently of this mind, since they allow the soul to have no remaining consciousness of what it did in that pre-existent state, either wholly separate from body, or informing any other body; and if they should not, it is plain experience would be against them. So that personal identity reaching no farther than consciousness reaches, a pre-existent spirit not having continued so many ages in a state of silence, must needs make different persons. Suppose a Christian, Platonist, or Pythagorean, should, upon God's having ended all his works of creation the seventh day, think his soul hath existed ever since; and should imagine it has revolved in several human bodies, as I once met with one who was persuaded his had been the soul of Socrates: (how reasonably I will not dispute: this I know, that in the post he filled, which was no inconsiderable one, he passed for a very rational man; and the press has shown that he wanted not parts or learning:) would any one say, that he, being not conscious of any of Socrates's actions or thoughts, could be the same person with Socrates? Let any one reflect upon himself, and conclude, that he has in himself an immaterial spirit, which is that which thinks in him, and in the constant change of his body keeps him the same; and is that which he calls himself: let

him also suppose it to be the same soul that was in Nestor or Thersites, at the siege of Troy (for souls being, as far as we know anything of them, in their nature indifferent to any parcel of matter, the supposition has no apparent absurdity in it), which it may have been as well as it is now the soul of any other man: but he now having no consciousness of any of the actions either of Nestor or Thersites, does or can he conceive himself the same person with either of them? Can he be concerned in either of their actions? attribute them to himself, or think them his own, more than the actions of any other man that ever existed? So that this consciousness not reaching to any of the actions of either of those men, he is no more one self with either of them, than if the soul or immaterial spirit that now informs him had been created and began to exist when it began to inform his present body, though it were ever so true that the same spirit that informed Nestor's or Thersites's body were numerically the same that now informs his. For this would no more make him the same person with Nestor, than if some of the particles of matter that were once a part of Nestor, were now a part of this man; the same immaterial substance, without the same consciousness, no more making the same person by being united to any body, than the same particle of matter, without consciousness, united to any body, makes the same person. But let him once find himself conscious of any of the actions of Nestor, he then finds himself the same person with Nestor.

15. And thus we may be able, without any difficulty, to conceive the same person at the resurrection, though in a body not exactly in make or parts the same which he had here, the same consciousness going along with the soul that inhabits it. But yet the soul alone, in the change of bodies, would scarce to any one, but to him that makes the soul the man, be enough to make the same man. For, should the soul of a prince, carrying with it the consciousness of the prince's past life, enter and inform the body of a cobbler, as soon as deserted by his own soul, every one sees he would be the same person with the prince, accountable only for the prince's actions:

but who would say it was the same man? The body too goes to the making of the man, and would, I guess, to everybody determine the man in this case, wherein the soul, with all its princely thoughts about it, would not make another man; but he would be the same cobbler to every one besides himself. I know that, in the ordinary way of speaking, the same person and the same man stand for one and the same thing. And, indeed, every one will always have a liberty to speak as he pleases, and to apply what articulate sounds to what ideas he thinks fit, and change them as often as he pleases. But yet, when we will inquire what makes the same spirit, man, or person, we must fix the ideas of spirit, man, or person in our minds; and having resolved with ourselves what we mean by them, it will not be hard to determine in either of them, or the like, when it is the same and when not.

16. *Consciousness makes the same person.*—But though the same immaterial substance or soul does not alone, wherever it be, and in whatsoever state, make the same man; yet it is plain, consciousness, as far as ever it can be extended, should it be to ages past, unites existences and actions, very remote in time, into the same person, as well as it does the existence and actions of the immediately preceding moment: so that whatever has the consciousness of present and past actions is the same person to whom they both belong. Had I the same consciousness that I saw the ark and Noah's flood, as that I saw an overflowing of the Thames last winter, or as that I write now, I could no more doubt that I who write this now, that saw the Thames overflowed last winter, and that viewed the flood at the general deluge, was the same self, place that self in what substance you please, than that I who write this am the same myself now whilst I write (whether I consist of all the same substance, material or immaterial, or no) that I was yesterday. For, as to this point of being the same self, it matters not whether this present self be made up of the same or other substances, I being as much concerned and as justly accountable for any action [that] was done a thousand

years since, and appropriated to me now by this self-consciousness, as I am for what I did the last moment.

17. *Self depends on consciousness.*—Self is that conscious thinking thing (whatever substance made up of, whether spiritual or material, simple or compounded, it matters not) which is sensible or conscious of pleasure and pain, capable of happiness or misery, and so is concerned for itself, as far as that consciousness extends. Thus every one finds, that whilst comprehended under that consciousness, the little finger is as much a part of itself as what is most so. Upon separation of this little finger, should this consciousness go along with the little finger, and leave the rest of the body, it is evident the little finger would be the person, the same person; and self then would have nothing to do with the rest of the body. As in this case it is the consciousness that goes along with the substance, when one part is separate from another, which makes the same person, and constitutes this inseparable self, so it is in reference to substances remote in time. That with which the consciousness of this present thinking thing can join itself makes the same person, and is one self with it, and with nothing else; and so attributes to itself and owns all the actions of that thing as its own, as far as that consciousness reaches, and no farther; as every one who reflects will perceive.

18. *Object of reward and punishment.*—In this personal identity is founded all the right and justice of reward and punishment; happiness and misery being that for which every one is concerned for himself, not mattering what becomes of any substance not joined to or affected with that consciousness. For as it is evident in the instance I gave but now, if the consciousness went along with the little finger when it was cut off, that would be the same self which was concerned for the whole body yesterday, as making a part of itself, whose actions then it cannot but admit as its own now. Though, if the same body should still live, and immediately from the separation of the little finger have its own peculiar consciousness, whereof the little finger knew nothing, it

would not at all be concerned for it, as a part of itself, or could own any of its actions, or have any of them imputed to him.

19. This may show us wherein personal identity consists, not in the identity of substance, but, as I have said, in the identity of consciousness; wherein if Socrates and the present mayor of Queenborough agree, they are the same person. If the same Socrates waking and sleeping do not partake of the same consciousness, Socrates waking and sleeping is not the same person; and to punish Socrates waking for what sleeping Socrates thought, and waking Socrates was never conscious of, would be no more of right than to punish one twin for what his brother-twin did, whereof he knew nothing, because their outsides were so like that they could not be distinguished; for such twins have been seen.

20. But yet possibly it will still be objected, "Suppose I wholly lose the memory of some parts of my life, beyond the possibility of retrieving them, so that perhaps I shall never be conscious of them again; yet am I not the same person that did those actions, had those thoughts, that I was once conscious of, though I have now forgot them?" To which I answer, That we must here take notice what the word "I" is applied to; which, in this case, is the man only. And the same man being presumed to be the same person, "I" is easily here supposed to stand also for the same person. But if it be possible for the same man to have distinct incommunicable consciousnesses at different times, it is past doubt the same man would at different times make different persons; which, we see, is the sense of mankind in the solemnest declaration of their opinions, human laws not punishing the mad man for the sober man's actions, nor the sober man for what the mad man did, thereby making them two persons; which is somewhat explained by our way of speaking in English, when we say, "Such an one is not himself, or is beside himself;" in which phrases it is insinuated as if those who now or, at least, first used them, thought that self was changed, the self-same person was no longer in that man.

21. *Difference between identity of man and person.*—But yet it is hard to conceive that Socrates, the same individual man, should be two persons. To help us a little in this, we must consider what is meant by Socrates, or the same individual man.

First, It must be either the same individual, immaterial, thinking substance; in short, the same numerical soul, and nothing else.

Secondly, Or the same animal, without any regard to an immaterial soul.

Thirdly, Or the same immaterial spirit united to the same animal.

Now, take which of these suppositions you please, it is impossible to make personal identity to consist in anything but consciousness, or reach any farther than that does.

For by the first of them, it must be allowed possible that a man born of different women, and in distant times, may be the same man. A way of speaking which, whoever admits, must allow it possible for the same man to be two distinct persons, as any two that have lived in different ages, without the knowledge of one another's thoughts.

By the second and third, Socrates in this life and after it cannot be the same man any way but by the same consciousness; and so, making human identity to consist in the same thing wherein we place personal identity, there will be no difficulty to allow the same man to be the same person. But then they who place human identity in consciousness only, and not in something else, must consider how they will make the infant Socrates the same man with Socrates after the resurrection. But whatsoever to some men makes a man, and consequently the same individual man, wherein perhaps few are agreed, personal identity can by us be placed in nothing but consciousness (which is that alone which makes what we call "self"), without involving us in great absurdities.

22. "But is not a man drunk and sober the same person? Why else is he punished for the fact he commits when drunk, though he be never afterwards conscious of it?" Just as

much the same person as a man that walks and does other things in his sleep is the same person, and is answerable for any mischief he shall do in it. Human laws punish both with a justice suitable to their way of knowledge; because in these cases they cannot distinguish certainly what is real, what counterfeit; and so the ignorance in drunkenness or sleep is not admitted as a plea. For, though punishment be annexed to personality, and personality to consciousness, and the drunkard perhaps be not conscious of what he did; yet human judicatures justly punish him, because the fact is proved against him, but want of consciousness cannot be proved for him. But in the great day, wherein the secrets of all hearts shall be laid open, it may be reasonable to think, no one shall be made to answer for what he knows nothing of; but shall receive his doom, his conscience accusing or excusing.

23. *Consciousness alone makes self.*—Nothing but consciousness can unite remote existences into the same person; the identity of substance will not do it. For, whatever substance there is, however framed, without consciousness there is no person: and a carcass may be a person, as well as any sort of substance be so without consciousness.

Could we suppose two distinct incommunicable consciousnesses acting the same body, the one constantly by day, the other by night; and, on the other side, the same consciousness acting by intervals two distinct bodies: I ask, in the first case, whether the day and the night man would not be two as distinct persons as Socrates and Plato? and whether, in the second case, there would not be one person in two distinct bodies, as much as one man is the same in two distinct clothings? Nor is it at all material to say, that this same and this distinct consciousness, in the cases above mentioned, is owing to the same and distinct immaterial substances, bringing it with them to those bodies; which, whether true or no, alters not the case: since it is evident the personal identity would equally be determined by the consciousness, whether that consciousness were annexed to some individual immaterial substance or no. For, granting that the thinking substance in man must be necessarily supposed immaterial, it is evident that immaterial thinking thing may sometimes part with its past consciousness, and be restored to it again, as appears in the forgetfulness men often have of their past actions, and the mind many times recovers the memory of a past consciousness which it had lost for twenty years together. Make these intervals of memory and forgetfulness to take their turns regularly by day and night, and you have two persons with the same immaterial spirit, as much as in the former instance two persons with the same body. So that self is not determined by identity or diversity of substance, which it cannot be sure of, but only by identity of consciousness.

24. Indeed, it may conceive the substance whereof it is now made up to have existed formerly, united in the same conscious being: but, consciousness removed, that substance is no more itself, or makes no more a part of it, than any other substance; as is evident in the instance we have already given of a limb cut off, of whose heat, or cold, or other affections, having no longer any consciousness, it is no more of a man's self than any other matter of the universe. In like manner it will be in reference to any immaterial substance, which is void of that consciousness whereby I am myself to myself: if there be any part of its existence which I cannot upon recollection join with that present consciousness whereby I am now myself, it is in that part of its existence no more myself than any other immaterial being. For, whatsoever any substance has thought or done, which I cannot recollect, and by my consciousness make my own thought and action, it will no more belong to me, whether a part of me thought or did it, than if it had been thought or done by any other immaterial being anywhere existing.

25. I agree, the more probable opinion is, that this consciousness is annexed to, and the affection of, one individual immaterial substance.

But let men, according to their diverse hypotheses, resolve

of that as they please. This every intelligent being, sensible of happiness or misery, must grant, that there is something that is himself that he is concerned for, and would have happy; that this self has existed in a continued duration more than one instant, and therefore it is possible may exist, as it has done, months and years to come, without any certain bounds to be set to its duration; and may be the same self, by the same consciousness, continued on for the future. And thus, by this consciousness, he finds himself to be the same self which did such or such an action some years since, by which he comes to be happy or miserable now. In all which account of self, the same numerical substance is not considered as making the same self: but the same continued consciousness, in which several substances may have been united, and again separated from it, which, whilst they continued in a vital union with that wherein this consciousness then resided, made a part of that same self. Thus any part of our bodies vitally united to that which is conscious in us, makes a part of ourselves; but upon separation from the vital union by which that consciousness is communicated, that which a moment since was part of ourselves is now no more so than a part of another man's self is a part of me, and it is not impossible but in a little time may become a real part of another person. And so we have the same numerical substance become a part of two different persons, and the same person preserved under the change of various substances. Could we suppose any spirit wholly stripped of all its memory or consciousness of past actions, as we find our minds always are of a great part of ours, and sometimes of them all, the union or separation of such a spiritual substance would make no variation of personal identity, any more than that of any particle of matter does. Any substance vitally united to the present thinking being, is a part of that very same self which now is: anything united to it by a consciousness of former actions, makes also a part of the same self, which is the same both then and now.

26. "*Person,*" *a forensic term.*—"Person," as I take it, is the name for this self. Wherever a man finds what he calls

"himself," there, I think, another may say is the same person. It is a forensic term appropriating actions and their merit; and so belongs only to intelligent agents capable of a law, and happiness and misery. This personality extends itself beyond present existence to what is past, only by consciousness; whereby it becomes concerned and accountable, owns and imputes to itself past actions, just upon the same ground and for the same reason that it does the present. All which is founded in a concern for happiness, the unavoidable concomitant of consciousness; that which is conscious of pleasure and pain desiring that *that* self that is conscious should be happy. And therefore whatever past actions it cannot reconcile or appropriate to that present self by consciousness, it can be no more concerned in, than if they had never been done: and to receive pleasure or pain, *i.e.*, reward or punishment, on the account of any such action, is all one as to be made happy or miserable in its first being without any demerit at all. For, supposing a man punished now for what he had done in another life, whereof he could be made to have no consciousness at all, what difference is there between that punishment and being created miserable? And therefore, conformable to this, the apostle tells us, that at the great day, when every one shall "receive according to his doings, the secrets of all hearts shall be laid open." The sentence shall be justified by the consciousness all persons shall have that they themselves, in what bodies soever they appear, or what substances soever that consciousness adheres to, are the same that committed those actions, and deserve that punishment for them.

27. I am apt enough to think I have, in treating of this subject, made some suppositions that will look strange to some readers, and possibly they are so in themselves. But yet, I think, they are such as are pardonable in this ignorance we are in of the nature of that thinking thing that is in us, and which we look on as ourselves. Did we know what it was, or how it was tied to a certain system of fleeting animal spirits; or whether it could or could not perform its opera-

tions of thinking and memory out of a body organised as ours is; and whether it has pleased God that no one such spirit shall ever be united to any but one such body, upon the right constitution of whose organs its memory should depend, we might see the absurdity of some of those suppositions I have made. But taking, as we ordinarily now do (in the dark concerning these matters), the soul of a man for an immaterial substance, independent from matter, and indifferent alike to it all, there can from the nature of things be no absurdity at all to suppose that the same soul may, at different times, be united to different bodies, and with them make up, for that time, one man: as well as we suppose a part of a sheep's body yesterday should be a part of a man's body to-morrow, and in that union make a vital part of Melibæus himself, as well as it did of his ram.

28. *The difficulty from ill use of names.*—To conclude: Whatever substance begins to exist, it must, during its existence, necessarily be the same: whatever compositions of substances begin to exist, during the union of those substances the concrete must be the same: whatever mode begins to exist, during its existence it is the same: and so if the composition be of distinct substances and different modes, the same rule holds. Whereby it will appear, that the difficulty or obscurity that has been about this matter rather rises from the names ill used, than from any obscurity in things themselves. For whatever makes the specific idea to which the name is applied, if that idea be steadily kept to, the distinction of anything into the same and diverse will easily be conceived, and there can arise no doubt about it.

29. *Continued existence makes identity.*—For supposing a rational spirit be the idea of a man, it is easy to know what is the same man; viz., the same spirit, whether separate or in a body, will be the same man. Supposing a rational spirit vitally united to a body of a certain conformation of parts to make a man, whilst that rational spirit, with that vital conformation of parts, though continued in a fleeting successive body, remains, it will be the same man. But if to any one

the idea of a man be but the vital union of parts in a certain shape, as long as that vital union and shape remains, in a concrete no otherwise the same but by a continued succession of fleeting particles, it will be the same man. For, whatever be the composition whereof the complex idea is made, whenever existence makes it one particular thing under any denomination, the same existence, continued, preserves it the same individual under the same denomination.

NOTE ON PERSONAL IDENTITY.

The above chapter is remarkable for the great precision and perspicuity with which Locke has distinguished the various kinds of identity from each other; and for the striking manner in which he has shown that our idea of personal identity depends entirely upon consciousness, this including the operation of memory. In fact, it may well be doubted whether any subsequent dissertation upon the same subject has ever exhibited an equal array of lucid exposition or cogent reasoning; and it is certain that he who wishes to obtain an eminent example of easy and elegant discussion, cannot do better than study the foregoing chapter from Locke's Essay.

But while the general features and style of this chapter are thus competent to excite our admiration, it cannot be denied that Locke's doctrine, as far as *personal* identity is concerned, was doomed to a speedy and complete refutation. Bishop Butler, the author of the justly celebrated "Analogy," is generally credited with having been Locke's earliest opponent upon this point; but such an opinion is without any foundation, as to John Serjeant, a contemporary of Locke, belongs the merit of priority in redarguing the faulty doctrine. The other principal iconoclasts are Buffier, Dr. Reid, and M. Cousin.

In briefly discussing the merit of Locke's theory, I shall consider,—first, the manner in which he gives two contradictory accounts of personal identity; secondly, the contradictions involved in his doctrine; and, thirdly, the causes which led to his adopting an erroneous conclusion.

In the first place, then, it is to be remarked that Locke gives two accounts of personal identity; one implicitly, the other explicitly. This latter, which he openly adheres to, and which is universally associated with his name, consists in the opinion that it is consciousness alone which makes, which constitutes, personal identity. That is to say, if a man perform some action and afterwards lose all consciousness of it, he is no longer the same person that did it. So far all is clear: we have a precise, if a paradoxical statement of that in which personal identity consists. But let us now proceed to Locke's implied doctrine, which is to be found in the account that he gives separately of "person" and "identity." A "person" we find (§ 9) to be a "thinking intelligent being;" and "identity," or individuality, is (§ § 3, 29) neither more nor less than "continued existence." Accordingly, putting these together, we find that personal identity is merely the continued existence of a thinking intelligent being. Thus, we arrive at something very different from the first statement: on the one hand we have existence, on the other, consciousness; in one place the continuity of being, in another a phenomenon of the mind. I am not aware of this discrepancy having been ever pointed out, although it is of great importance, as showing that Locke had in reality more correct notions upon the subject than the shackles of his system would allow him to develop.

In the second place it will only be necessary to exhibit *some* of the contradictions which inhere in the explicit doctrine of Locke; and for this purpose I shall select the two following:—

a. Since it is consciousness alone that makes personal identity, it follows that those who existed during times of which we retain no memory or consciousness, were not the same persons as ourselves. But I have no remembrance of my birth; therefore, I am not the same person as him who was then born; *i.e.* I never commenced to exist, or was born.

b. "Suppose a brave officer to have been flogged, when a boy at school, for robbing an orchard, to have taken a standard from the enemy in his first campaign, and to have been made a general in advanced life: suppose also, which must be admitted to be possible, that, when he took the standard he was conscious of his having been flogged at school; and that when made a general he was conscious of his taking the standard, but had absolutely lost the consciousness of his flogging.

"These things being supposed, it follows from Mr. Locke's doctrine, that he who was flogged at school is the same person who took the standard; and that he who took the standard, is the same person who was made a general. Whence it follows, if there be any truth in logic, that the general is the same person with him who was flogged at school. But the general's consciousness does not reach so far back as his flogging; therefore, according to Mr. Locke's doctrine, he is not the person who was flogged. Therefore the general is, and at the same time is not, the same person with him who was flogged at school." *

Thirdly.—The cause of Locke's maintaining so erroneous a doctrine is to be found in his theory as to the origin of all our knowledge. This, it will be remembered, is that every idea arises either from sensation or reflection; and, consequently, since it was

* Reid's "Essays on the Intellectual Powers," III. chap. vi.

evident that sensation could never produce the idea of personal identity, Locke resorted to reflection as its source. Reflection, however, can give nothing beyond the idea of consciousness, and this Locke was, therefore, compelled to regard as constituting the idea of personal identity.

Now, throwing aside for a moment all theory as to the source of our knowledge, let us consider what it is that the idea of personal identity really comprehends, with especial reference to consciousness and memory. First, it is evident that, as thought or consciousness is merely a phenomenon of mind, it requires mind to exist before it can take place; and we can have no idea of thought unless as inhering in a thinking subject. Secondly, memory, in like manner, requires the continued existence of mind, as an essential condition of its occurrence; and no idea of memory can be had, unless a duration of mental being forms part of it. From this it follows that a consciousness of remembrance necessitates, as a condition, the idea of the same existence continued from past to present time; or, in other words, whenever I am conscious of remembering anything, I am also conscious of myself as now existing, and of myself as having existed at some prior period. But what is this second idea of which I am conscious? It is the idea of *personal identity;* which is thus seen to be *distinct from* both consciousness and memory. At the same time it is sufficiently obvious that we could have no idea of personal identity until *after* perceiving a present consciousness, and remembering a past one. Thus the ideas of consciousness and memory, with reference to that of personal identity, are first in order of time, but last in order of reason; while the idea of personal identity is first in order of reason, but last in order of time. These modes of succession are respectively termed the logical and chronological orders.*

We are thus in a position to fully understand the nature of Locke's error upon this subject. It was twofold, and consisted, first, in confining his attention exclusively to the chronological order of ideas; and, secondly, in confusing the occasion of an idea with the idea itself. The former of these phases was produced by his reference of all knowledge to experience; this leading him merely to remark the various times at which the faculties of sensation and reflection were enabled to present the mind with ideas. The latter was a consequence of his assuming that the mind has no innate knowledge; this compelling him to treat the ideas of consciousness and personal identity as the same.

In the above discussion we have another illustration of the true doctrine respecting innate ideas, to which reference has been made in former notes. It will be perceived that the key to the whole question is the recognition of a distinction between the logical and chronological orders of ideas and their originals—between actual existence and the knowledge of existence.

* Compare Cousin's *Cours de Philosophie,* 2_e, tom. iii., xviii.

OF THE IMPERFECTION OF WORDS.

1. *Words are used for recording and communicating our thoughts.*—From what has been said in the foregoing chapters, it is easy to perceive what imperfection there is in language, and how the very nature of words makes it almost unavoidable for many of them to be doubtful and uncertain in their significations. To examine the perfection or imperfection of words, it is necessary first to consider their use and end: for as they are more or less fitted to attain that, so they are more or less perfect. We have, in the former part of this discourse, often, upon occasion, mentioned a double use of words.

First, One for the recording of our own thoughts.

Secondly, The other for the communicating of our thoughts to others.

2. *Any words will serve for recording.*—As to the first of these, for the recording our own thoughts for the help of our own memories, whereby, as it were, we talk to ourselves, any words will serve the turn. For, since sounds are voluntary and indifferent signs of any ideas, a man may use what words he pleases to signify his own ideas to himself: and there will be no imperfection in them if he constantly use the same sign for the same idea: for then he cannot fail of having his meaning understood, wherein consists the right use and perfection of language.

3. *Communication by words civil or philosophical.*—Secondly, As to communication of words, that too has a double use.

I. Civil.

II. Philosophical.

First, By their civil use, I mean such a communication of thoughts and ideas by words as may serve for the upholding common conversation and commerce about the ordinary affairs and conveniences of civil life, in the societies of men one amongst another.

Secondly, By the philosophical use of words, I mean such an use of them as may serve to convey the precise notions of things, and to express, in general propositions, certain and undoubted truths which the mind may rest upon and be satisfied with, in its search after true knowledge. These two uses are very distinct; and a great deal less exactness will serve in the one than in the other, as we shall see in what follows.

4. *The imperfection of words is the doubtfulness of their signification.*—The chief end of language in communication being to be understood, words serve not well for that end, neither in civil nor philosophical discourse, when any word does not excite in the hearer the same idea which it stands for in the mind of the speaker. Now since sounds have no natural connexion with our ideas, but have all their signification from the arbitrary imposition of men, the doubtfulness and uncertainty of their signification, which is the imperfection we here are speaking of, has its cause more in the ideas they stand for, than in any incapacity there is in one sound more than in another to signify any idea: for in that regard they are all equally perfect.

That then which makes doubtfulness and uncertainty in the signification of some more than other words, is the difference of ideas they stand for.

5. *Causes of their imperfection.*—Words having naturally no signification, the idea which each stands for must be learned and retained by those who would exchange thoughts and hold intelligible discourse with others, in any language. But this is hardest to be done, where,

First, The ideas they stand for are very complex, and made up of a great number of ideas put together.

Secondly, Where the ideas they stand for have no certain connection in nature; and so no settled standard anywhere in nature existing to rectify and adjust them by.

Thirdly, Where the signification of the word is referred to a standard, which standard is not easy to be known.

Fourthly, Where the signification of the word, and the real essence* of the thing, are not exactly the same.

These are difficulties that attend the signification of several

---

* By "real essence" Locke understands that peculiar internal constitution of a thing upon which its perceptible qualities are dependent.—Ed.

words that are intelligible. Those which are not intelligible at all, such as names standing for any simple ideas, which another has not organs or faculties to attain, as the names of colours to a blind man, or sounds to a deaf man, need not here be mentioned.

In all these cases we shall find an imperfection in words; which I shall more at large explain, in their particular application to our several sorts of ideas: for if we examine them, we shall find that the names of mixed modes* are most liable to doubtfulness and imperfection for the two first of these reasons; and the names of substances chiefly for the two latter.

6. *The names of mixed modes doubtful.*—First, The names of mixed modes are many of them liable to great uncertainty and obscurity in their signification.

First, Because the ideas they stand for are so complex.— I. Because of that great composition these complex ideas are often made up of. To make words serviceable to the end of communication, it is necessary (as has been said) that they excite in the hearer exactly the same idea they stand for in the mind of the speaker. Without this, men fill one another's heads with noise and sounds; but convey not thereby their thoughts, and lay not before one another their ideas, which is the end of discourse and language. But when a word stands for a very complex idea, that is compounded and decompounded, it is not easy for men to form and retain that idea so exactly as to make the name in common use stand for the same precise idea without any the least variation. Hence it comes to pass, that men's names of very compound ideas, such as for the most part are moral words, have seldom, in two different men, the same precise signification; since one man's complex idea seldom agrees with another's, and often differs from his own, from that which he had yesterday, or will have to-morrow.

7. *Secondly, Because they have no standards.*—II. Because the names of mixed modes, for the most part, want standards

* "*Mixed* modes" are ideas compounded of several simple notions or modes.—ED.

in nature, whereby men may rectify and adjust their significations; therefore they are very various and doubtful. They are assemblages of ideas put together at the pleasure of the mind, pursuing its own ends of discourse, and suited to its own notions, whereby it designs not to copy anything really existing, but to denominate and rank things, as they come to agree with those archetypes or forms it has made. He that first brought the word "sham," "wheedle," or "banter" in use, put together, as he thought fit, those ideas he made it stand for: and as it is with any new names of modes that are now brought into any language, so was it with the old ones when they were first made use of. Names, therefore, that stand for collections of ideas which the mind makes at pleasure, must needs be of doubtful signification when such collections are nowhere to be found constantly united in nature, nor any patterns to be shown whereby men may adjust them. What the word "murder" or "sacrilege," &c., signifies, can never be known from things themselves. There be many of the parts of those complex ideas which are not visible in the action itself: the intention of the mind, or the relation of holy things, which make a part of murder or sacrilege, have no necessary connection with the outward and visible action of him that commits either: and the pulling the trigger of the gun, with which the murder is committed, and is all the action that perhaps is visible, has no natural connection with those other ideas that make up the complex one, named "murder." They have their union and combination only from the understanding which unites them under one name: but, uniting them without any rule or pattern, it cannot be but that the signification of the name that stands for such voluntary collections should be often various in the minds of different men, who have scarce any standing rule to regulate themselves and their notions by any such arbitrary ideas.

8. *Propriety not a sufficient remedy.*—It is true, common use, that is, the rule of propriety, may be supposed here to afford some aid to settle the signification of language; and it cannot be denied but that in some measure it does. Common

use regulates the meaning of words pretty well for common conversation; but nobody having an authority to establish the precise signification of words, nor determine to what ideas any one shall annex them, common use is not sufficient to adjust them to philosophical discourses; there being scarce any name, of any very complex idea (to say nothing of others), which in common use has not a great latitude, and which, keeping within the bounds of propriety, may not be made the sign of far different ideas. Besides, the rule and measure of propriety itself being nowhere established, it is often matter of dispute whether this or that way of using a word be propriety of speech or no. From all which it is evident, that the names of such kind of very complex ideas are naturally liable to this imperfection, to be of doubtful and uncertain signification; and, even in men that have a mind to understand one another, do not always stand for the same idea in speaker and hearer. Though the names "glory" and "gratitude" be the same in every man's mouth through a whole country, yet the complex collective idea, which every one thinks on or intends by that name, is apparently very different in men using the same language.

9. *The way of learning these names contributes also to their doubtfulness.*—The way also wherein the names of mixed modes are ordinarily learned, does not a little contribute to the doubtfulness of their signification. For if we will observe how children learn languages, we shall find that, to make them understand what the names of simple ideas or substances stand for, people ordinarily show them the thing whereof they would have the idea; and then repeat to them the name that stands for it, as, "white, sweet, milk, sugar, cat, dog." But as for mixed modes, especially the most material of them, moral words, the sounds are usually learned first; and then, to know what complex ideas they stand for, they are either beholden to the explication of others, or (which happens for the most part) are left to their own observation and industry; which being little laid out in the search of the true and precise meaning of names, these moral words are, in most men's

mouths, little more than bare sounds; or, when they have any, it is for the most part but a very loose and undetermined, and consequently obscure and confused, signification. And even those themselves, who have with more attention settled their notions, do yet hardly avoid the inconvenience to have them stand for complex ideas, different from those which other, even intelligent and studious, men make them the signs of. Where shall one find any either controversial debate or familiar discourse concerning "honour, faith, grace, religion, church," &c., wherein it is not easy to observe the different notions men have of them? which is nothing but this, that they are not agreed in the signification of those words; nor have in their minds the same complex ideas which they make them stand for: and so all the contests that follow thereupon are only about the meaning of a sound. And hence we see that, in the interpretation of laws, whether divine or human, there is no end; comments beget comments, and explications make new matter for explications: and of limiting, distinguishing, varying the signification of these moral words, there is no end. These ideas of men's making are, by men still having the same power, multiplied *in infinitum*. Many a man, who was pretty well satisfied of the meaning of a text of Scripture, or clause in the code, at first reading, has, by consulting commentators, quite lost the sense of it, and by those elucidations given rise or increase to his doubts, and drawn obscurity upon the place. I say not this, that I think commentaries needless; but to show how uncertain the names of mixed modes naturally are, even in the mouths of those who had both the intention and the faculty of speaking as clearly as language was capable to express their thoughts.

10. *Hence unavoidable obscurity in ancient authors.*—What obscurity this has unavoidably brought upon the writings of men who have lived in remote ages and different countries, it will be needless to take notice; since the numerous volumes of learned men, employing their thoughts that way, are proofs more than enough to show what attention, study, sagacity, and reasoning are required to find out the true

meaning of ancient authors. But, there being no writings we have any great concernment to be very solicitous about the meaning of, but those that contain either truths we are required to believe or laws we are to obey, and draw inconveniences on us when we mistake or transgress, we may be less anxious about the sense of other authors; who writing but their own opinions, we are under no greater necessity to know them than they to know ours. Our good or evil depending not on their decrees, we may safely be ignorant of their notions: and therefore in the reading of them, if they do not use their words with a due clearness and perspicuity, we may lay them aside, and, without any injury done them, resolve thus with ourselves,

Si non vis intelligi, debes negligi.*

11. *Names of substances of doubtful signification.*—If the signification of the names of mixed modes are uncertain because there be no real standards existing in nature to which those ideas are referred and by which they may be adjusted, the names of substances are of a doubtful signification for a contrary reason, viz., because the ideas they stand for are supposed conformable to the reality of things, and are referred to standards made by nature. In our ideas of substances we have not the liberty, as in mixed modes, to frame what combinations we think fit to be the characteristical notes to rank and denominate things by. In these we must follow nature, suit our complex ideas to real existences, and regulate the signification of their names by the things themselves, if we will have our names to be the signs of them, and stand for them. Here, it is true, we have patterns to follow; but patterns that will make the signification of their names very uncertain: for, names must be of a very unsteady and various meaning, if the ideas they stand for be referred to standards without us, that either cannot be known at all, or can be known but imperfectly and uncertainly.

* "If you are not willing to be understood, you ought to be neglected."—ED.

12. *Names of substances referred, First, to real essences that cannot be known.*—The names of substances have, as has been showed, a double reference in their ordinary use.

First, Sometimes they are made to stand for, and so their signification is supposed to agree to, the real constitution of things from which all their properties flow, and in which they all centre. But this real constitution, or (as it is apt to be called) essence, being utterly unknown to us, any sound that is put to stand for it must be very uncertain in its application; and it will be impossible to know what things are or ought to be called "an horse," or "antimony," when those words are put for real essences that we have no ideas of at all. And therefore, in this supposition, the names of substances being referred to standards that cannot be known, their significations can never be adjusted and established by those standards.

13. *Secondly, To co-existing qualities which are known but imperfectly.*—Secondly, The simple ideas that are found to co-exist in substances being that which their names immediately signify, these, as united in the several sorts of things, are the proper standards to which their names are referred, and by which their significations may best be rectified. But neither will these archetypes so well serve to this purpose, as to leave these names without very various and uncertain significations. Because these simple ideas that co-exist, and are united in the same subject, being very numerous, and having all an equal right to go into the complex specific idea, which the specific name is to stand for, men, though they propose to themselves the very same subject to consider, yet frame very different ideas about it: and so the name they use for it unavoidably comes to have, in several men, very different significations. The simple qualities which make up the complex ideas being most of them powers, in relation to changes which they are apt to make in or receive from other bodies, are almost infinite. He that shall but observe what a great variety of alterations any one of the baser metals is apt to receive from the different application only of fire, and how much a greater number of changes any of them will receive in the hands of a chemist by the application of other bodies, will not think it strange that I count the properties of any sort of bodies not easy to be collected and completely known by the ways of inquiry which our faculties are capable of. They being therefore at least so many that no man can know the precise and definite number, they are differently discovered by different men, according to their various skill, attention, and ways of handling; who therefore cannot choose but have different ideas of the same substance, and therefore make the signification of its common name very various and uncertain. For the complex ideas of substances being made up of such simple ones as are supposed to co-exist in nature, every one has a right to put into his complex idea those qualities he has found to be united together. For though, in the substance, gold, one satisfies himself with colour and weight, yet another thinks solubility in *aqua regia** as necessary to be joined with that colour in his idea of gold, as any one does its fusibility; solubility in *aqua regia* being a quality as constantly joined with its colour and weight, as fusibility or any other: others put in its ductility, or fixedness, &c., as they have been taught by tradition or experience. Who of all these has established the right signification of the word "gold?" or who shall be the judge to determine? Each has his standard in nature which he appeals to, and with reason thinks he has the same right to put into his complex idea signified by the word "gold" those qualities which upon trial he has found united; as another, who has not so well examined, has to leave them out; or a third, who has made other trials, has to put in others. For, the union in nature of these qualities being the true ground of their union in one complex idea, who can say one of them has more reason to be put in or left out than another? From whence it will always unavoidably follow, that the complex ideas of substances, in men using the same name for them, will be very various; and so the significations of those names very uncertain.

* A mixture of nitric with hydrochloric acid.—ED.

14. Besides, there is scarce any particular thing existing, which, in some of its simple ideas, does not communicate with a greater, and in others with a less, number of particular beings: who shall determine in this case, which are those that are to make up the precise collection that is to be signified by the specific name; or can with any just authority prescribe which obvious or common qualities are to be left out, or which more secret or more particular are to be put into the signification of the name of any substance? All which together seldom or never fail to produce that various and doubtful signification in the names of substances, which causes such uncertainty, disputes, or mistakes, when we come to a philosophical use of them.

15. *With this imperfection, they may serve for civil, but not well for philosophical use.*—It is true, as to civil and common conversation, the general names of substances, regulated in their ordinary signification by some obvious qualities (as by the shape and figure in things of known seminal propagation, and in other substances for the most part by colour, joined with some other sensible qualities), do well enough to design the things men would be understood to speak of; and so they usually conceive well enough the substances meant by the word "gold" or "apple," to distinguish the one from the other. But in philosophical inquiries and debates, where general truths are to be established, and consequences drawn from positions laid down, there the precise signification of the names of substances will be found not only not to be well established, but also very hard to be so. For example: He that shall make malleableness, or a certain degree of fixedness, a part of his complex idea of gold, may make propositions concerning gold, and draw consequences from them, that will truly and clearly follow from gold taken in such a signification : but yet such as another man can never be forced to admit, nor be convinced of their truth, who makes not malleableness, or the same degree of fixedness, part of that complex idea that the name "gold," in his use of it, stands for.

16. *Instance, liquor.*—This is a natural and almost unavoid-

able imperfection in almost all the names of substances, in all languages whatsoever, which men will easily find when, once passing from confused or loose notions, they come to more strict and close inquiries. For then they will be convinced how doubtful and obscure those words are in their signification, which in ordinary use appeared very clear and determined. I was once in a meeting of very learned and ingenious physicians, where by chance there arose a question, Whether any liquor passed through the filaments of the nerves? The debate having been managed a good while, by variety of arguments on both sides, I (who had been used to suspect that the greatest part of disputes were more about the signification of words, than a real difference in the conception of things) desired, that before they went any farther on in this dispute, they would first examine and establish amongst them what the word "liquor" signified. They at first were a little surprised at the proposal; and had they been persons less ingenious, they might perhaps have taken it for a very frivolous or extravagant one: since there was no one there that thought not himself to understand very perfectly what the word "liquor" stood for; which I think, too, none of the most perplexed names of substances. However, they were pleased to comply with my motion; and, upon examination, found that the signification of that word was not so settled and certain as they had all imagined; but that each of them made it a sign of a different complex idea. This made them perceive that the main of their dispute was about the signification of that term; and that they differed very little in their opinions concerning some fluid and subtile matter passing through the conduits of the nerves, though it was not so easy to agree whether it was to be called "liquor" or no; a thing which when each considered, he thought it not worth the contending about.

17. *Instance, gold.*—How much this is the case in the greatest part of disputes that men are engaged so hotly in, I shall, perhaps, have an occasion in another place to take notice. Let us only here consider a little more exactly the

fore-mentioned instance of the word "gold," and we shall see how hard it is precisely to determine its signification. I think all agree to make it stand for a body of a certain yellow shining colour; which being the idea to which children have annexed that name, the shining yellow part of a peacock's tail is properly to them gold. Others finding fusibility joined with that yellow colour in certain parcels of matter, make of that combination a complex idea to which they give the name "gold," to denote a sort of substances; and so exclude from being gold all such yellow shining bodies as by fire will be reduced to ashes; and admit to be of that species, or to be comprehended under that name "gold," only such substances as having that shining yellow colour will by fire be reduced to fusion, and not to ashes. Another by the same reason adds the weight, which being a quality as straitly joined with that colour as its fusibility, he thinks has the same reason to be joined in its idea, and to be signified by its name: and therefore the other, made up of body of such a colour, and fusibility, to be imperfect; and so on of all the rest: wherein no one can show a reason why some of the inseparable qualities, that are always united in nature, should be put into the nominal essence,* and others left out: or why the word "gold," signifying that sort of body the ring on his finger is made of, should determine that sort rather by its colour, weight, and fusibility, than by its colour, weight, and solubility in *aqua regia:* since the dissolving it by that liquor is as inseparable from it as the fusion by fire; and they are both of them nothing but the relation which that substance has to two other bodies, which have a power to operate differently upon it. For by what right is it that fusibility comes to be a part of the essence signified by the word "gold," and solubility but a property of it? Or why is its colour part of the essence, and its malleableness but a property? That which I mean is this, that these being all but properties, depending on its real constitution, and nothing but powers either active

---

* A "nominal essence" is the abstract idea to which a general name, such as "man," "metal," "body," &c., is applied.—ED.

or passive in reference to other bodies, no one has authority to determine the signification of the word "gold" (as referred to such a body existing in nature) more to one collection of ideas to be found in that body than to another: whereby the signification of that name must unavoidably be very uncertain: since, as has been said, several people observe *several* properties in the same substance; and I think I may say, nobody *all*. And therefore we have but very imperfect descriptions of things, and words have very uncertain significations.

18. *The names of simple ideas the least doubtful.*—From what has been said it is easy to observe, what has been before remarked, viz., that the names of simple ideas are, of all others, the least liable to mistakes, and that for these reasons: First, Because the ideas they stand for, being each but one single perception, are much easier got and more clearly retained than the more complex ones; and therefore are not liable to the uncertainty which usually attends those compounded ones of substances and mixed modes, in which the precise number of simple ideas that make them up are not easily agreed, and so readily kept in mind. And, Secondly, Because they are never referred to any other essence but barely that perception they immediately signify: which reference is that which renders the significations of the names of substances naturally so perplexed, and gives occasion to so many disputes. Men that do not perversely use their words, or on purpose set themselves to cavil, seldom mistake, in any language which they are acquainted with, the use and signification of the names of simple ideas: white and sweet, yellow and bitter, carry a very obvious meaning with them, which every one precisely comprehends, or easily perceives he is ignorant of, and seeks to be informed. But what precise collection of simple ideas modesty or frugality stands for in another's use, is not so certainly known. And, however we are apt to think we well enough know what is meant by "gold" or "iron," yet the precise complex idea others make them the signs of is not so certain: and I believe it is very seldom that in speaker or hearer they stand for exactly the same collec-

tion. Which must needs produce mistakes and disputes, when they are made use of in discourses wherein men have to do with universal propositions, and would settle in their minds universal truths, and consider the consequences that follow from them.

19. *And next to them, simple modes.*—By the same rule, the names of simple modes are, next to those of simple ideas, least liable to doubt and uncertainty, especially those of figure and number, of which men have so clear and distinct ideas. Whoever, that had a mind to understand them, mistook the ordinary meaning of "seven," or "a triangle?" And in general the least compounded ideas in every kind have the least dubious names.

20. *The most doubtful are the names of very compounded mixed modes and substances.*—Mixed modes therefore, that are made up but of a few and obvious simple ideas, have usually names of no very uncertain signification. But the names of mixed modes, which comprehend a great number of simple ideas, are commonly of a very doubtful and undetermined meaning, as has been shown. The names of substances, being annexed to ideas that are neither the real essences nor exact representations of the patterns they are referred to, are liable yet to greater imperfection and uncertainty, especially when we come to a philosophical use of them.

21. *Why this imperfection charged upon words.*—The great disorder that happens in our names of substances proceeding for the most part from our want of knowledge and inability to penetrate into their real constitutions, it may probably be wondered why I charge this as an imperfection rather upon our words than understandings. This exception has so much appearance of justice, that I think myself obliged to give a reason why I have followed this method. I must confess, then, that when I first began this discourse of the understanding, and a good while after, I had not the least thought that any consideration of words was at all necessary to it. But when, having passed over the original and composition of our ideas, I began to examine the extent and certainty of our knowledge, I found it had so near a connection with

words, that unless their force and manner of signification were first well observed, there could be very little said clearly and pertinently concerning knowledge: which, being conversant about truth, had constantly to do with propositions. And though it terminated in things, yet it was for the most part so much by the intervention of words, that they seemed scarce separable from our general knowledge. At least, they interpose themselves so much between our understandings and the truth which it would contemplate and apprehend, that, like the medium through which visible objects pass, their security and disorder does not seldom cast a mist before our eyes, and impose upon our understandings. If we consider, in the fallacies men put upon themselves as well as others, and the mistakes in men's disputes and notions, how great a part is owing to words and their uncertain or mistaken significations, we shall have reason to think this no small obstacle in the way to knowledge; which I conclude we are the more carefully to be warned of, because it has been so far from being taken notice of as an inconvenience, that the arts of improving it have been made the business of men's study, and obtained the reputation of learning and subtilty, as we shall see in the following chapter. But I am apt to imagine that, were the imperfections of language, as the instrument of knowledge, more thoroughly weighed, a great many of the controversies that make such a noise in the world would of themselves cease; and the way to knowledge, and perhaps peace too, lie a great deal opener than it does.

22. *This should teach us moderation in imposing our own sense of old authors.*—Sure I am, that the signification of words, in all languages, depending very much on the thoughts, notions, and ideas of him that uses them, must unavoidably be of great uncertainty to men of the same language and country. This is so evident in the Greek authors, that he that shall peruse their writings will find, in almost every one of them, a distinct language, though the same words. But when to this natural difficulty in every country there shall be added different countries and remote ages, wherein the speakers and

writers had very different notions, tempers, customs, ornaments and figures of speech, &c., every one of which influenced the signification of their words then, though to us now they are lost and unknown, it would become us to be charitable one to another in our interpretations or misunderstanding of those ancient writings; which, though of great concernment to be understood, are liable to the unavoidable difficulties of speech, which (if we except the names of simple ideas, and some very obvious things) is not capable, without a constant defining the terms, of conveying the sense and intention of the speaker without any manner of doubt and uncertainty to the hearer. And in discourses of religion, law, and morality, as they are matters of the highest concernment, so there will be the greatest difficulty.

23. The volumes of interpreters and commentators on the Old and New Testament are but too manifest proofs of this. Though everything said in the text be infallibly true, yet the reader may be, nay, cannot choose but be, very fallible in the understanding of it. Nor is it to be wondered that the will of God, when clothed in words, should be liable to that doubt and uncertainty which unavoidably attends that sort of conveyance, when even His Son, whilst clothed in flesh, was subject to all the frailties and inconveniences of human nature, sin excepted. And we ought to magnify His goodness, that He hath spread before all the world such legible characters of His works and providence, and given all mankind so sufficient a light of reason, that they to whom this written word never came, could not (whenever they set themselves to search) either doubt of the being of a God, or of the obedience due to Him. Since, then, the precepts of natural religion are plain, and very intelligible to all mankind, and seldom come to be controverted; and other revealed truths, which are conveyed to us by books and languages, are liable to the common and natural obscurities and difficulties incident to words: methinks it would become us to be more careful and diligent in observing the former, and less magisterial, positive, and imperious in imposing our own sense and interpretations of the latter.

OF THE ABUSE OF WORDS.

1. *Abuse of words.*—Besides the imperfection that is naturally in language, and the obscurity and confusion that is so hard to be avoided in the use of words, there are several wilful faults and neglects which men are guilty of in this way of communication, whereby they render these signs less clear and distinct in their signification than naturally they need to be.

2. *First, Words without any, or without clear, ideas.*—First, In this kind, the first and most palpable abuse is, the using of words without clear and distinct ideas; or, which is worse, signs without anything signified. Of these there are two sorts:—

I. One may observe, in all languages, certain words that, if they be examined, will be found, in their first original and their appropriated use, not to stand for any clear and distinct ideas. These, for the most part, the several sects of philosophy and religion have introduced. For their authors or promoters, either affecting something singular, and out of the way of common apprehensions, or to support some strange opinions, or cover some weakness of their hypothesis, seldom fail to coin new words, and such as, when they come to be examined, may justly be called, "insignificant terms." For, having either had no determinate collection of ideas annexed to them when they were first invented, or at least such as, if well examined, will be found inconsistent, it is no wonder if afterwards, in the vulgar use of the same party, they remain empty sounds with little or no signification, amongst those who think it enough to have them often in their mouths, as the distinguishing characters of their church or school, without much troubling their heads to examine what are the precise ideas they stand for. I shall not need here to heap up instances; every one's reading and conversation will sufficiently furnish him: or if he wants to be better stored, the great mint masters of these kind of terms, I mean the schoolmen and metaphysicians (under which, I think, the disputing natural and moral philosophers of these latter ages may be comprehended), have wherewithal abundantly to content him.

3. II. Others there be who extend this abuse yet farther, who take so little care to lay by words which, in their primary notation, have scarce any clear and distinct ideas which they are annexed to, that, by an unpardonable negligence, they familiarly use words which the propriety of language has affixed to very important ideas, without any distinct meaning at all. "Wisdom, glory, grace," &c., are words frequent enough in every man's mouth; but if a great many of those who use them should be asked what they mean by them, they would be at a stand, and not know what to answer: a plain proof that, though they have learned those sounds, and have them ready at their tongues' end, yet there are no determined ideas laid up in their minds, which are to be expressed to others by them.

4. *Occasioned by learning names before the ideas they belong to.*—Men having been accustomed from their cradles to learn words which are easily got and retained, before they knew or had framed the complex ideas to which they were annexed, or which were to be found in the things they were thought to stand for, they usually continue to do so all their lives; and, without taking the pains necessary to settle in their minds determined ideas, they use their words for such unsteady and confused notions as they have, contenting themselves with the same words other people use; as if their very sound necessarily carried with it constantly the same meaning. This though men make a shift with in the ordinary occurrences of life, where they find it necessary to be understood, and therefore they make signs till they are so; yet this insignificancy in their words, when they come to reason concerning either their tenets or interest, manifestly fills their discourse with abundance of empty, unintelligible noise and jargon, especially in moral matters where the words for the most part, standing for arbitrary and numerous collections of ideas, not regularly and permanently united in nature, their

bare sounds are often only thought on, or at least very obscure and uncertain notions annexed to them. Men take the words they find in use amongst their neighbours; and that they may not seem ignorant what they stand for, use them confidently, without much troubling their heads about a certain fixed meaning; whereby, besides the ease of it, they obtain this advantage, that as in such discourses they seldom are in the right, so they are as seldom to be convinced that they are in the wrong; it being all one to go about to draw those men out of their mistakes who have no settled notions, as to dispossess a vagrant of his habitation, who has no settled abode. This I guess to be so; and every one may observe in himself and others whether it be or no.

5. *Secondly, Unsteady application of them.* — Secondly, Another great abuse of words is, inconsistency in the use of them. It is hard to find a discourse written of any subject, especially of controversy, wherein one shall not observe, if he read with attention, the same words (and those commonly the most material in the discourse, and upon which the argument turns) used sometimes for one collection of simple ideas, and sometimes for another, which is a perfect abuse of language. Words being intended for signs of my ideas, to make them known to others, not by any natural signification, but by a voluntary imposition, it is plain cheat and abuse when I make them stand sometimes for one thing and sometimes for another: the wilful doing whereof can be imputed to nothing but great folly or greater dishonesty. And a man, in his accounts with another, may, with as much fairness, make the characters of numbers stand sometimes for one and sometimes for another collection of units (*v.g.*, this character 3 stands sometimes for three, sometimes for four, and sometimes for eight), as in his discourse or reasoning, make the same words stand for different collections of simple ideas. If men should do so in their reckonings, I wonder who would have to do with them! One who would speak thus in the affairs and business of the world, and call eight sometimes seven, and sometimes nine, as best served his advantage, would presently have clapped upon him

one of the two names men constantly are disgusted with. And yet in arguings and learned contests the same sort of proceeding passes commonly for wit and learning: but to me it appears a greater dishonesty than the misplacings of counters in the casting up a debt; and the cheat the greater by how much truth is of greater concernment and value than money.

6. *Thirdly, Affected obscurity by wrong application.*—Another abuse of language is an affected obscurity, by either applying old words to new and unusual significations, or introducing new and ambiguous terms without defining either: or else putting them so together as may confound their ordinary meaning. Though the peripatetic philosophy has been most eminent in this way, yet other sects have not been wholly clear of it. There is scarce any of them that are not cumbered with some difficulties (such is the imperfection of human knowledge), which they have been fain to cover with obscurity of terms and to confound the signification of words, which, like a mist before people's eyes, might hinder their weak parts from being discovered. That "body" and "extension" in common use, stand for two distinct ideas, is plain to any one that will but reflect a little. For, were their signification precisely the same, it would be properand as intelligible to say "the body of an extension," as "the extension of a body;" and yet there are those who find it necessary to confound their signification. To this abuse, and the mischiefs of confounding the signification of words, logic and the liberal sciences, as they have been handled in the Schools, have given reputation; and the admired art of disputing hath added much to the natural imperfection of languages, whilst it has been made use of and fitted to perplex the signification of words more than to discover the knowledge and truth of things: and he that will look into that sort of learned writings, will find the words there much more obscure, uncertain, and undetermined in their meaning than they are in ordinary conversation.*

---

* In this Locke does the Schools an injustice; for the language of the mediæval philosophers is, generally speaking, characterised by great clearness and precision.—ED.

7. *Logic and dispute has much contributed to this.*—This is unavoidably to be so, where men's parts and learning are estimated by their skill in disputing. And if reputation and reward shall attend these conquests, which depend mostly on the fineness and niceties of words, it is no wonder if the wit of men so employed should perplex, involve, and subtilize the significations of sounds, so as never to want something to say in opposing or defending any question; the victory being adjudged not to him who had truth on his side, but the last word in the dispute.

8. *Calling it "subtilty."*—This, though a very useless skill, and that which I think the direct opposite to the ways of knowledge, hath yet passed hitherto under the laudable and esteemed names of "subtilty" and "acuteness;" and has had the applause of the Schools, and encouragement of one part of the learned men of the world. And no wonder since the philosophers of old (the disputing and wrangling philosophers I mean, such as Lucian wittily and with reason taxes), and the Schoolmen since, aiming at glory and esteem for their great and universal knowledge, easier a great deal to be pretended to than really acquired, found this a good expedient to cover their ignorance with a curious and inexplicable web of perplexed words, and procure to themselves the admiration of others by unintelligible terms, the apter to produce wonder because they could not be understood: whilst it appears in all history that these profound doctors were no wiser nor more useful than their neighbours,* and brought but small advantage to human life, or the societies wherein they lived: unless the coining of new words, where they produced no new things to apply them to, or the perplexing or obscuring the signification of old ones, and so bringing all things into question and dispute, were a thing profitable to the life of man, or worthy commendation and reward.

9. *This learning very little benefits society.*—For, notwithstanding these learned disputants, these all-knowing doctors,

* Their metaphysical knowledge and acumen have not yet been surpassed.—ED.

it was to the unscholastic statesman that the governments of the world owed their peace, defence, and liberties; and from the illiterate and contemned mechanic (a name of disgrace) that they received the improvements of useful arts. Nevertheless, this artificial ignorance and learned gibberish prevailed mightily in these last ages, by the interest and artifice of those who found no easier way to that pitch of authority and dominion they have attained, than by amusing the men of business and ignorant with hard words, or employing the ingenious and idle in intricate disputes about unintelligible terms, and holding them perpetually entangled in that endless labyrinth. Besides, there is no such way to gain admittance, or give defence to strange and absurd doctrines, as to guard them round about with legions of obscure, doubtful, and undefined words; which yet make these retreats more like the den of robbers, or holes of foxes, than the fortresses of fair warriors: which if it be hard to get them out of, it is not for the strength that is in them, but the briers and thorns, and the obscurity of the thickets they are beset with. For, untruth being unacceptable to the mind of man, there is no other defence left for absurdity but obscurity.

10. *But destroys the instruments of knowledge and communication.*—Thus learned ignorance, and this art of keeping even inquisitive men from true knowledge, hath been propagated in the world, and hath much perplexed whilst it pretended to inform the understanding. For we see that other well-meaning and wise men, whose education and parts had not acquired that acuteness, could intelligibly express themselves to one another, and in its plain use make a benefit of language. But though unlearned men well enough understood the words "white" and "black," &c., and had constant notions of the ideas signified by those words; yet there were philosophers found who had learning and subtilty enough to prove that snow was black; *i.e.*, to prove that white was black. Whereby they had the advantage to destroy the instruments and means of discourse, conversation, instruction, and society; whilst, with great art and subtilty, they did no more but per-

plex and confound the signification of words, and thereby render language less useful than the real defects of it had made it; a gift which the illiterate had not attained to.

11. *As useful as to confound the sound of the letters.*—These learned men did equally instruct men's understandings and profit their lives, as he who should alter the signification of known characters, and, by a subtile device of learning, far surpassing the capacity of the illiterate, dull, and vulgar, should, in his writing, show that he could put A for B, and D for E, &c., to the no small admiration and benefit of his reader; it being as senseless to put "black," which is a word agreed on to stand for one sensible idea, to put it, I say, for another or the contrary idea, *i.e.*, to call snow "black," as to put this mark, A, which is a character agreed on to stand for one modification of sound made by a certain motion of the organs of speech, for B, which is agreed on to stand for another modification of sound made by another certain motion of the organs of speech.

12. *This art has perplexed religion and justice.*—Nor hath this mischief stopped in logical niceties or curious empty speculations; it hath invaded the great concernments of human life and society, obscured and perplexed the material truths of law and divinity, brought confusion, disorder, and uncertainty into the affairs of mankind, and, if not destroyed, yet in great measure rendered useless, those two great rules, religion and justice. What have the greatest part of the comments and disputes upon the laws of God and man served for, but to make the meaning more doubtful, and perplex the sense? What has been the effect of those multiplied curious distinctions and acute niceties, but obscurity and uncertainty, leaving the words more unintelligible, and the reader more at a loss? How else comes it to pass that princes, speaking or writing to their servants, in their ordinary commands, are easily understood? speaking to their people, in their laws, are not so? And, as I remarked before, doth it not often happen that a man of an ordinary capacity very well understands a text or a law that he reads, till he consults an expositor, or

goes to counsel; who, by that time he hath done explaining them, makes the words signify either nothing at all, or what he pleases?

13. *And ought not to pass for learning.*—Whether any by-interests of these professions have occasioned this, I will not here examine; but I leave it to be considered, whether it would not be well for mankind, whose concernment it is to know things as they are and to do what they ought, and not to spend their lives in talking about them, or tossing words to and fro: whether it would not be well, I say, that the use of words were made plain and direct; and that language, which was given us for the improvement of knowledge and bond of society should not be employed to darken truth, and unsettle people's rights; to raise mists, and render unintelligible both morality and religion; or that at least, if this will happen, it should not be thought learning or knowledge to do so.

14. *Fourthly, Taking them for things.*—Fourthly, Another great abuse of words is the taking them for things. This, though it, in some degree, concerns all names in general, yet more particularly affects those of substances. To this abuse those men are most subject who confine their thoughts to any one system, and give themselves up into a firm belief of the perfection of any received hypothesis: whereby they come to be persuaded, that the terms of that sect are so suited to the nature of things that they perfectly correspond with their real existence. Who is there that has been bred up in the peripatetic philosophy, who does not think the ten names, under which are ranked the ten predicaments,* to be exactly conformable to the nature of things? Who is there of that school that is not persuaded, that "substantial forms,"† "vegetative souls," "abhorrence of a vacuum," "intentional species,"‡

---

* The "predicaments" or "categories" of the Aristotelic philosophy were the manners or modes in which all things were supposed to exist. Their enumeration is as follows:—1° Substance; 2° Quantity; 3° Quality; 4° Relation; 5° Action; 6° Passion; 7° Where; 8° When; 9° Posture; 10° Habit.—ED.

† *i. e.* The qualities of bodies, which were said to be real separate existences, occasionally conjoined to matter.—ED.

‡ *Vide* note to third selection.—ED.

&c., are something real? These words men have learned from their very entrance upon knowledge, and have found their masters and systems lay great stress upon them: and therefore they cannot quit the opinion that they are conformable to nature, and are the representations of something that really exists. The Platonists have their " soul of the world," and the Epicureans their "endeavour towards motion" in their "atoms when at rest." There is scarce any sect in philosophy has not a distinct set of terms that others understand not. But yet this gibberish, which, in the weakness of human understanding, serves so well to palliate men's ignorance and cover their errors, comes by familiar use amongst those of the same tribe to seem the most important part of language, and of all other the terms the most significant: and should aërial and ethereal vehicles* come once, by the prevalency of that doctrine, to be generally received anywhere, no doubt those terms would make impressions on men's minds, so as to establish them in the persuasion of the reality of such things, as much as peripatetic forms and intentional species have heretofore done.

15. *Instance in matter.*—How much names taken for things are apt to mislead the understanding, the attentive reading of philosophical writers would abundantly discover; and that, perhaps, in words little suspected of any such misuse. I shall instance in one only, and that a very familiar one. How many intricate disputes have there been about matter, as if there were some such thing really in nature distinct from body; as it is evident the word "matter" stands for an idea distinct from the idea of body! For, if the idea these two terms stood for were precisely the same, they might indifferently in all places be put one for another. But we see, that though it be proper to say, "There is one matter of all bodies," one cannot say, "There is one body of all matters:" we familiarly say, "One body is bigger than another;" but

---

* That is, as a means of communication between mind and matter—a doctrine not very far removed from that which now obtains as regards the existence of "ether."—Ed

it sounds harsh (and I think is never used) to say, "One matter is bigger than another." Whence comes this then? Viz., from hence, that though matter and body be not really distinct, but wherever there is the one there is the other; yet "matter" and "body" stand for two different conceptions, whereof the one is incomplete, and but a part of the other. For, "body" stands for a solid, extended, figured substance, whereof "matter" is but a partial and more confused conception, it seeming to me to be used for the substance and solidity of body, without taking in its extension and figure: and therefore it is that, speaking of matter, we speak of it always as one, because, in truth, it expressly contains nothing but the idea of a solid substance, which is everywhere the same, everywhere uniform. This being our idea of matter, we no more conceive or speak of different matters in the world, than we do of different solidities; though we both conceive and speak of different bodies, because extension and figure are capable of variation. But since solidity cannot exist without extension and figure, the taking "matter" to be the name of something really existing under that precision, has no doubt produced those obscure and unintelligible discourses and disputes which have filled the heads and books of philosophers concerning *materia prima;* which imperfection or abuse, how far it may concern a great many other general terms, I leave to be considered. This, I think, I may at least say, that we should have a great many fewer disputes in the world, if words were taken for what they are, the signs of our ideas only, and not for things themselves. For when we argue about "matter," or any the like term, we truly argue only about the idea we express by that sound, whether that precise idea agree to anything really existing in nature or no. And if men would tell what ideas they make their words stand for, there could not be half that obscurity or wrangling in the search or support of truth that there is.

16. *This makes errors lasting.*—But whatever inconvenience follows from this mistake of words, this, I am sure, that by constant and familiar use they charm men into notions far

remote from the truth of things. It would be a hard matter to persuade any one that the words which his father or schoolmaster, the parson of the parish, or such a reverend doctor used, signified nothing that really existed in nature: which, perhaps, is none of the least causes that men are so hardly drawn to quit their mistakes, even in opinions purely philosophical, and where they have no other interest but truth. For the words they have a long time been used to remaining firm in their minds, it is no wonder that the wrong notions annexed to them should not be removed.

17. *Fifthly, Setting them for what they cannot signify.*— Fifthly, Another abuse of words is the setting them in the place of things which they do or can by no means signify. We may observe that, in the general names of substances, whereof the nominal essences are only known to us, when we put them into propositions, and affirm or deny anything about them, we do most commonly tacitly suppose or intend they should stand for the real essence of a certain sort of substances. For when a man says, "Gold is malleable," he means and would insinuate something more than this, that what I call "gold" is malleable (though truly it amounts to no more), but would have this understood, viz., that gold, *i. e.*, what has the real essence of gold, is malleable; which amounts to thus much, that malleableness depends on, and is inseparable from, the real essence of gold. But a man, not knowing wherein that real essence consists, the connection in his mind of malleableness is not truly with an essence he knows not, but only with the sound "gold" he puts for it. Thus when we say, that *animal rationale* is, and *animal implume, bipes, latis unguibus** is not, a good definition of a man; it is plain we suppose the name "man" in this case to stand for the real essence of a species, and would signify that "a rational animal" better described that real essence than "a two-legged animal with

---

* This is the celebrated definition of "man," as given by Plato. It was at first merely "a two-legged animal without feathers;" but when a rival philosopher introduced a plucked cock to the assembled sages, and called it Plato's "man," it was found necessary to add the epithet "broad-nailed" to the definition.—ED.

broad nails, and without feathers." For else, why might not Plato as properly make the word ἄνθρωπος, or "man," stand for his complex idea, made up of the ideas of a body distinguished from others by a certain shape, and other outward appearances, as Aristotle make the complex idea, to which he gave the name ἄνθρωπος, or "man," of body and the faculty of reasoning joined together; unless the name ἄνθρωπος, or "man," were supposed to stand for something else than what it signifies; and to be put in the place of some other thing than the idea a man professes he would express by it?

18. *V. g., Putting them for the real essences of substances.*—It is true, the names of substances would be much more useful, and propositions made in them much more certain, were the real essences of substances the ideas in our minds which those words signified. And it is for want of those real essences that our words convey so little knowledge or certainty in our discourses about them: and therefore the mind, to remove that imperfection as much as it can, makes them, by a secret supposition, to stand for a thing having that real essence, as if thereby it made some nearer approaches to it. For though the word "man" or "gold" signify nothing truly but a complex idea of properties united together in one sort of substances: yet there is scarce anybody, in the use of these words, but often supposes each of those names to stand for a thing having the real essence on which those properties depend. Which is so far from diminishing the imperfection of our words, that by a plain abuse it adds to it, when we would make them stand for something which, not being in our complex idea, the name we use can no ways be the sign of.

19. *Hence we think every change of our idea in substances, not to change the species.*—This shows us the reason why, in mixed modes, any of the ideas that make the composition of the complex one being left out or changed, it is allowed to be another thing, *i. e.*, to be of another species, as is plain in chance-medley, manslaughter, murder, parricide, &c. The reason whereof is, because the complex idea, signified by that

name, is the real as well as nominal essence; and there is no secret reference of that name to any other essence but that. But in substances it is not so. For, though in that called "gold" one puts into his complex idea what another leaves out, and *vice versâ;* yet men do not usually think that therefore the species is changed: because they secretly in their minds refer that name, and suppose it annexed, to a real immutable essence of a thing existing, on which those properties depend. He that adds to his complex idea of gold that of fixedness or solubility in *aqua regia,* which he put not in it before, is not thought to have changed the species; but only to have a more perfect idea by adding another simple idea, which is always, in fact, joined with those other of which his former complex idea consisted. But this reference of the name to a thing whereof we have not the idea, is so far from helping at all, that it only serves the more to involve us in difficulties. For, by this tacit reference to the real essence of that species of bodies, the word "gold" (which, by standing for a more or less perfect collection of simple ideas, serves to design that sort of body well enough in civil discourse) comes to have no signification at all, being put for somewhat whereof we have no idea at all, and so can signify nothing at all when the body itself is away. For, however it may be thought all one; yet, if well considered, it will be found a quite different thing to argue about "gold" in name, and about a parcel of the body itself, *v. g.*, a piece of leaf-gold laid before us: though in discourse we are fain to substitute the name for the thing.

20. *The cause of the abuse, a supposition of nature's working always regularly.*—That which, I think, very much disposes men to substitute their names for the real essences of species, is the supposition before mentioned, that nature works regularly in the production of things, and sets the boundaries to each of those species by giving exactly the same real internal constitution to each individual, which we rank under one general name. Whereas any one who observes their different qualities can hardly doubt that many of the individuals called

by the same name are, in their internal constitution, as different one from another as several of those which are ranked under different specific names. This supposition, however, that the same precise internal constitution goes always with the same specific name, makes men forward to take those names for the representatives of those real essences, though indeed they signify nothing but the complex ideas they have in their minds when they use them. So that, if I may so say, signifying one thing, and being supposed for or put in the place of another, they cannot but in such a kind of use cause a great deal of uncertainty in men's discourses; especially in those who have thoroughly imbibed the doctrine of substantial forms, whereby they firmly imagine the several species of things to be determined and distinguished.

21. *This abuse contains two false suppositions.*—But, however preposterous and absurd it be to make our names stand for ideas we have not, or (which is all one) essences that we know not, it being in effect to make our words the signs of nothing; yet it is evident to any one, who reflects ever so little on the use men make of their words, that there is nothing more familiar. When a man asks whether this or that thing he sees, let it be a drill* or a monstrous fœtus, be a man or no, it is evident the question is not whether that particular thing agree to his complex idea expressed by the name "man," but whether it has in it the real essence of a species of things which he supposes his name "man" to stand for. In which way of using the names of substances there are these false suppositions contained:—

First, That there are certain precise essences according to which nature makes all particular things, and by which they are distinguished into species. That everything has a real constitution whereby it is what it is, and on which its sensible qualities depend, is past doubt; but I think it has been proved that this makes not the distinction of species as we rank them, nor the boundaries of their names.

Secondly, This tacitly also insinuates as if we had the ideas

* A baboon.—Ed.

of these proposed essences. For to what purpose else is it to inquire, whether this or that thing have the real essence of the species man, if we did not suppose that there were such a specific essence known? Which yet is utterly false: and therefore such application of names, as would make them stand for ideas which we have not, must needs cause great disorder in discourses and reasonings about them, and be a great inconvenience in our communication by words.

22. *Sixthly, A supposition that words have a certain and evident signification.*—Sixthly, There remains yet another more general, though perhaps less observed, abuse of words; and that is, that men having by a long and familiar use annexed to them certain ideas, they are apt to imagine so near and necessary a connection between the names and the signification they use them in, that they forwardly suppose one cannot but understand what their meaning is, and therefore one ought to acquiesce in the words delivered; as if it were past doubt that, in the use of those common received sounds, the speaker and hearer had necessarily the same precise ideas. Whence, presuming that when they have in discourse used any term, they have thereby, as it were, set before others the very thing they talk of; and so likewise taking the words of others as naturally standing for just what they themselves have been accustomed to apply them to; they never trouble themselves to explain their own or understand clearly others' meaning. From whence commonly proceeds noise and wrangling, without improvement or information; whilst men take words to be the constant, regular marks of agreed notions, which, in truth, are no more but the voluntary and unsteady signs of their own ideas. And yet men think it strange if, in discourse or (where it is often absolutely necessary) in dispute, one sometimes asks the meaning of their terms: though the arguings one may every day observe in conversation make it evident that there are few names of complex ideas which any two men use for the same just precise collection. It is hard to name a word which will not be a clear instance of this; "life" is a term, none more familiar. Any one almost would take it for an

affront to be asked what he meant by it. And yet if it comes in question whether a plant, that lies ready formed in the seed, have life; whether the embryo in an egg before incubation, or a man in a swoon without sense or motion, be alive or no; it is easy to perceive, that a clear, distinct, settled idea does not always accompany the use of so known a word as that of "life" is. Some gross and confused conceptions men indeed ordinarily have, to which they apply the common words of their language; and such a loose use of their words serves them well enough in their ordinary discourses or affairs. But this is not sufficient for philosophical inquiries. Knowledge and reasoning require precise determinate ideas. And though men will not be so importunately dull as not to understand what others say, without demanding an explication of their terms, nor so troublesomely critical as to correct others in the use of the words they receive from them; yet where truth and knowledge are concerned in the case, I know not what fault it can be to desire the explication of words whose sense seems dubious: or why a man should be ashamed to own his ignorance in what sense another man uses his words, since he has no other way of certainly knowing it but by being informed. This abuse of taking words upon trust has nowhere spread so far, nor with so ill effects, as amongst men of letters. The multiplication and obstinacy of disputes which has so laid waste the intellectual world, is owing to nothing more than this ill use of words. For, though it be generally believed that there is great diversity of opinions in the volumes and variety of controversies the world is distracted with, yet the most I can find that the contending learned men of different parties do in their arguings one with another, is, that they speak different languages. For I am apt to imagine, that when any of them, quitting terms, think upon things, and know what they think, they think all the same: though perhaps what they would have, be different.

23. *The ends of language: First: To convey our ideas.*—To conclude this consideration of the imperfection and abuse of language: The ends of language, in our discourse with others,

being chiefly these three: First, To make known one man's thoughts or ideas to another: Secondly, To do it with as much ease and quickness as is possible; and, Thirdly, Thereby to convey the knowledge of things. Language is either abused or deficient when it fails of any of these three.

First, Words fail in the first of these ends, and lay not open one man's ideas to another's view: First, When men have names in their mouths without any determined ideas in their minds whereof they are the signs: or, Secondly, When they apply the common received names of any language to ideas, to which the common use of that language does not apply them: or, Thirdly, When they apply them very unsteadily, making them stand now for one and by-and-by for another idea.

24. *Secondly, To do it with quickness.*—Secondly, Men fail of conveying their thoughts with all the quickness and case that may be, when they have complex ideas without having distinct names for them. This is sometimes the fault of the language itself, which has not in it a sound yet applied to such a signification: and sometimes the fault of the man, who has not yet learned the name for that idea he would show another.

25. *Thirdly, Therewith to convey the knowledge of things.*—Thirdly, There is no knowledge of things conveyed by men's words, when their ideas agree not to the reality of things. Though it be a defect that it has its original in our ideas, which are not so conformable to the nature of things as attention, study, and application might make them; yet it fails not to extend itself to our words, too, when we use them as signs of real beings which yet never had any reality or existence.

26. *How men's words fail in all these.*—First, He that hath words of any language without distinct ideas in his mind to which he applies them, does, so far as he uses them in discourse, only make a noise without any sense or signification; and, how learned soever he may seem by the use of hard words, or learned terms, is not much more advanced thereby in knowledge, than he would be in learning who had nothing

in his study but the bare titles of books, without possessing the contents of them. For all such words, however put into discourse according to the right construction of grammatical rules, or the harmony of well-turned periods, do yet amount to nothing but bare sounds, and nothing else.

27. Secondly, He that has complex ideas without particular names for them, would be in no better a case than a bookseller who had in his warehouse volumes that lay there unbound, and without titles, which he could therefore make known to others only by showing the loose sheets, and communicate them only by tale. This man is hindered in his discourse for want of words to communicate his complex ideas, which he is therefore forced to make known by an enumeration of the simple ones that compose them; and so is fain often to use twenty words to express what another man signifies in one.

28. Thirdly, He that puts not constantly the same sign for the same idea, but uses the same words sometimes in one and sometimes in another signification, ought to pass in the schools and conversation for as fair a man as *he* does in the market and exchange *who* sells several things under the same name.

29. Fourthly, He that applies the words of any language to ideas different from those to which the common use of that country applies them, however his own understanding may be filled with truth and light, will not by such words be able to convey much of it to others without defining his terms. For, however the sounds are such as are familiarly known and easily enter the ears of those who are accustomed to them, yet, standing for other ideas than those they usually are annexed to, and are wont to excite in the minds of the hearers, they cannot make known the thoughts of him who thus uses them.

30. Fifthly, He that hath imagined to himself substances such as never have been, and filled his head with ideas which have not any correspondence with the real nature of things, to which yet he gives settled and defined names, may fill his discourse, and perhaps another man's head, with the fantastical

imaginations of his own brain, but will be very far from advancing thereby one jot in real and true knowledge.

31. He that hath names without ideas, wants meaning in his words, and speaks only empty sounds. He that hath complex ideas without names for them, wants liberty and despatch in his expressions, and is necessitated to use periphrases. He that uses his words loosely and unsteadily will either be not minded or not understood. He that applies his names to ideas different from their common use, wants propriety in his language, and speaks gibberish. And he that hath ideas of substances disagreeing with the real existence of things, so far wants the materials of true knowledge in his understanding, and hath, instead thereof, chimeras.

32. *How in substances.*—In our notions concerning substances we are liable to all the former inconveniences: *v. g.*, (1) He that uses the word "tarantula," without having any imagination or idea of what it stands for, pronounces a good word: but so long means nothing at all by it. (2) He that in a new-discovered country shall see several sorts of animals and vegetables unknown to him before, may have as true ideas of them as of a horse or a stag; but can speak of them only by a description, till he shall either take the names the natives call them by, or give them names himself. (3) He that uses the word "body" sometimes for pure extension, and sometimes for extension and solidity together, will talk very fallaciously. (4) He that gives the name "horse" to that idea which common usage calls "mule," talks improperly, and will not be understood. (5) He that thinks the name "centaur" stands for some real being, imposes on himself, and mistakes words for things.

33. *How in modes and relations.*—In modes and relations generally, we are liable only to the four first of these inconveniences, viz., (1) I may have in my memory the names of modes, as "gratitude" or "charity," and yet not have any precise ideas annexed in my thoughts to those names. (2) I may have ideas, and not know the names that belong to them; *v. g.*, I may have the idea of a man's drinking till his colour

and humour be altered, till his tongue trips, and his eyes look red, and his feet fail him, and yet not know that it is to be called "drunkenness." (3) I may have the ideas of virtues or vices, and names also, but apply them amiss; *v. g.*, when I apply the name "frugality" to that idea which others call and signify by this sound, "covetousness." (4) I may use any of those names with inconstancy. (5) But in modes and relations, I cannot have ideas disagreeing to the existence of things: for, modes being complex ideas made by the mind at pleasure, and relation being but my way of considering or comparing two things together, and so also an idea of my own making, these ideas can scarce be found to disagree with anything existing; since they are not in the mind as the copies of things regularly made by nature, nor as properties inseparably flowing from the internal constitution or essence of any substance; but, as it were, patterns lodged in my memory, with names annexed to them to denominate actions and relations by, as they come to exist. But the mistake is commonly in my giving a wrong name to my conceptions; and so using words in a different sense from other people, I am not understood but am thought to have wrong ideas of them, when I give wrong names to them. Only if I put in my ideas of mixed modes or relations any inconsistent ideas together, I fill my head also with chimeras; since such ideas, if well examined, cannot so much as exist in the mind, much less any real being be ever denominated from them.

34. *Seventhly, Figurative speech also an abuse of language.*— Since wit and fancy finds easier entertainment in the world than dry truth and real knowledge, figurative speeches and allusion in language will hardly be admitted as an imperfection or abuse of it. I confess, in discourses where we seek rather pleasure and delight, than information and improvement, such ornaments as are borrowed from them can scarce pass for faults. But yet, if we would speak of things as they are, we must allow that all the art of rhetoric, besides order and clearness, all the artificial and figurative application of words eloquence hath invented, are for nothing else but to

insinuate wrong ideas, move the passions, and thereby mislead the judgment; and so indeed are perfect cheats: and therefore, however laudable or allowable oratory may render them in harangues and popular addresses, they are certainly, in all discourses that pretend to inform or instruct, wholly to be avoided; and, where truth and knowledge are concerned, cannot but be thought a great fault either of the language or person that makes use of them. What and how various they are, will be superfluous here to take notice; the books of rhetoric which abound in the world will instruct those who want to be informed. Only I cannot but observe how little the preservation and improvement of truth and knowledge is the care and concern of mankind; since the arts of fallacy are endowed and preferred. It is evident how much men love to deceive and be deceived, since rhetoric, that powerful instrument of error and deceit, has its established professors, is publicly taught, and has always been had in great reputation; and I doubt not but it will be thought great boldness, if not brutality, in me to have said thus much against it. Eloquence, like the fair sex, has too prevailing beauties in it to suffer itself ever to be spoken against. And it is in vain to find fault with those arts of deceiving wherein men find pleasure to be deceived.

NOTES.

A. The Schoolmen.

In the preceding article Locke has taken occasion to animadvert in strong terms upon the philosophy of the Schoolmen. This censure, however, is, for the most part, very unfounded; and it is most probable that whilst apparently speaking of the metaphysicians who flourished in the middle ages, Locke was in reality alluding to the alchemists and natural philosophers of those times. In any case it is certain that he adopted—although unwittingly—many of his own doctrines from the systems of philosophy which had found place in those very Schools that he condemned.

At the same time it must not be denied that the discussions which occupied the attention of the Schoolmen were oftentimes

of a very trivial and ridiculous character. Theology formed the great staple of these debates, and the disputants shrank not from investigating questions the most inapproachable and absurd. Thus, the dress of the angel Gabriel became an object of much research; it being doubtful as to whether he wore clean or dirty linen, and as to whether his garment were white or of two colours. With regard also to the Virgin Mary, it was sought to ascertain precisely the colour of her hair, and the extent of her knowledge. But the most insoluble difficulty which came under the notice of the Schoolmen, and which never was disposed of, lay in the following question:—" When a hog is carried to market with a rope tied about his neck, which is held at the other end by a man, whether is the *hog* carried to market by the *rope* or the *man?*" *
These debates, however, were engaged in merely for the purpose of recreation.

The similarity of black and white to which Locke alludes had reference to the real essences of these colours, it being contended by the Schoolmen that the only difference was in the sensations, and not in the colours themselves. But, indeed, if it be granted that black can be *seen*, or that black is something different from absolute darkness, it can easily be shown that black is white. For, a black body reflects the same kind of light as a white body, as may be seen when polished surfaces are employed; and, therefore, since it is by light that vision is alone possible, it follows that in both cases the same colour is seen: *i.e.*, black is white,— the difference being one of degree, not of kind.

Taken as a whole, the scholastic philosophy may be justly considered as one of the most stupendous monuments of human acuteness and wisdom that have ever existed; and the time is rapidly approaching when, freed from the crust of prejudice and ignorance accumulated during so many ages of unmerited neglect, it will shine forth in pristine splendour, and will reveal to the world such beauties of structure and detail as cannot fail to inspire all beholders with sentiments of the liveliest admiration.

B. Locke's notion of Logic.

When speaking of logic, Locke invariably betrays his entire misconception of that science; and, guided through the night of ignorance by an *ignis fatuus* of his own providing, he jousts madly against those forms which he takes to be giants of deceit and fraud, but which in reality are the massive towers of truth and reason. It is in no small degree astonishing that this should be the case, for it consorts but ill with that consummate acumen and penetration which are so evident in the remainder of Locke's writings; but it may doubtless be ascribed to his scanty know-

---

* Compare Disraeli's *Curiosities of Literature*, vol. i. p. 65.

ledge of the scholastic philosophy; a cause which, as we saw in the preceding note, led him into many errors respecting the metaphysicians of the middle ages.

But, whilst thus attributing Locke's attacks upon logic to his misapprehension and ignorance of the spirit which animated the scholastic speculations, I would be held merely to allude to the cause of his animosity against logicians, and not to the cause of this cause,—*i.e.*, the cause of the misapprehension referred to; and this will appear plain if I enter a little more into detail. The lamp, then, by whose light Locke examined the subject of logic was his erroneous idea as to the aim of the scholastic doctrines; and the source from whence its flame was fed, is to be found in his own system of Sensualism. With respect to the former of these it may be briefly stated that Locke looked upon the Schoolmen as mere disputants for the sake of victory and applause; as caring in nowise for the foundation and veracity of the propositions which they advanced, providing that they succeeded in silencing their adversaries; and as occupied solely in logomachies, whose only possible result was the overthrow of all qualities whereby language might be adapted to its proper purpose of useful intercommunication. In this, however, Locke was altogether wrong, and to his authority may be charged much of the foolish abuse with which it has, till lately, been the fashion to attack the Schools.

As regards the second point mentioned above, it will be sufficient to recall the fact that, in Locke's system, all the products of thought, or, in other words, all knowledges, are derived entirely from experience; from sensation, and from reflection depending upon sensation; no such thing as mental laws being imagined or admitted. From this it results that thought is, tacitly at least, held to be a faculty or phenomenon of the mind which proceeds in an arbitrary manner; and since it is thus subservient to no rigorous and necessary laws, the idea of any science which should investigate the nature and working of such laws is at once dismissed, or, rather, is never entertained. Accordingly, it is evident that, bound by the fetters of an incomplete and vicious psychology, Locke was never free to grasp the vital principle of logic: for him, the harmonious symmetry of that noble science was as a thing of naught; and the sure guide through the whole universe of thought became, in his regard, nothing more than a paltry means of equivocation and dispute. Logic, in fact, the science of the laws of thought, was by Locke imagined to be but a form, a method of argumentation; and this mistake, while caused by, yet at the same time served to perpetuate, the fundamental error of his system; for by it he was deprived of access to a science which would have shown him that our knowledge cannot be altogether dependent on experience.

OF THE REMEDIES OF THE FOREGOING IMPERFECTIONS AND ABUSES.

1. *They are worth seeking.*—The natural and improved imperfections of languages we have seen above at large; and speech being the great bond that holds society together, and the common conduit whereby the improvements of knowledge are conveyed from one man and one generation to another; it would well deserve our most serious thoughts to consider what remedies are to be found for these inconveniences above mentioned.

2. *Are not easy.*—I am not so vain to think that any one can pretend to attempt the perfect reforming the languages of the world, no, not so much as of his own country, without rendering himself ridiculous. To require that men should use their words constantly in the same sense, and for none but determined and uniform ideas, would be to think that all men should have the same notions, and should talk of nothing but what they have clear and distinct ideas of. Which is not to be expected by any one, who hath not vanity enough to imagine he can prevail with men to be very knowing or very silent. And he must be very little skilled in the world who thinks that a voluble tongue shall accompany only a good understanding; or that men's talking much or little shall hold proportion only to their knowledge.

3. *But yet necessary to philosophy.*—But though the market and exchange must be left to their own ways of talking, and gossippings not be robbed of their ancient privilege; though the Schools and men of argument would perhaps take it amiss to have anything offered to abate the length or lessen the number of their disputes; yet, methinks, those who pretend seriously to search after or maintain truth, should think themselves obliged to study how they might deliver themselves without obscurity, doubtfulness, or equivocation, to which men's words are naturally liable, if care be not taken.

4. *Misuse of words the cause of great errors.*—For he that shall well consider the errors and obscurity, the mistakes and confusion, that are spread in the world by an ill use of words, will find some reason to doubt whether language, as it has been employed, has contributed more to the improvement or hinderance of knowledge amongst mankind. How many are there, that, when they would think on things, fix their thoughts only on words, especially when they would apply their minds to moral matters! And who then can wonder, if the result of such contemplations and reasonings, about little more than sounds, whilst the ideas they annexed to them are very confused, or very unsteady, or perhaps none at all; who can wonder, I say, that such thoughts and reasonings end in nothing but obscurity and mistake, without any clear judgment or knowledge?

5. *Obstinacy.*—This inconvenience, in an ill use of words, men suffer in their own private meditations; but much more manifest are the disorders which follow from it in conversation, discourse, and arguings with others. For, language being the great conduit whereby men convey their discoveries, reasonings, and knowledge, from one to another, he that makes an ill use of it, though he does not corrupt the fountains of knowledge which are in things themselves, yet he does, as much as in him lies, break or stop the pipes whereby it is distributed to the public use and advantage of mankind. He that uses words without any clear and steady meaning, what does he but lead himself and others into errors? And he that designedly does it, ought to be looked on as an enemy to truth and knowledge. And yet who can wonder, that all the sciences and parts of knowledge have been so overcharged with obscure and equivocal terms and insignificant and doubtful expressions, capable to make the most attentive or quick-sighted very little, or not at all, the more knowing or orthodox; since subtilty, in those who make profession to teach or defend truth, hath passed so much for a virtue? a virtue indeed which consisting, for the most part, in nothing but the fallacious and illusory use of obscure or deceitful terms. is

only fit to make men more conceited in their ignorance, and obstinate in their errors.

6. *And wrangling.*—Let us look into the books of controversy, of any kind, there we shall see that the effect of obscure, unsteady, or equivocal terms, is nothing but noise and wrangling about sounds, without convincing or bettering a man's understanding. For, if the idea be not agreed on betwixt the speaker and hearer for which the words stand, the argument is not about things, but names. As often as such a word whose signification is not ascertained betwixt them comes in use, their understandings have no other object wherein they agree but barely the sound; the things that they think on at that time, as expressed by that word, being quite different.

7. *Instance bat, and bird.*—Whether a bat be a bird or not, is not a question whether a bat be another thing than indeed it is, or have other qualities than indeed it has; for that would be extremely absurd to doubt of: but the question is, (1) Either between those that acknowledged themselves to have but imperfect ideas of one or both of those sorts of things, for which these names are supposed to stand; and then it is a real inquiry concerning the nature of a bird or a bat, to make their yet imperfect ideas of it more complete, by examining whether all the simple ideas to which, combined together, they both give the name "bird" be all to be found in a bat: but this is a question only of inquirers (not disputers), who neither affirm nor deny, but examine. Or, (2.) It is a question between disputants; whereof the one affirms, and the other denies, that a bat is a bird. And then the question is barely about the signification of one or both these words; in that, they not having both the same complex ideas to which they give the two names, one holds and the other denies that these two names may be affirmed one of another. Where they agree in the signification of these two names, it were impossible they should dispute about them. For they would presently and clearly see (were that adjusted between them) whether all the simple ideas of the more

general name "bird" were found in the complex idea of a bat or no; and so there could be no doubt, whether a bat were a bird or no. And here I desire it may be considered, and carefully examined, whether the greatest part of the disputes in the world are not merely verbal and about the signification of words; and whether if the terms they are made in were defined, and reduced in their signification (as they must be where they signify anything) to determined collections of the simple ideas they do or should stand for, those disputes would not end of themselves and immediately vanish. I leave it then to be considered what the learning of disputation is, and how well they are employed for the advantage of themselves or others whose business is only the vain ostentation of sounds; *i.e.*, those who spend their lives in disputes and controversies. When I shall see any of those combatants strip all his terms of ambiguity and obscurity (which every one may do in the words he uses himself), I shall think him a champion for knowledge, truth, and peace, and not the slave of vain-glory, ambition, or a party.

8. To remedy the defects of speech before mentioned to some degree, and to prevent the inconveniences that follow from them, I imagine the observation of these following rules may be of use till somebody better able shall judge it worth his while to think more maturely on this matter, and oblige the world with his thoughts on it.

First remedy: To use no word without an idea.—First, A man should take care to use no word without a signification, no name without an idea for which he makes it stand. This rule will not seem altogether needless to any one who shall take the pains to recollect how often he has met with such words as "instinct," "sympathy," and "antipathy," &c., in the discourse of others, so made use of as he might easily conclude, that those that used them had no ideas in their minds to which they applied them; but spoke them only as sounds, which usually served instead of reasons on the like occasions. Not but that these words and the like have very proper significations in which they may be used; but there being no natural connection between any words and any ideas, these and any other may be learned by rote, and pronounced or writ by men, who have no ideas in their minds to which they have annexed them, and for which they make them stand; which is necessary they should, if men would speak intelligibly even to themselves alone.

9. *Secondly, To have distinct ideas annexed to them in modes.* — Secondly, It is not enough a man uses his words as signs of some ideas: those ideas he annexes them to, if they be simple, must be clear and distinct; if complex, must be determinate; *i. e.*, the precise collection of simple ideas settled in the mind, with that sound annexed to it as the sign of that precise determined collection, and no other. This is very necessary in names of modes, and especially moral words; which, having no settled objects in nature from whence their ideas are taken as from their original, are apt to be very confused. "Justice" is a word in every man's mouth, but most commonly with a very undetermined, loose signification: which will always be so unless a man has in his mind a distinct comprehension of the component parts that complex idea consists of: and if it be decompounded, must be able to resolve it still on till he at last comes to the simple ideas that make it up.: and unless this be done, a man makes an ill use of the word, let it be "justice," for example, or any other. I do not say, a man needs stand to recollect, and make this analysis at large, every time the word "justice" comes in his way: but this, at least, is necessary, that he have so examined the signification of that name, and settled the idea of all its parts, in his mind, that he can do it when he pleases. If one who makes this complex idea of justice to be such a treatment of the person or goods of another as is according to law, hath not a clear and distinct idea what law is, which makes a part of his complex idea of justice, it is plain his idea of justice itself will be confused and imperfect. This exactness will, perhaps, be judged very troublesome; and therefore most men will think they may be excused from settling the complex ideas of mixed modes so precisely in their minds. But yet I

must say, ti'l this be done it must not be wondered that they have a great deal of obscurity and confusion in their own minds, and a great deal of wrangling in their discourses with others.

10. *And conformable in substances.*—In the names of substances, for a right use of them something more is required than barely determined ideas. In these the names must also be conformable to things as they exist: but of this, I shall have occasion to speak more at large by-and-by. This exactness is absolutely necessary in inquiries after philosophical knowledge, and in controversies about truth. And though it would be well, too, if it extended itself to common conversation and the ordinary affairs of life, yet, I think, that is scarce to be expected. Vulgar notions suit vulgar discourses: and both, though confused enough, yet serve pretty well the market and the wake. Merchants and lovers, cooks and tailors, have words wherewithal to despatch their ordinary affairs; and so, I think, might philosophers and disputants, too, if they had a mind to understand, and to be clearly understood.

11. *Thirdly, Propriety.*—Thirdly, It is not enough that men have ideas, determined ideas, for which they make these signs stand; but they must also take care to apply their words, as near as may be, to such ideas as common use has annexed them to. For, words, especially of languages already framed, being no man's private possession, but the common measure of commerce and communication, it is not for any one, at pleasure, to change the stamp they are current in, nor alter the ideas they are affixed to; or at least when there is a necessity to do so, he is bound to give notice of it. Men's intentions in speaking are, or at least should be, to be understood; which cannot be without frequent explanations, demands, and other the like incommodious interruptions, where men do not follow common use. Propriety of speech is that which gives our thoughts entrance into other men's minds with the greatest ease and advantage; and therefore deserves some part of our care and study, especially in the names of

moral words. The proper signification and use of terms is best to be learned from those who in their writings and discourses appear to have had the clearest notions, and applied to them their terms with the exactest choice and fitness. This way of using a man's words according to the propriety of the language, though it have not always the good fortune to be understood, yet most commonly leaves the blame of it on him who is so unskilful in the language he speaks as not to understand it, when made use of as it ought to be.

12. *Fourthly, To make known their meaning.*—Fourthly, But because common use has not so visibly annexed any signification to words, as to make men know always certainly what they precisely stand for; and because men in the improvement of their knowledge come to have ideas different from the vulgar and ordinary received ones, for which they must either make new words (which men seldom venture to do, for fear of being thought guilty of affectation or novelty), or else must use old ones in a new signification; therefore after the observation of the foregoing rules, it is sometimes necessary for the ascertaining the signification of words, to declare their meaning; where either common use has left it uncertain and loose (as it has in most names of very complex ideas), or where the term, being very material in the discourse, and that upon which it chiefly turns, is liable to any doubtfulness or mistake.

13. *And that three ways.*—As the ideas men's words stand for are of different sorts, so the way of making known the ideas they stand for, when there is occasion, is also different. For though defining be thought the proper way to make known the proper signification of words; yet there are some words that will not be defined, as there be others whose precise meaning cannot be made known but by definition; and perhaps a third, which partake somewhat of both the other, as we shall see in the names of simple ideas, modes, and substances.

14. *First, In simple ideas, by synonymous terms or showing.*—First, When a man makes use of the name of any simple

idea, which he perceives is not understood, or is in danger to be mistaken, he is obliged, by the laws of ingenuity and the end of speech, to declare his meaning, and make known what idea he makes it stand for. This, as has been shown, cannot be done by definition; and therefore when a synonymous word fails to do it, there is but one of these ways left. (First,) Sometimes the naming the subject, wherein that simple idea is to be found, will make its name be understood by those who are acquainted with that subject, and know it by that name. So to make a countryman understand what *feuille-morte* colour signifies, it may suffice to tell him, it is the colour of withered leaves falling in autumn. (Secondly,) But the only sure way of making known the signification of the name of any simple idea, is, by presenting to his senses that subject which may produce it in his mind, and make him actually have the idea that word stands for.

15. *Secondly, In mixed modes, by definition.* — Secondly, Mixed modes, especially those belonging to morality, being most of them such combinations of ideas as the mind puts together of its own choice, and whereof there are not always standing patterns to be found existing, the signification of their names cannot be made known as those of simple ideas, by any showing; but, in recompense thereof, may be perfectly and exactly defined. For, they being combinations of several ideas that the mind of man has arbitrarily put together without reference to any archetypes, men may, if they please, exactly know the ideas that go to each composition, and so both use these words in a certain and undoubted signification, and perfectly declare, when there is occasion, what they stand for. This, if well considered, would lay great blame on those who make not their discourses about moral things very clear and distinct. For since the precise signification of the names of mixed modes, or, which is all one, the real essence of each species, is to be known, they being not of nature's but man's making, it is a great negligence and perverseness to discourse of moral things with uncertainty and obscurity; which is more pardonable in treating of natu-

ral substances, where doubtful terms are hardly to be avoided, for a quite contrary reason, as we shall see by-and-by.

16. *Morality capable of demonstration.*—Upon this ground it is that I am bold to think, that morality is capable of demonstration, as well as mathematics; since the precise real essence of the things moral words stand for may be perfectly known; and so the congruity or incongruity of the things themselves be certainly discovered, in which consists perfect knowledge. Nor let any one object, that the names of substances are often to be made use of in morality, as well as those of modes, from which will arise obscurity. For as to substances, when concerned in moral discourses, their divers natures are not so much inquired into as supposed; *v. g.*, when we say that "man is subject to law," we mean nothing by "man" but a corporeal, rational creature: what the real essence or other qualities of that creature are in this case, is no way considered. And therefore, whether a child or changeling be a man in a physical sense, may amongst the naturalists be as disputable as it will, it concerns not at all "the moral man," as I may call him, which is this immoveable, unchangeable idea, a corporeal, rational being. For, were there a monkey or any other creature to be found, that had the use of reason to such a degree as to be able to understand general signs, and to deduce consequences about general ideas, he would no doubt be subject to law, and, in that sense, be a man, how much soever he differed in shape from others of that name. The names of substances, if they be used in them as they should, can no more disturb moral than they do mathematical discourses: where, if the mathematician speaks of a cube or globe of gold, or any other body, he has his clear settled idea, which varies not, though it may, by mistake, be applied to a particular body to which it belongs not.

17. *Definitions can make moral discourses clear.*—This I have here mentioned by-the-bye, to show of what consequence it is for men, in their names of mixed modes, and consequently in all their moral discourses, to define their words when there is occasion: since thereby moral knowledge may be brought to

so great clearness and certainty. And it must be great want of ingenuity (to say no worse of it) to refuse to do it: since a definition is the only way whereby the precise meaning of moral words can be known; and yet a way whereby their meaning may be known certainly, and without leaving any room for any contest about it. And therefore the negligence or perverseness of mankind cannot be excused, if their discourses in morality be not much more clear than those in natural philosophy: since they are about ideas in the mind, which are none of them false or disproportionate; they having no external beings for the archetypes which they are referred to, and must correspond with. It is far easier for men to frame in their minds an idea which shall be the standard to which they will give the name "justice," with which pattern, so made, all actions that agree shall pass under that denomination; than, having seen Aristides, to frame an idea that shall in all things be exactly like him, who is as he is, let men make what idea they please of him. For the one, they need but know the combination of ideas that are put together within in their own minds; for the other, they must inquire into the whole nature and abstruse, hidden constitution, and various qualities of a thing existing without them.

18. *And is the only way.*—Another reason that makes the defining of mixed modes so necessary, especially of moral words, is what I mentioned a little before, viz., that it is the only way whereby the signification of the most of them can be known with certainty. For the ideas they stand for, being for the most part such whose component parts nowhere exist together, but scattered and mingled with others, it is the mind alone that collects them and gives them the union of one idea: and it is only by words, enumerating the several simple ideas which the mind has united, that we can make known to others what their names stand for; the assistance of the senses in this case not helping us by the proposal of sensible objects, to show the ideas which our names of this kind stand for, as it does often in the names of sensible simple ideas, and also to some degree in those of substances.

19. *Thirdly, In substances, by showing and defining.*—Thirdly, For the explaining the signification of the names of substances as they stand for the ideas we have of their distinct species, both the fore-mentioned ways, viz., of showing and defining, are requisite in many cases to be made use of. For there being ordinarily in each sort some leading qualities, to which we suppose the other ideas which make up our complex idea of that species annexed, we forwardly give the specific name to that thing wherein that characteristical mark is found, which we take to be the most distinguishing idea of that species. These leading or characteristical (as I may so call them) ideas, in the sorts of animals and vegetables, is . . . . mostly figure, and in inanimate bodies colour, and in some both together. Now,

20. *Ideas of the leading qualities of substances are best got by showing.*—These leading sensible qualities are those which make the chief ingredients of our specific ideas, and consequently the most observable and invariable part in the definitions of our specific names, as attributed to sorts of substances coming under our knowledge. For though the sound "man," in its own nature, be as apt to signify a complex idea made up of animality and rationality united in the same subject, as to signify any other combination; yet used as a mark to stand for a sort of creatures we count of our own kind, perhaps the outward shape is as necessary to be taken into our complex idea signified by the word "man," as any other we find in it; and therefore why Plato's *animal implume, bipes, latis unguibus*, should not be as good a definition of the name "man," standing for that sort of creatures, will not be easy to show: for it is the shape, as the leading quality, that seems more to determine that species than a faculty of reasoning, which appears not at first, and in some never. And if this be not allowed to be so, I do not know how they can be excused from murder who kill monstrous births (as we call them), because of an unordinary shape, without knowing whether they have a rational soul or no; which can be no more discerned in a well-formed than ill-shaped infant as soon as born. And who is it

has informed us, that a rational soul can inhabit no tenement, unless it has just such a sort of frontispiece, or can join itself to and inform no sort of body but one that is just of such an outward structure?

21. Now these leading qualities are best made known by showing, and can hardly be made known otherwise. For, the shape of a horse or cassiowary will be but rudely and imperfectly imprinted on the mind by words: the sight of the animals doth it a thousand times better. And the idea of the particular colour of gold is not to be got by any description of it, but only by the frequent exercise of the eyes about it; as is evident in those who are used to this metal, who will frequently distinguish true from counterfeit, pure from adulterate, by the sight; where others (who have as good eyes, but yet by use have not got the precise nice idea of that peculiar yellow) shall not perceive any difference. The like may be said of those other simple ideas, peculiar in their kind to any substance; for which precise ideas there are no peculiar names. The particular ringing sound there is in gold, distinct from the sound of other bodies, has no particular name annexed to it, no more than the particular yellow that belongs to that metal.

22. *The ideas of their powers best by definition.*—But because many of the simple ideas that make up our specific ideas of substances, are powers which lie not obvious to our senses in the things as they ordinarily appear: therefore, in the signification of our names of substances, some part of the signification will be better made known by enumerating those simple ideas, than in showing the substance itself. For he that, to the yellow shining colour of gold got by sight, shall, from my enumerating them, have the ideas of great ductility, fusibility, fixedness, and solubility in *aqua regia*, will have a perfecter idea of gold than he can have by seeing a piece of gold, and thereby imprinting in his mind only its obvious qualities. But if the former constitution of this shining, heavy, ductile thing (from whence all these its properties flow) lay open to our senses, as the formal constitution or

essence of a triangle does, the signification of the word "gold" might as easily be ascertained as that of "triangle."

23. *A reflection on the knowledge of spirits.*—Hence we may take notice how much the foundation of all our knowledge of corporeal things lies in our senses. For how spirits, separate from bodies (whose knowledge and ideas of these things are certainly much more perfect than ours), know them, we have no notion, no idea at all. The whole extent of our knowledge or imagination reaches not beyond our own ideas, limited to our ways of perception: though yet it be not to be doubted that spirits of a higher rank than those immersed in flesh may have as clear ideas of the radical constitution of substances as we have of a triangle, and so perceive how all their properties and operations flow from thence: but the manner how they come by that knowledge exceeds our conceptions.

24. *Ideas also of substances must be conformable to things.*— But though definitions will serve to explain the names of substances as they stand for our ideas, yet they leave them not without great imperfection as they stand for things. For, our names of substances being not put barely for our ideas, but being made use of ultimately to represent things, and so are put in their place, their signification must agree with the truth of things, as well as with men's ideas. And therefore in substances we are not always to rest in the ordinary complex idea commonly received as the signification of that word, but must go a little farther, and inquire into the nature and properties of the things themselves, and thereby perfect, as much as we can, our ideas of their distinct species; or else learn them from such as are used to that sort of things, and are experienced in them. For since it is intended their names should stand for such collections of simple ideas as do really exist in things themselves, as well as for the complex idea in other men's minds, which in their ordinary acceptation they stand for: therefore to define their names right, natural history is to be inquired into; and their properties are, with care and examination, to be found out. For it is

not enough, for the avoiding inconveniences in discourses and arguings about natural bodies and substantial things, to have learned, from the propriety of the language, the common but confused or very imperfect idea to which each word is applied, and to keep them to that idea in our use of them: but we must, by acquainting ourselves with the history of that sort of things, rectify and settle our complex idea belonging to each specific name; and in discourse with others (if we find them mistake us) we ought to tell what the complex idea is that we make such a name stand for. This is the more necessary to be done by all those who search after knowledge and philosophical verity, in that children being taught words whilst they have but imperfect notions of things, apply them at random and without much thinking, and seldom frame determined ideas to be signified by them. Which custom (it being easy, and serving well enough for the ordinary affairs of life and conversation) they are apt to continue when they are men: and so begin at the wrong end, learning words first and perfectly, but make the notions to which they apply those words afterwards very overtly. By this means it comes to pass, that men speaking the proper language of their country, *i.e.*, according to grammar rules of that language, do yet speak very improperly of things themselves; and, by their arguing one with another, make but small progress in the discoveries of useful truths, and the knowledge of things, as they are to be found in themselves, and not in our imaginations; and it matters not much, for the improvement of our knowledge, how they are called.

25. *Not easy to be made so.*—It were therefore to be wished that men versed in physical inquiries, and acquainted with the several sorts of natural bodies, would set down those simple ideas wherein they observe the individuals of each sort constantly to agree. This would remedy a great deal of that confusion which comes from several persons applying the same name to a collection of a smaller or greater number of sensible qualities, proportionably as they have been more or less acquainted with or accurate in examining the qualities of any

sort of things which come under one denomination. But a dictionary of this sort containing, as it were, a natural history, requires too many hands, as well as too much time, cost, pains, and sagacity, ever to be hoped for; and till that be done, we must content ourselves with such definitions of the names of substances as explain the sense men use them in. And it would be well, where there is occasion, if they would afford us so much. This yet is not usually done; but men talk to one another, and dispute in words whose meaning is not agreed between them, out of a mistake that the significations of common words are certainly established, and the precise ideas they stand for perfectly known; and that it is a shame to be ignorant of them. Both which suppositions are false: no names of complex ideas having so settled, determined significations, that they are constantly used for the same precise ideas. Nor is it a shame for a man not to have a certain knowledge of any thing but by the necessary ways of attaining it; and so it is no discredit not to know what precise idea any sound stands for in another man's mind without he declare it to me by some other way than barely using that sound, there being no other way without such a declaration, certainly to know it. Indeed, the necessity of communication by language brings men to an agreement in the signification of common words, within some tolerable latitude, that may serve for ordinary conversation: and so a man cannot be supposed wholly ignorant of the ideas which are annexed to words by common use, in a language familiar to him. But common use, being but a very uncertain rule, which reduces itself at last to the ideas of particular men, proves often but a very variable standard. But though such a dictionary as I have above mentioned will require too much time, cost, and pains to be hoped for in this age, yet, methinks, it is not unreasonable to propose, that words standing for things which are known and distinguished by their outward shapes, should be expressed by little draughts and prints made of them. A vocabulary made after this fashion would, perhaps, with more ease and in less time, teach the true signification of many terms, especially in languages of remote countries or ages, and settle truer ideas in men's minds of several things, whereof we read the names in ancient authors, than all the large and laborious comments of learned critics. Naturalists that treat of plants and animals, have found the benefit of this way: and he that has had occasion to consult them, will have reason to confess that he has a clearer idea of *apium* or *ibex* from a little print of that herb or beast, than he could have from a long definition of the names of either of them. And so no doubt he would have of *strigil* and *sistrum*, if, instead of " a curry-comb " and " cymbal," which are the English names dictionaries render them by, he could see stamped in the margin small pictures of these instruments, as they were in use amongst the ancients. *Toga, tunica, pallium*, are words easily translated by " gown," " coat," and " cloak : " but we have thereby no more true ideas of the fashion of those habits amongst the Romans, than we have of the faces of the tailors who made them. Such things as these, which the eye distinguishes by their shapes, would be best let into the mind by draughts made of them, and more determine the signification of such words than any other words set for them, or made use of to define them. But this only by-the-bye.

26. *Fifthly, By constancy in their signification.*—Fifthly, If men will not be at the pains to declare the meaning of their words, and definition of their terms are not to be had; yet this is the least can be expected, that, in all discourses wherein one man pretends to instruct or convince another, he should use the same word constantly in the same sense. If this were done (which nobody can refuse without great disingenuity), many of the books extant might be spared; many of the controversies in dispute would be at an end; several of those great volumes, swollen with ambiguous words now used in one sense and by-and-by in another, would shrink into a very narrow compass; and many of the philosophers' (to mention no other) as well as poets' works might be contained in a nut-shell.

27. *When the variation is to be explained.*—But, after all, the provision of words is so scanty in respect of that infinite

variety of thoughts, that men wanting terms to suit their precise notion, will, notwithstanding their utmost caution, be forced often to use the same word in somewhat different senses. And though in the continuation of a discourse, or the pursuit of an argument, there be hardly room to digress into a particular definition, as often as a man varies the signification of any term; yet the import of the discourse will, for the most part, if there be no designed fallacy, sufficiently lead candid and intelligent readers into the true meaning of it: but where that is not sufficient to guide the reader, there it concerns the writer to explain his meaning, and show in what sense he there uses that term.

NOTE.

ARE DISPUTES MERELY VERBAL?

With reference to this question which Locke, for the most part, answers in the affirmative, it may be well if I quote the following passage from M. Cousin's *Cours de Philosophie*, 2e, tome iii., 20.

"Everywhere Locke attributes to words the greatest part of our errors; and if you expound the master by the pupils, you will find in all the writers of the school of Locke that all disputes are disputes of words; that science is nothing but a language, and consequently, that a well-constructed science is a well-constructed language. I declare my opposition to the exaggerations of these assertions. No doubt words have a great influence; no doubt they have much to do with our errors, and we should strive to make the best language possible. Who questions this? But the question is to know whether every error is derived from language, and whether science is merely a well-constructed language. No; the causes of our errors are very different; they are both more extended and more profound. Levity, presumption, indolence, precipitation, pride, a multitude of moral causes influence our judgments. The vices of language may be added to natural causes, and aggravate them, but they do not constitute them. If you look more closely, you will see that the greater part of disputes, which seem at first disputes of words, are, at bottom, disputes of things. Humanity is too serious to become excited and often shed its best blood, for the sake of words. Wars do not turn upon verbal disputes; I say as much of other quarrels, of theological quarrels, and of scientific quarrels, the profundity and importance of which are misconceived when they are resolved into pure logomachies."

OF THE DEGREES OF OUR KNOWLEDGE.

1. *Intuitive.*—All our knowledge consisting. as I have said, in the view the mind has of its own ideas, which is the utmost light and greatest certainty we, with our faculties and in our way of knowledge, are capable of, it may not be amiss to consider a little the degrees of its evidence. The different clearness of our knowledge seems to me to lie in the different way of perception the mind has of the agreement or disagreement of any of its ideas. For if we will reflect on our own ways of thinking, we shall find that sometimes the mind perceives the agreement or disagreement of two ideas immediately by themselves, without the intervention of any other: and this, I think, we may call "intuitive knowledge." For in this the mind is at no pains of proving or examining, but perceives the truth, as the eye doth light, only by being directed towards it. Thus the mind perceives that white is not black, that a circle is not a triangle, that three are more than two, and equal to one and two. Such kind of truths the mind perceives at the first sight of the ideas together, by bare intuition, without the intervention of any other idea; and this kind of knowledge is the clearest and most certain that human frailty is capable of. This part of knowledge is irresistible, and, like bright sunshine, forces itself immediately to be perceived as soon as ever the mind turns its view that way; and leaves no room for hesitation, doubt, or examination, but the mind is presently filled with the clear light of it. It is on this intuition that depends all the certainty and evidence of all our knowledge, which certainty every one finds to be so great, that he cannot imagine, and therefore cannot require, a greater: for a man cannot conceive himself capable of a greater certainty, than to know that any idea in his mind is such as he perceives it to be; and that two ideas, wherein he perceives a difference, are different, and not precisely the same. He that demands a greater certainty than this demands he knows not what, and shows

only that he has a mind to be a sceptic without being able to be so. Certainty depends so wholly on this intuition, that in the next degree of knowledge, which I call "demonstrative," this intuition is necessary in all the connections of the intermediate ideas, without which we cannot attain knowledge and certainty.

2 *Demonstrative.*—The next degree of knowledge is, where the mind perceives the agreement or disagreement of any ideas, but not immediately. Though wherever the mind perceives the agreement or disagreement of any of its ideas, there be certain knowledge; yet it does not always happen that the mind sees that agreement or disagreement which there is between them, even where it is discoverable; and in that case remains in ignorance, and at most gets no farther than a probable conjecture. The reason why the mind cannot always perceive presently the agreement or disagreement of two ideas, is, because those ideas concerning whose agreement or disagreement the inquiry is made, cannot by the mind be so put together as to show it. In this case then, when the mind cannot so bring its ideas together as, by their immediate comparison and, as it were, juxtaposition or application one to another, to perceive their agreement or disagreement, it is fain, by the intervention of other ideas (one or more, as it happens), to discover the agreement or disagreement which it searches; and this is that which we call "reasoning." Thus the mind, being willing to know the agreement or disagreement in bigness between the three angles of a triangle and two right ones, cannot, by an immediate view and comparing them, do it: because the three angles of a triangle cannot be brought at once, and be compared with any one or two angles; and so of this the mind has no immediate, no intuitive knowledge. In this case the mind is fain to find out some other angles, to which the three angles of a triangle have an equality; and finding those equal to two right ones, comes to know their equality to two right ones.

3. *Depends on proofs.*—Those intervening ideas which serve to show the agreement of any two others, are called "proofs;"

and where the agreement or disagreement is by this means plainly and clearly perceived, it is called "demonstration," it being shown to the understanding, and the mind made to see that it is so. A quickness in the mind to find out these intermediate ideas (that shall discover the agreement or disagreement of any other), and to apply them right, is, I suppose, that which is called "sagacity."

4. *But not so easy.*—This knowledge by intervening proofs, though it be certain, yet the evidence of it is not altogether so clear and bright, nor the assent so ready, as in intuitive knowledge. For though in demonstration the mind does at last perceive the agreement or disagreement of the ideas it considers, yet it is not without pains and attention: there must be more than one transient view to find it. A steady application and pursuit is required to this discovery: and there must be a progression by steps and degrees before the mind can in this way arrive at certainty, and come to perceive the agreement or repugnancy between two ideas that need proofs and the use of reason to show it.

5. *Not without precedent doubt.*—Another difference between intuitive and demonstrative knowledge, is, that though in the latter all doubt be removed, when by the intervention of the intermediate ideas the agreement or disagreement is perceived; yet before the demonstration there was a doubt; which in intuitive knowledge cannot happen to the mind that has its faculty of perception left to a degree capable of distinct ideas, no more than it can be a doubt to the eye (that can distinctly see white and black), whether this ink and this paper be all of a colour. If there be sight in the eyes, it will at first glimpse, without hesitation, perceive the words printed on this paper, different from the colour of the paper: and so, if the mind have the faculty of distinct perception, it will perceive the agreement or disagreement of those ideas that produce intuitive knowledge. If the eyes have lost the faculty of seeing, or the mind of perceiving, we in vain inquire after the quickness of sight in one, or clearness of perception in the other.

6. *Not so clear.*—It is true, the perception produced by demonstration is also very clear; yet it is often with a great abatement of that evident lustre and full assurance that always accompany that which I call "intuitive;" like a face reflected by several mirrors one to another, where, as long as it retains the similitude and agreement with the object, it produces a knowledge; but it is still in every successive reflection with a lessening of that perfect clearness and distinctness which is in the first, till at last, after many removes, it has a great mixture of dimness, and is not at first sight so knowable, especially to weak eyes. Thus it is with knowledge made out by a long train of proofs.

7. *Each step must have intuitive evidence.*—Now, in every step reason makes in demonstrative knowledge, there is an intuitive knowledge of that agreement or disagreement it seeks with the next intermediate idea, which it uses as a proof: for if it were not so, that yet would need a proof; since without the perception of such agreement or disagreement there is no knowledge produced. If it be perceived by itself, it is intuitive knowledge: if it cannot be perceived by itself, there is need of some intervening idea, as a common measure, to show their agreement or disagreement. By which it is plain, that every step in reasoning that produces knowledge has intuitive certainty; which when the mind perceives, there is no more required but to remember it, to make the agreement or disagreement of the ideas, concerning which we inquire, visible and certain. So that to make anything a demonstration, it is necessary to perceive the immediate agreement of the intervening ideas, whereby the agreement or disagreement of the two ideas under examination (whereof the one is always the first, and the other the last in the account) is found. This intuitive perception of the agreement or disagreement of the intermediate ideas, in each step and progression of the demonstration, must also be carried exactly in the mind, and a man must be sure that no part is left out: which, because in long deductions, and the use of many proofs, the memory does not always so readily and exactly retain; there-

fore it comes to pass, that this is more imperfect than intuitive knowledge, and men embrace often falsehood for demonstrations.

* * * * * * *

14. *Sensitive knowledge of particular existence.*—These two, viz., intuition and demonstration, are the degrees of our knowledge; whatever comes short of one of these, with what assurance soever embraced, is but faith or opinion, but not knowledge, at least in all general truths. There is, indeed, another perception of the mind employed about the particular existence of finite beings without us; which, going beyond bare probability, and yet not reaching perfectly to either of the foregoing degrees of certainty, passes under the name of "knowledge." There can be nothing more certain, than that the idea we receive from an external object is in our minds; this is intuitive knowledge. But whether there be anything more than barely that idea in our minds, whether we can thence certainly infer the existence of anything without us which corresponds to that idea, is that whereof some men think there may be a question made; because men may have such ideas in their minds when no such thing exists, no such object affects their senses. But yet here, I think, we are provided with an evidence that puts us past doubting; for I ask any one, whether he be not invincibly conscious to himself of a different perception when he looks on the sun by day, and thinks on it by night; when he actually tastes wormwood, or smells a rose, or only thinks on that savour or odour? We as plainly find the difference there is between any idea revived in our minds by our own memory, and actually coming into our minds by our senses, as we do between any two distinct ideas. If any one say, "A dream may do the same thing, and all these ideas may be produced in us without any external objects;" he may please to dream that I make him this answer: (1) That it is no great matter whether I remove his scruple or no: where all is but dream, reasoning and arguments are of no use, truth and knowledge nothing. (2) That I believe he will allow a very manifest difference between

dreaming of being in the fire, and being actually in it. But yet if he be resolved to appear so sceptical as to maintain, that what I call "being actually in the fire" is nothing but a dream; and that we cannot thereby certainly know that any such thing as fire actually exists without us; I answer, that we certainly finding that pleasure or pain follows upon the application of certain objects to us, whose existence we perceive, or dream that we perceive, by our senses; this certainly is as great as our happiness or misery, beyond which we have no concernment to know or to be. So that, I think, we may add to the two former sorts of knowledge this also, of the existence of particular external objects by that perception and consciousness we have of the actual entrance of ideas from them, and allow these three degrees of knowledge, viz., intuitive, demonstrative, and sensitive: in each of which there are different degrees and ways of evidence and certainty.

15. *Knowledge not always clear, where the ideas are so.*—But since our knowledge is founded on and employed about our ideas only, will it not follow from thence that it is conformable to our ideas; and that where our ideas are clear and distinct, or obscure and confused, our knowledge will be so too? To which I answer, No: for our knowledge consisting in the perception of the agreement or disagreement of any two ideas, its clearness or obscurity consists in the clearness or obscurity of that perception, and not in the clearness or obscurity of the ideas themselves; *v. g.*, a man that has as clear ideas of the angles of a triangle, and of equality to two right ones, as any mathematician in the world, may yet have but a very obscure perception of their agreement, and so have but a very obscure knowledge of it. But ideas which by reason of their obscurity or otherwise are confused, cannot produce any clear or distinct knowledge; because as far as any ideas are confused, so far the mind cannot perceive clearly whether they agree or disagree. Or, to express the same thing in a way less apt to be misunderstood, he that hath not determined the ideas to the words he uses cannot make propositions of them, of whose truth he can be certain.

NOTE.
ON SENSITIVE KNOWLEDGE.

Locke's general theory of knowledge, as knowledge, will most properly fall to be considered at the end of the next Selection: but it is necessary in the present place to say a few words respecting that *sensitive* knowledge of which mention is made in § 14 of the preceding article.

Since, in § 1, Locke asserts that all knowledge consists " in the view the mind has of its own ideas," and since, in § 14, he admits that ideas are something different both from mind and from external objects; it follows that for him a *sensitive* knowledge involves a contradiction. This is evident from a consideration of the elements into which this sensitive knowledge may be resolved; for, by his own account, it is a knowledge " of the existence of particular external objects" acquired " by that perception and consciousness we have of the actual entrance of ideas from them;" in which " perception and consciousness" three terms are known; first, the external objects themselves; secondly, the ideas produced in the mind; and, thirdly, the act of production or entrance. There is, indeed, a fourth term, viz., the mind, but this may for present purposes be omitted. Accordingly, we see that this *sensitive* knowledge implies, *inter alia*, a pre-existence and separate knowledge of external objects, *i.e.*, a knowledge of something different from ideas; which is in direct contradiction to the theory that *all* knowledge consists " in the view the mind has of its own ideas." Thus have I proved my point; but worse remains behind: this being that the doctrine of *sensitive* knowledge as exhibited by Locke, founds upon a gross paralogism, and is, therefore, utterly inadmissible. For, we have already seen that the " perception and consciousness" by means of which a *sensitive* knowledge is acquired, cannot take place without a previous, or, at all events a co-ordinate and distinct knowledge of external objects. But what *is* this sensitive knowledge? It is " a knowledge of the existence of particular external objects." Behold, then, the circle in which this reasoning revolves! A knowledge is asserted to exist, because it must follow from a certain supposed action of the mind, which action, when duly analysed, is discovered to imply the very knowledge whose existence is in question.

From the general tone of § 14, it may be seen that Locke has some little presentiment of the results to which the theory of ideas as advocated by him must necessarily lead; that is to say, he saw that those who should accept his doctrines might legitimately doubt the existence of an external world, unless some saving clause were introduced. To meet this difficulty he proposed, with evident hesitation, the theory of " sensitive knowledge." We have seen the result.

OF THE EXTENT OF HUMAN KNOWLEDGE.

1. KNOWLEDGE, as has been said, lying in the perception of the agreement or disagreement of any of our ideas, it follows from hence, that,

First, No farther than we have ideas.—First, We can have knowledge no farther than we have ideas.

2. *Secondly, No farther than we can perceive their agreement or disagreement.*—Secondly, That we can have no knowledge farther than we can have perception of that agreement or disagreement: which perception being, (1) Either by intuition, or the immediate comparing any two ideas; or, (2) By reason, examining the agreement or disagreement of two ideas by the intervention of some others; or, (3) By sensation, perceiving the existence of particular things; hence it also follows,

3. *Thirdly, Intuitive knowledge extends itself not to all the relations of all our ideas.*—Thirdly, that we cannot have an intuitive knowledge that shall extend itself to all our ideas, and all that we would know about them; because we cannot examine and perceive all the relations they have one to another by juxtaposition, or an immediate comparison one with another. Thus having the ideas of an obtuse and an acute-angled triangle, both drawn from equal bases, and between parallels, I can by intuitive knowledge perceive the one not to be the other; but cannot that way know whether they be equal or no: because their agreement or disagreement in equality can never be perceived by an immediate comparing them; the difference of figure makes their parts uncapable of an exact immediate application; and therefore there is need of some intervening qualities to measure them by, which is demonstration or rational knowledge.

4. *Fourthly, Nor demonstrative knowledge.*—Fourthly, It follows also, from what is above observed, that our rational knowledge cannot reach to the whole extent of our ideas: because between two different ideas we would examine, we cannot always find such mediums as we can connect one to another with an intuitive knowledge, in all the parts of the

deduction; and wherever that fails, we come short of knowledge and demonstration.

5. *Fifthly, Sensitive knowledge narrower than either.* — Fifthly, Sensitive knowledge, reaching no farther than the existence of things actually present to our senses, is yet much narrower than either of the former.

6. *Sixthly, Our knowledge therefore narrower than our ideas.* —From all which it is evident, that the extent of our knowledge comes not only short of the reality of things, but even of the extent of our own ideas. Though our knowledge be limited to our ideas, and cannot exceed them either in extent or perfection: and though these be very narrow bounds in respect of the extent of all being, and far short of what we may justly imagine to be in some even created understandings not tied down to the dull and narrow information [which] is to be received from some few and not very acute ways of perception, such as are our senses; yet it would be well with us if our knowledge were but as large as our ideas, and there were not many doubts and inquiries concerning the ideas we have, whereof we are not, nor I believe ever shall be in this world, resolved. Nevertheless, I do not question but that human knowledge, under the present circumstances of our beings and constitutions, may be carried much farther than it hitherto has been, if men would sincerely, and with freedom of mind, employ all that industry and labour of thought in improving the means of discovering truth which they do for the colouring or support of falsehood, to maintain a system, interest, or party they are once engaged in. But yet, after all, I think I may, without injury to human perfection, be confident that our knowledge would never reach to all we might desire to know concerning those ideas we have; nor be able to surmount all the difficulties, and resolve all the questions, [which] might arise concerning any of them. We have the ideas of a square, a circle, and equality: and yet, perhaps, shall never be able to find a circle equal to a square, and certainly know that it is so. We have the ideas of matter and thinking, but possibly shall never be able to know

whether any mere material being thinks or no; it being impossible for us, by the contemplation of our own ideas without revelation, to discover whether Omnipotency has not given to some systems of matter, fitly disposed, a power to perceive and think, or else joined and fixed to matter, so disposed, a thinking immaterial substance: it being, in respect of our notions, not much more remote from our comprehension to conceive that God can, if he pleases, superadd to matter a faculty of thinking, than that he should superadd to it another substance with a faculty of thinking; since we know not wherein thinking consists, nor to what sort of substances the Almighty has been pleased to give that power which cannot be in any created being but merely by the good pleasure and bounty of the Creator. For I see no contradiction in it, that the first eternal thinking Being should, if he pleased, give to certain systems of created senseless matter, put together as he thinks fit, some degrees of sense, perception, and thought: though, as I think I have proved . . . . it is no less than a contradiction to suppose matter (which is evidently in its own nature void of sense and thought) should be that eternal first thinking Being. What certainty of knowledge can any one have that some perceptions, such as, *v. g.*, pleasure and pain, should not be in some bodies themselves, after a certain manner modified and moved, as well as that they should be in an immaterial substance upon the motion of the parts of body? body, as far as we can conceive, being able only to strike and affect body; and motion, according to the utmost reach of our ideas, being able to produce nothing but motion: so that when we allow it to produce pleasure or pain, or the idea of a colour or sound, we are fain to quit our reason, go beyond our ideas, and attribute it wholly to the good pleasure of our Maker. For, since we must allow he has annexed effects to motion, which we can no way conceive motion able to produce, what reason have we to conclude that he could not order them as well to be produced in a subject we cannot conceive capable of them, as well as in a subject we cannot conceive the motion of matter can any way operate upon? I say not this that I would any way lessen the belief of the soul's immateriality: I am not here speaking of probability, but knowledge: and I think, not only that it becomes the modesty of philosophy not to pronounce magisterially, where we want that evidence that can produce knowledge; but also, that it is of use to us to discern how far our knowledge does reach; for the state we are at present in, not being that of vision, we must, in many things, content ourselves with faith and probability: and in the present question about the immateriality of the soul, if our faculties cannot arrive at demonstrative certainty, we need not think it strange. All the great ends of morality and religion are well enough secured, without philosophical proofs of the soul's immateriality; since it is evident that he who made us at first begin to subsist here sensible intelligent beings, and for several years continued us in such a state, can and will restore us to the like state of sensibility in another world, and make us capable there to receive the retribution he has designed to men according to their doings in this life. And therefore it is not of such mighty necessity to determine one way or the other, as some, over zealous for or against the immateriality of the soul, have been forward to make the world believe: who either, on the one side, indulging too much their thoughts immersed altogether in matter, can allow no existence to what is not material: or who, on the other side, finding not cogitation within the natural powers of matter, examined over and over again by the utmost intension of mind, have the confidence to conclude that Omnipotency itself cannot give perception and thought to a substance which has the modification of solidity. He that considers how hardly sensation is, in our thoughts, reconcileable to extended matter, or existence to anything that hath no extension at all, will confess that he is very far from certainly knowing what his soul is. It is a point which seems to me to be put out of the reach of our knowledge: and he who will give himself leave to consider freely, and look into the dark and intricate part of each hypothesis, will scarce find his reason able to determine him fixedly for or against the soul's materiality; since on which side soever he views it, either as an unextended substance, or as a thinking extended matter, the difficulty to conceive either will, whilst either alone is in his thoughts, still drive him to the contrary side: an unfair way which some men take with themselves: who, because of the unconceivableness of something they find in one, throw themselves violently into the contrary hypothesis, though altogether as unintelligible to an unbiassed understanding. This serves not only to show the weakness and the scantiness of our knowledge, but the insignificant triumph of such sort of arguments which, drawn from our own views, may satisfy us that we can find no certainty on one side of the question; but do not at all thereby help us to truth by running into the opposite opinion, which on examination will be found clogged with equal difficulties. For what safety, what advantage to any one is it, for the avoiding the seeming absurdities and, to him, insurmountable rubs he meets with in one opinion, to take refuge in the contrary, which is built on something altogether as inexplicable, and as far remote from his comprehension? It is past controversy, that we have in us something that thinks; our very doubts about what it is confirm the certainty of its being, though we must content ourselves in the ignorance of what kind of being it is: and it is as vain to go about to be sceptical in this, as it is unreasonable in most other cases to be positive against the being of anything, because we cannot comprehend its nature. For I would fain know, what substance exists that has not something in it which manifestly baffles our understandings. Other spirits, who see and know the nature and inward constitution of things, how much must they exceed us in knowledge? To which if we add larger comprehension, which enables them at one glance to see the connection and agreement of very many ideas, and readily supplies to them the intermediate proofs, which we, by single and slow steps, and long poring in the dark, hardly at last find out, and are often ready to forget one before we have hunted out another. we may guess at some part of the happiness of superior ranks of spirits, who have a quicker and more penetrating sight, as well as a larger field of knowledge. But, to return to the argument in hand: our knowledge, I say, is not only limited to the paucity and imperfections of the ideas we have, and which we employ it about, but even comes short of that too: but how far it reaches, let us now inquire.

7. *How far our knowledge reaches.*—The affirmations or negations we make concerning the ideas we have, may, as I have before intimated in general, be reduced to these four sorts, viz., identity, co-existence, relation, and real existence. I shall examine how far our knowledge extends in each of these:—

8. *First. Our knowledge of identity and diversity, as far as our ideas.*—First, As to identity and diversity, in this way of the agreement or disagreement of ideas, our intuitive knowledge is as far extended as our ideas themselves: and there can be no idea in the mind which does not presently, by an intuitive knowledge, perceive to be what it is, and to be different from any other.

9. *Secondly. Of co-existence, a very little way.*—Secondly, As to the second sort, which is the agreement or disagreement of our ideas in co-existence, in this our knowledge is very short, though in this consists the greatest and most material part of our knowledge concerning substances. For our ideas of the species of substances being, as I have showed, nothing but certain collections of simple ideas united in one subject, and so co-existing together;—*v. g.*, our idea of "flame" is a body hot, luminous, and moving upward; of "gold," a body heavy to a certain degree, yellow, malleable, and fusible. These, or some such complex ideas as these in men's minds, do these two names of the different substances, "flame" and "gold," stand for. When we would know anything farther concerning these, or any other sort of substances, what do we inquire but what other qualities or powers these substances have or have not? which is nothing else but to know what other simple ideas do or do not co-exist with those that make up that complex idea.

10. *Because the connection between most simple ideas is unknown*.—This, how weighty and considerable a part soever of human science, is yet very narrow, and scarce any at all. The reason whereof is, that the simple ideas whereof our complex ideas of substances are made up are, for the most part, such as carry with them, in their own nature, no visible necessary* connection or inconsistency with any other simple ideas, whose co-existence with them we should inform ourselves about.

11. *Especially of secondary qualities*.—The ideas that our complex ones of substances are made up of, and about which our knowledge concerning substances is most employed, are those of their secondary qualities; which depending all (as has been shown) upon the primary qualities of their minute and insensible parts, or, if not upon them, upon something yet more remote from our comprehension, it is impossible we should know which have a necessary union or inconsistency one with another: for, not knowing the root they spring from, not knowing what size, figure, and texture of parts they are on which depend and from which result those qualities which make our complex idea of gold, it is impossible we should know what other qualities result from or are incompatible with the same constitution of the insensible parts of gold; and so, consequently, must always co-exist with that complex idea we have of it, or else are inconsistent with it.

12. *Because all connection between any secondary and primary qualities is undiscoverable*.—Besides this ignorance of the primary qualities of the insensible parts of bodies, on which depend all their secondary qualities, there is yet another and more incurable part of ignorance, which sets us more remote from a certain knowledge of the co-existence or in-co-existence (if I may so say) of different ideas in the same subject; and that is, that there is no discoverable connection between any secondary quality and those primary qualities that it depends on.

13. That the size, figure, and motion of one body should

---

* This hint, if rightly followed up, might have led Locke to perceive the grand distinction between *necessary* and *contingent* truth; and so might have altered his entire system.—ED.

cause a change in the size, figure, and motion of another body, is not beyond our conception. The separation of the parts of one body upon the intrusion of another, and the change from rest to motion upon impulse; these, and the like, seem to us to have some connection one with another. And if we knew these primary qualities of bodies, we might have reason to hope we might be able to know a great deal more of these operations of them one upon another: but our minds not being able to discover any connection betwixt these primary qualities of bodies, and the sensations that are produced in us by them, we can never be able to establish certain and undoubted rules of the consequence or co-existence of any secondary qualities, though we could discover the size, figure, or motion of those invisible parts which immediately produce them. We are so far from knowing what figure, size, or motion of parts produce a yellow colour, a sweet taste, or a sharp sound, that we can by no means conceive how any size, figure, or motion of any particles can possibly produce in us the idea of any colour, taste, or sound whatsoever; there is no conceivable connection betwixt the one and the other.

14. In vain therefore shall we endeavour to discover by our ideas (the only true way of certain and universal knowledge) what other ideas are to be found constantly joined with that of our complex idea of any substance: since we neither know the real constitution of the minute parts on which their qualities do depend; nor, did we know them, could we discover any necessary connection between them and any of the secondary qualities; which is necessary to be done before we can certainly know their necessary co-existence. So that, let our complex idea of any species of substances be what it will, we can hardly, from the simple ideas contained in it, certainly determine the necessary co-existence of any other quality whatsoever. Our knowledge in all these inquiries reaches very little farther than our experience. Indeed some few of the primary qualities have a necessary dependence and visible connection one with another, as figure necessarily supposes extension, receiving or communicating motion by impulse

supposes solidity. But though these and perhaps some others of our ideas have, yet there are so few of them that have, a visible connection one with another, that we can by intuition or demonstration discover the co-existence of very few of the qualities [which] are to be found united in substances : and we are left only to the assistance of our senses to make known to us what qualities they contain. For, of all the qualities that are co-existent in any subject, without this dependence and evident connection of their ideas one with another, we cannot know certainly any two to co-exist any farther than experience, by our senses, informs us. Thus though we see the yellow colour, and upon trial find the weight, malleableness, fusibility, and fixedness that are united in a piece of gold : yet, because no one of these ideas has any evident dependence or necessary connection with the other, we cannot certainly know that where any four of these are, the fifth will be there also, how highly probable soever it may be ; because the highest probability amounts not to certainty ; without which there can be no true knowledge. For this co-existence can be no farther known than it is perceived : and it cannot be perceived but either in particular subjects by the observation of our senses, or in general by the necessary connection of the ideas themselves.

15. *Of repugnancy to co-existence, larger.*—As to incompatibility or repugnancy to co-existence, we may know that any subject can have of each sort of primary qualities but one particular at once *v. g.*, each particular extension, figure, number of parts, motion, excludes all other of each kind. The like also is certain of all sensible ideas peculiar to each sense : for whatever of each kind is present in any subject, excludes all other of that sort ; *v. g.*, no one subject can have two smells or two colours at the same time. To this, perhaps, will be said, "Has not an *opal* or the infusion of *lignum nephriticum* two colours at the same time ?" To which I answer, that these bodies, to eyes differently placed, may at the same time afford different colours : but I take liberty also to say, that to eyes differently placed it is different parts of the object that

reflect the particles of light: and therefore it is not the same part of the object, and so not the very same subject, which at the same time appears both yellow and azure. For it is as impossible that the very same particle of any body should at the same time differently modify or reflect the rays of light, as that it should have two different figures and textures at the same time.

16. *Of the co-existence of powers, a very little way.*—But as to the power of substances to change the sensible qualities of other bodies, which makes a great part of our inquiries about them, and is no inconsiderable branch of our knowledge; I doubt, as to these, whether our knowledge reaches much farther than our experience; or whether we can come to the discovery of most of these powers, and be certain that they are in any subject, by the connection with any of those ideas which to us make its essence. Because the active and passive powers of bodies, and their ways of operating, consisting in a texture and motion of parts which we cannot by any means come to discover, it is but in very few cases we can be able to perceive their dependence on or repugnance to any of those ideas which make our complex one of that sort of things. I have here instanced in the corpuscularian hypothesis, as that which is thought to go farthest in an intelligible explication of the qualities of bodies; and I fear the weakness of human understanding is scarce able to substitute another, which will afford us a fuller and clearer discovery of the necessary connection and co-existence of the powers which are to be observed united in several sorts of them. This at least is certain, that whichever hypothesis be clearest and truest (for of that it is not my business to determine), our knowledge concerning corporeal substances will be very little advanced by any of them, till we are made to see what qualities and powers of bodies have a necessary connection or repugnancy one with another; which, in the present state of philosophy, I think, we know but to a very small degree: and I doubt whether, with those faculties we have, we shall ever be able to carry our general knowledge (I say not particular experi-

ence) in this part much farther. Experience is that which in this part we must depend on. And it were to be wished that it were more improved. We find the advantages some men's generous pains have this way brought to the stock of natural knowledge. And if others, especially the philosophers by fire, who pretend to it, had been so wary in their observations and sincere in their reports as those who call themselves philosophers ought to have been, our acquaintance with the bodies here about us, and our insight into their powers and operations, had been yet much greater.

17. *Of spirits yet narrower.*—If we are at a loss in respect of the powers and operations of bodies, I think it easy to conclude we are much more in the dark in reference to spirits, whereof we naturally have no ideas but what we draw from that of our own, by reflecting on the operations of our own souls within us, as far as they can come within our observation. But how inconsiderable a rank the spirits that inhabit our bodies hold amongst those various, and possibly innumerable, kinds of nobler beings; and how far short they come of the endowments and perfections of cherubims and seraphims, and infinite sorts of spirits above us, is what by a transient hint, in another place, I have offered to my reader's consideration.

18. *Thirdly, Of other relations, it is not easy to say how far.*—As to the third sort of our knowledge, viz., the agreement or disagreement of any of our ideas in any other relation: this, as it is the largest field of our knowledge, so it is hard to determine how far it may extend: because the advances that are made in this part of knowledge depending on our sagacity in finding intermediate ideas that may show the relations and habitudes of ideas, whose co-existence is not considered, it is a hard matter to tell when we are at an end of such discoveries, and when reason has all the helps it is capable of for the finding of proofs, or examining the agreement or disagreement of remote ideas. They that are ignorant of algebra, cannot imagine the wonders in this kind are to be done by it: and what farther improvements and helps, advantageous to other

parts of knowledge, the sagacious mind of man may yet find out, it is not easy to determine. This at least I believe, that the ideas of quantity are not those alone that are capable of demonstration and knowledge; and that other, and perhaps more useful, parts of contemplation would afford us certainty, if vices, passions, and domineering interest did not oppose or menace such endeavours.

Morality capable of demonstration.—The idea of a Supreme Being, infinite in power, goodness, and wisdom, whose workmanship we are, and on whom we depend; and the idea of ourselves, as understanding, rational beings, being such as are clear in us, would, I suppose, if duly considered and pursued, afford such foundations of our duty and rules of action as might place morality amongst the sciences capable of demonstration: wherein I doubt not, but from self-evident propositions, by necessary consequences, as incontestable as those in mathematics, the measures of right and wrong might be made out, to any one that will apply himself with the same indifferency and attention to the one as he does to the other of these sciences. The relation of other modes may certainly be perceived, as well as those of number and extension: and I cannot see why they should not also be capable of demonstration, if due methods were thought on to examine or pursue their agreement or disagreement. "Where there is no property, there is no injustice," is a proposition as certain as any demonstration in Euclid: for, the idea of property being a right to anything, and the idea to which the name "injustice" is given being the invasion or violation of that right; it is evident that these ideas being thus established, and these names annexed to them, I can as certainly know this proposition to be true as that a triangle has three angles equal to two right ones. Again: "No government allows absolute liberty:" the idea of government being the establishment of society upon certain rules or laws, which require conformity to them; and the idea of absolute liberty being for any one to do whatever he pleases: I am as capable of being certain of the truth of this proposition as of any in the mathematics.

19. *Two things have made moral ideas thought uncapable of demonstration: their complexedness, and want of sensible representation.*—That which, in this respect, has given the advantage to the ideas of quantity, and made them thought more capable of certainty and demonstration, is,

First, That they can be set down and represented by sensible marks, which have a greater and nearer correspondence with them than any words or sounds whatsoever. Diagrams drawn on paper are copies of the ideas in the mind, and not liable to the uncertainty that words carry in their signification. An angle, circle, or square, drawn in lines, lies open to the view, and cannot be mistaken: it remains unchangeable, and may at leisure be considered and examined, and the demonstration be revised, and all the parts of it may be gone over more than once, without any danger of the least change in the ideas. This cannot be thus done in moral ideas: we have no sensible marks that resemble them, whereby we can set them down: we have nothing but words to express them by; which though, when written, they remain the same, yet the ideas they stand for may change in the same man; and it is very seldom that they are not different in different persons.

Secondly, Another thing that makes the greater difficulty in ethics is, that moral ideas are commonly more complex than those of the figures ordinarily considered in mathematics. From whence these two inconveniences follow: First, that their names are of more uncertain signification; the precise collection of simple ideas they stand for not being so easily agreed on, and so the sign that is used for them, in communication always, and in thinking often, does not steadily carry with it the same idea. Upon which the same disorder, confusion, and error follows as would if a man, going to demonstrate something of an heptagon, should, in the diagram he took to do it, leave out one of the angles, or by oversight make the figure with one angle more than the name ordinarily imported, or he intended it should when at first he thought of his demonstration. This often happens, and is hardly avoidable in very complex moral ideas, where, the same name being retained, one angle, *i.e.*, one simple idea, is left out or put in in the complex one (still called by the same name) more at one time than another. Secondly, From the complexedness of these moral ideas there follows another inconvenience, viz., that the mind cannot easily retain those precise combinations so exactly and perfectly as is necessary in the examination of the habitudes and correspondencies, agreements or disagreements, of several of them one with another; especially where it is to be judged of by long deductions, and the intervention of several other complex ideas, to show the agreement or disagreement of two remote ones.

The great help against this which mathematicians find in diagrams and figures, which remain unalterable in their draughts, is very apparent; and the memory would often have great difficulty otherwise to retain them so exactly, whilst the mind went over the parts of them, step by step, to examine their several correspondencies. And though, in casting up a long sum, either in addition, multiplication, or division, every part be only a progression of the mind taking a view of its own ideas, and considering their agreement or disagreement, and the resolution of the question be nothing but the result of the whole, made up of such particulars whereof the mind has a clear perception; yet without setting down the several parts by marks whose precise significations are known, and by marks that last and remain in view when the memory had let them go, it would be almost impossible to carry so many different ideas in mind, without confounding or letting slip some parts of the reckoning, and thereby making all our reasonings about it useless. In which case, the cyphers or marks help not the mind at all to perceive the agreement of any two or more numbers, their equalities or proportions: *that* the mind has only by intuition of its own ideas of the numbers themselves. But the numerical characters are helps to the memory to record and retain the several ideas about which the demonstration is made, whereby a man may know how far his intuitive knowledge in surveying several of the particulars has proceeded; that so he may, without confusion, go on to what is yet unknown, and, at last, have in view before him the result of all his perceptions and reasonings.

20. *Remedies of those difficulties.*—One part of these disadvantages in moral ideas, which has made them be thought not capable of demonstration, may in a good measure be remedied by definitions, setting down that collection of simple ideas which every term shall stand for, and then using the terms steadily and constantly for that precise collection. And what methods algebra, or something of that kind, may hereafter suggest, to remove the other difficulties, is not easy to foretell. Confident I am, that if men would in the same method, and with the same indifferency, search after moral as they do mathematical truths, they would find them to have a stronger connection one with another, and a more necessary consequence from our clear and distinct ideas, and to come nearer perfect demonstration, than is commonly imagined. But much of this is not to be expected, whilst the desire of esteem, riches, or power makes men espouse the well-endowed opinions in fashion, and then seek arguments either to make good their beauty, or varnish over and cover their deformity: nothing being so beautiful to the eye as truth is to the mind, nothing so deformed and irreconcileable to the understanding as a lie. For, though many a man can with satisfaction enough own a no-very-handsome wife in his bosom, yet who is bold enough openly to avow that he has espoused a falsehood, and received into his breast so ugly a thing as a lie? Whilst the parties of men cram their tenets down all men's throats whom they can get into their power, without permitting them to examine their truth or falsehood; and will not let truth have fair play in the world, nor men the liberty to search after it; what improvements can be expected of this kind? what greater light can be hoped for in the moral sciences? The subject part of mankind, in most places, might, instead thereof, with Egyptian bondage, expect Egyptian darkness, were not the candle of the Lord set up by himself in men's

minds, which it is impossible for the breath or power of man wholly to extinguish.

21. *Fourthly, Of real existence. We have an* INTUITIVE *knowledge of our own,* DEMONSTRATIVE *of God's,* SENSITIVE *of some few other things'*.—As to the fourth sort of our knowledge, viz., of the real actual existence of things, we have an intuitive knowledge of our own existence; a demonstrative knowledge of the existence of a God; of the existence of anything else, we have no other but a sensitive knowledge, which extends not beyond the objects present to our senses.

22. *Our ignorance great.*—Our knowledge being so narrow, as I have showed, it will, perhaps, give us some light into the present state of our minds, if we look a little into the dark side, and take a view of our ignorance: which, being infinitely larger than our knowledge, may serve much to the quieting of disputes and improvement of useful knowledge, if, discovering how far we have clear and distinct ideas, we confine our thoughts within the contemplation of those things that are within the reach of our understandings, and launch not out into that abyss of darkness (where we have not eyes to see, nor faculties to perceive anything), out of a presumption that nothing is beyond our comprehension. But to be satisfied of the folly of such a conceit, we need not go far. He that knows anything, knows this in the first place, that he need not seek long for instances of his ignorance. The meanest and most obvious things that come in our way have dark sides, that the quickest sight cannot penetrate into. The clearest and most enlarged understandings of thinking men find themselves puzzled and at a loss in every particle of matter. We shall the less wonder to find it so when we consider the causes of our ignorance, which, from what has been said, I suppose, will be found to be chiefly these three:

FIRST, Want of ideas.

SECONDLY, Want of a discoverable connection between the ideas we have.

THIRDLY, Want of tracing and examining our ideas.

23. *First, One cause of it, want of ideas, either such as we*

have no conception of.—FIRST, There are some things, and those not a few, that we are ignorant of for want of ideas.

First, All the simple ideas we have are confined (as I have shown) to those we receive from corporeal objects by sensation, and from the operations of our own minds as the objects of reflection. But how much these few and narrow inlets are disproportionate to the vast whole extent of all beings, will not be hard to persuade those who are not so foolish as to think their span the measure of all things. What other simple ideas it is possible the creatures in other parts of the universe may have by the assistance of senses and faculties more or perfecter than we have, or different from ours, it is not for us to determine; but to say or think there are no such because we conceive nothing of them, is no better an argument than if a blind man should be positive in it, that there was no such thing as sight and colours because he had no manner of idea of any such thing, nor could by any means frame to himself any notions about seeing. The ignorance and darkness that is in us no more hinders nor confines the knowledge that is in others, than the blindness of a mole is an argument against the quicksightedness of an eagle. He that will consider the infinite power, wisdom, and goodness of the Creator of all things, will find reason to think it was not all laid out upon so inconsiderable, mean, and impotent a creature as he will find man to be, who, in all probability, is one of the lowest of all intellectual beings. What faculties therefore other species of creatures have to penetrate into the nature and inmost constitutions of things, what ideas they may receive of them far different from ours, we know not. This we know and certainly find, that we want several other views of them besides those we have, to make discoveries of them more perfect. And we may be convinced that the ideas we can attain to by our faculties are very disproportionate to things themselves, when a positive, clear, distinct one of substance itself, which is the foundation of all the rest, is concealed from us. But want of ideas of this kind, being a part as well as cause of our ignorance, cannot be described.

Only this, I think, I may confidently say of it, that the intellectual and sensible world are in this perfectly alike—that that part which we see of either of them holds no proportion with what we see not; and whatsoever we can reach with our eyes or our thoughts of either of them, is but a point, almost nothing, in comparison of the rest.

24. *Or want of such ideas as particularly we have not, because of their remoteness.*—Secondly, Another great cause of ignorance is the want of ideas we are capable of. As the want of ideas which our faculties are not able to give us shuts us wholly from those views of things which it is reasonable to think other beings, perfecter than we, have, of which we know nothing; so the want of ideas I now speak of keeps us in ignorance of things we conceive capable of being known to us. Bulk, figure, and motion we have ideas of. But though we are not without ideas of these primary qualities of bodies in general, yet not knowing what is the particular bulk, figure, and motion, of the greatest part of the bodies of the universe, we are ignorant of the several powers, efficacies, and ways of operation, whereby the effects which we daily see are produced. These are hid from us in some things by being too remote; and, in others, by being too minute. When we consider the vast distance of the known and visible parts of the world, and the reasons we have to think that what lies within our ken is but a small part of the immense universe, we shall then discover a huge abyss of ignorance. What are the particular fabrics of the great masses of matter which make up the whole stupendous frame of corporeal beings, how far they are extended, what is their motion, and how continued or communicated, and what influence they have one upon another, are contemplations that, at first glimpse, our thoughts lose themselves in. If we narrow our contemplation, and confine our thoughts to this little canton, I mean this system of our sun, and the grosser masses of matter that visibly move about it, what several sorts of vegetables, animals, and intellectual corporeal beings, infinitely different from those of our little spot of earth, may there probably be in the

other planets, to the knowledge of which, even of their outward figures and parts, we can no way attain whilst we are confined to this earth, there being no natural means, either by sensation or reflection, to convey their certain ideas into our minds! They are out of the reach of those inlets of all our knowledge; and what sorts of furniture and inhabitants those mansions contain in them, we cannot so much as guess, much less have clear and distinct ideas of them.

25. *Or because of their minuteness.*—If a great, nay, far the greatest part of the several ranks of bodies in the universe escape our notice by their remoteness, there are others no less concealed from us by their minuteness. These insensible corpuscles being the active parts of matter and the great instruments of nature, on which depend not only all their secondary qualities, but also most of their natural operations, our want of precise, distinct ideas of their primary qualities keeps us in an incurable ignorance of what we desire to know about them. I doubt not but if we could discover the figure, size, texture, and motion of the minute constituent parts of any two bodies, we should know without trial several of their operations one upon another, as we do now the properties of a square or a triangle. Did we know the mechanical affections of the particles of rhubarb, hemlock, opium, and a man, as a watchmaker does those of a watch, whereby it performs its operations, and of a file, which, by rubbing on them, will alter the figure of any of the wheels, we should be able to tell beforehand that rhubarb will purge, hemlock kill, and opium make a man sleep, as well as a watchmaker can, that a little piece of paper laid on the balance will keep the watch from going till it be removed; or that some small part of it being rubbed by a file, the machine would quite lose its motion, and the watch go no more. The dissolving of silver in *aqua fortis*, and gold in *aqua regia*, and not *vice versâ*, would be then perhaps no more difficult to know, than it is to a smith to understand why the turning of one key will open a lock, and not the turning of another. But whilst we are destitute of senses acute enough to discover the minute particles of bodies,

and to give us ideas of their mechanical affections, we must be content to be ignorant of their properties and ways of operation; nor can we be assured about them any farther than some few trials we make are able to reach. But whether they will succeed again another time we cannot be certain. This hinders our certain knowledge of universal truths concerning natural bodies, and our reason carries us herein very little beyond particular matter of fact.

26. *Hence no science of bodies.*—And therefore I am apt to doubt, that how far soever human industry may advance useful and experimental philosophy in physical things, scientifical will still be out of our reach; because we want perfect and adequate ideas of those very bodies which are nearest to us and most under our command. Those which we have ranked into classes under names, and we think ourselves best acquainted with, we have but very imperfect and incomplete ideas of. Distinct ideas of the several sorts of bodies that fall under the examination of our senses perhaps we may have; but adequate ideas, I suspect, we have not of any one amongst them. And though the former of these will serve us for common use and discourse: yet whilst we want the latter, we are not capable of scientifical knowledge, nor shall ever be able to discover general instructive, unquestionable truths concerning them. Certainty and demonstration are things we must not, in these matters, pretend to. By the colour, figure, taste, and smell, and other sensible qualities, we have as clear and distinct ideas of sage and hemlock, as we have of a circle and a triangle; but having no ideas of the particular primary qualities of the minute parts of either of these plants, nor of other bodies which we would apply them to, we cannot tell what effects they will produce; nor when we see those effects can we so much as guess, much less know, their manner of production. Thus, having no ideas of the particular mechanical affections of the minute parts of bodies that are within our view and reach, we are ignorant of their constitutions, powers, and operations; and of bodies more remote we are yet more ignorant, not knowing so much as their very

outward shapes, or the sensible and grosser parts of their constitutions.

27. *Much less of spirits.*—This, at first sight, will show us how disproportionate our knowledge is to the whole extent even of material beings; to which if we add the consideration of that infinite number of spirits that may be, and probably are, which are yet more remote from our knowledge, whereof we have no cognizance, nor can frame to ourselves any distinct ideas of their several ranks and sorts, we shall find this cause of ignorance conceal from us, in an impenetrable obscurity, almost the whole intellectual world; a greater, certainly, and more beautiful world than the material. For, bating some very few, and those, if I may so call them, "superficial," ideas of spirit, which by reflection we get of our own, and from thence the best we can collect of the Father of all spirits, the eternal independent author of them and us and all things, we have no certain information so much as of the existence of other spirits but by revelation. Angels of all sorts are naturally beyond our discovery; and all those intelligencies whereof it is likely there are more orders than of corporeal substances, are things whereof our natural faculties give us no certain account at all. That there are minds and thinking beings in other men, as well as himself, every man has a reason, from their words and actions, to be satisfied; and the knowledge of his own mind cannot suffer a man that considers to be ignorant that there is a God. But that there are degrees of spiritual beings between us and the great God, who is there that by his own search and ability can come to know? Much less have we distinct ideas of their different natures, conditions, states, powers, and several constitutions, wherein they agree or differ from one another and from us. And therefore, in what concerns their different species and properties, we are under an absolute ignorance.

28. *Secondly, Want of a discoverable connection between ideas we have.*—Secondly, What a small part of the substantial beings that are in the universe the want of ideas leaves open

to our knowledge, we have seen. In the next place, another cause of ignorance of no less moment is a want of a discoverable connection between those ideas which we have. For wherever we want that, we are utterly uncapable of universal and certain knowledge; and are, as in the former case, left only to observation and experiment; which how narrow and confined it is, how far from general knowledge, we need not be told. I shall give some few instances of this cause of our ignorance, and so leave it. It is evident that the bulk, figure, and motion of several bodies about us, produce in us several sensations, as of colours, sounds, taste, smell, pleasure, and pain, &c. These mechanical affections of bodies having no affinity at all with those ideas they produce in us (there being no conceivable connection between any impulse of any sort of body, and any perception of a colour or smell which we find in our minds), we can have no distinct knowledge of such operations beyond our experience; and can reason no otherwise about them than as effects produced by the appointment of an infinitely wise Agent which perfectly surpass our comprehensions. As the ideas of sensible secondary qualities which we have in our minds can by us be no way deduced from bodily causes, nor any correspondence or connection be found between them and those primary qualities which experience shows us produce them in us; so, on the other side, the operation of our minds upon our bodies is as unconceivable. How any thought should produce a motion in body is as remote from the nature of our ideas, as how any body should produce any thought in the mind. That it is so, if experience did not convince us, the consideration of the things themselves would never be able in the least to discover to us. These and the like, though they have a constant and regular connection in the ordinary course of things; yet that connection being not discoverable in the ideas themselves, which appearing to have no necessary dependence one on another, we can attribute their connection to nothing else but the arbitrary determination of that all-wise Agent who has made them to be, and to operate as they do, in a way wholly above our weak understandings to conceive.

29. *Instances.*—In some of our ideas there are certain relations, habitudes, and connections so visibly included in the nature of the ideas themselves, that we cannot conceive them separable from them by any power whatsoever. And in these only we are capable of certain and universal knowledge. Thus the idea of a right-lined triangle necessarily carries with it an equality of its angles to two right ones. Nor can we conceive this relation, this connection of these two ideas, to be possibly mutable, or to depend on any arbitrary power, which of choice made it thus, or could make it otherwise. But the coherence and continuity of the parts of matter, the production of sensation in us of colours and sounds, &c., by impulse and motion, nay, the original rules and communications of motion, being such wherein we can discover no natural connection with any ideas we have, we cannot but ascribe them to the arbitrary will and good pleasure of the wise Architect. I need not, I think, here mention the resurrection of the dead, the future state of this globe of earth, and such other things which are by every one acknowledged to depend wholly on the determination of a free agent. The things that, as far as our observation reaches, we constantly find to proceed regularly, we may conclude do act by a law set them; but yet by a law that we know not; whereby, though causes work steadily, and effects constantly flow from them, yet their connections and dependencies being not discoverable in our ideas, we can have but an experimental knowledge of them. From all which it is easy to perceive what a darkness we are involved in, how little it is of being, and the things that are, that we are capable to know. And therefore we shall do no injury to our knowledge when we modestly think with ourselves, that we are so far from being able to comprehend the whole nature of the universe and all the things contained in it, that we are not capable of a philosophical knowledge of the bodies that are about us, and make a part

of us; concerning their secondary qualities, powers, and operations, we can have no universal certainty. Several effects come every day within the notice of our senses, of which we have so far sensitive knowledge; but the causes, manner, and certainty of their production, for the two foregoing reasons, we must be content to be ignorant of. In these we can go no farther than particular experience informs us of matter of fact, and by analogy to guess what effects the like bodies are, upon other trials, like to produce. But as to a perfect science of natural bodies (not to mention spiritual beings), we are, I think, so far from being capable of any such thing, that I conclude it lost labour to seek after it.*

30. *Thirdly, want of tracing our ideas.*—Thirdly, Where we have adequate ideas, and where there is a certain and discoverable connection between them, yet we are often ignorant for want of tracing those ideas which we have or may have; and for want of finding out those intermediate ideas which may show us what habitude of agreement or disagreement they have one with another. And thus many are ignorant of mathematical truths, not out of any imperfection of their faculties, or uncertainty in the things themselves; but for want of application in acquiring, examining, and by due ways comparing those ideas. That which has most contributed to hinder the due tracing of our ideas, and finding out their relations and agreements or disagreements one with another has been, I suppose, the ill use of words. It is impossible that men should ever truly seek, or certainly discover, the agreement or disagreement of ideas themselves, whilst their thoughts flutter about, or stick only in sounds of doubtful and uncertain significations. Mathematicians, abstracting their thoughts from names, and accustoming themselves to set before their minds the ideas themselves that they would consider, and

* In these modern times, however, a very near approach is being made to such a science as that which Locke mentions. Natural philosophy has emerged from the helplessness of infancy; and in the recently-developed doctrine of the Conservation of Force, we may recognise a foreshadowing of that Unity which is, as it were, the adolescence of science.—ED.

not sounds instead of them, have avoided thereby a great part of that perplexity, puddering, and confusion, which has so much hindered men's progress in other parts of knowledge. For whilst they stick in words of undetermined and uncertain signification, they are unable to distinguish true from false, certain from probable, consistent from inconsistent, in their own opinions. This having been the fate or misfortune of a great part of the men of letters, the increase brought into the stock of real knowledge has been very little in proportion to the schools, disputes, and writings, the world has been filled with; whilst students, being lost in the great wood of words, knew not whereabout they were, how far their discoveries were advanced, or what was wanting in their own or the general stock of knowledge. Had men, in the discoveries of the material, done as they have in those of the intellectual, world, involved all in the obscurity of uncertain and doubtful ways of talking, volumes writ of navigation and voyages, theories and stories of zones and tides multiplied and disputed, nay, ships built, and fleets set out, would never have taught us the way beyond the line; and the antipodes would be still as much unknown as when it was declared heresy to hold there were any. But having spoken sufficiently of words, and the ill or careless use that is commonly made of them, I shall not say anything more of it here.

NOTES.

A. Of Intuition.

Intuition, according to Locke, is the immediate perception of the agreement or disagreement betwixt two ideas; and it may be well to point out here that the knowledge thus acquired depends for its legitimacy upon those mental laws of which Locke was accustomed to speak in such disparaging terms, viz., "Whatever is, is;" and "It is impossible for the same thing at the same time to be and not to be." For, since no comparison between two ideas can take place without some analysis, it follows that an assertion of their agreement or disagreement is an assertion of their respective characters (*i. e.* the appearances which they present to the mind) being similar or dissimilar. But this proceeds upon the assumption that an idea viewed as a whole is the same thing as all its parts or characters when viewed together, and that two sets of characters which differ in any portion are not the same idea: such assumptions being merely other modes of expressing the laws, "Whatever is, is;" and "It is impossible for the same thing at the same time to be and not to be."

B. OF LOCKE'S THEORY CONCERNING KNOWLEDGE.

In this theory there are two points requiring discussion—first, the notion that all knowledge concerns ideas, and ideas only; and, secondly, the statement that every judgment, or act of knowledge, is a recognition of the agreement or disagreement existing between two ideas.

As regards the former of these, it has already (p. 67) been shown that representative ideas are now discarded from all legitimate psychologies; but yet it will be desirable to add a few words respecting the character of such knowledge as these ideas, if admitted to exist, are capable of imparting. That is to say, we seek to inquire whether the knowledge thus acquired be true or false; and the only method of doing so is to investigate that quality which constitutes real or valid knowledge. This is pointed out by Locke as follows:—"It is evident the mind knows not things immediately, but only by the intervention of the ideas it has of them. Our knowledge, therefore, is real only so far as there is a conformity between our ideas and the reality of things." In other words, when our ideas faithfully reflect the objects which produce them, our knowledge is true: when a dissimilarity exists between our ideas and their archetypes, we have only a false knowledge.

Now, ideas, admitting them, with Locke, to exist, are either material or immaterial. If they be material, they cannot resemble or represent mind, the Deity, time, space, &c.; and therefore, of these we can have no true knowledge: if they be immaterial, they cannot resemble or represent corporeal bodies; and therefore the world of matter is to us chimerical. Again, even if material, they cannot resemble the secondary qualities of bodies, *i. e.* colours, savours, odours, &c., which are sensations in nowise like the physical properties which produce them; nor can they represent primary qualities, such as solidity, figure, &c., which in this sense are abstractions; and still less can they represent matter *per se*, *i. e.* substance divested of all sensible qualities: it follows, therefore, that material ideas can give no true knowledge of matter; and, as we have before seen that they can give none of spirit, we are unable, while dependent upon them for knowledge, to believe in the existence or reality of either minds or bodies. So also, even if ideas be immaterial, they can in no manner represent any spiritual being, for it is only of matter that images or resemblances exist: and we have already seen that they cannot represent bodies; therefore we are led to the same result with immaterial as with material ideas—that is to say, we can have no valid belief in either souls or bodies. But, furthermore, if ideas be representative, they must be material, as otherwise they could not be images or resemblances: accordingly, the subject in which they inhere, *i. e.* the mind, must be material too, and also everything represented; so that we are compelled to adopt a complete system of Materialism, if we are so sparing as not to carry the doctrine to its logical result, that is, to Nihilism. And, finally, after having thus shown that the theory of representative ideas cannot on any supposition be saved, it remains to be pointed out that, although one should admit that we only perceive ideas, and that these ideas are representative of their archetypes, yet, in spite of all this, we should still remain without any means of discovering whether our knowledge were true or false. This follows from the same analysis as that performed in the note on "sensitive knowledge:" for, as the truth or error of our knowledge depends upon the agreement or disagreement of our ideas and the objects producing them, it is evident that we cannot judge whether such conformity or non-conformity exists, unless we perceive on the one hand the objects themselves, and on the other the ideas. But as we are only able to perceive ideas, we cannot be conscious of the objects themselves, and therefore cannot perceive whether the two things agree or disagree—that is, we cannot tell whether our knowledge be true or false.

The second of the points alluded to at the commencement of this note is that portion of Locke's doctrine which declares that every judgment, or act of knowledge, is a recognition of the agreement or disagreement existing between two ideas. The objection urged against this theory is that, whilst professing to account for *all* knowledge, it can only do so for *some* of our judgments. Take, for example (as is done by M. Cousin), this judgment, "I exist;" the question is whether such a knowledge as it expresses is the recognition of an agreement between two ideas; and the argument for a negative answer runs as follows:— If this judgment be the result of a comparison between two ideas, these ideas must evidently be those of a *me*, an *ego*, and of existence. But the *ego* must not be conceived as existing, for then there would be no necessity for the judgment: it must be imagined as separate from existence, as an abstract *me*, as *ego* in general. For similar reasons, the idea of existence must not be that of an existing *me*, but of existence in the abstract. Behold, then, the two terms which are to be compared; they are abstractions: it therefore follows that the agreement between them must be an abstract relation; that is to say, we can merely form the judgment that "Every *me* must exist"—a very different truth from that which we are investigating, viz. an assertion of personal existence, a statement of a single real fact, "I exist." not a mere generalisation of possible existence.

Again, since, according to Locke, the knowledge of personal existence is acquired from the comparison of two ideas, and since these ideas must, as we have shown, be abstractions, it follows that human knowledge commences with abstractions; whereas, in fact, it is things in the concrete which are first known, which are the subjects of primitive knowledge.

Once more: the theory in question is based upon a paralogism, a *petitio principii;* for the idea of abstract existence could only have been obtained from a previous knowledge of concrete existences; and therefore to attempt to derive the latter from the former is to attempt to prove a thing by means of something else which implies it.

"We thus have three radical objections against the theory of Locke:—

"1°. It sets out from abstractions; consequently it gives only an abstract result, and not that which you are seeking.

"2°. It sets out from abstractions; and, consequently, it does not set out from the true starting point, the human intelligence.

"3°. It sets out from abstractions which it could have obtained only by aid of this same concrete knowledge which it pretends to draw from abstractions which suppose it; consequently it takes for granted what is in question."

Such is a *résumé* of M. Cousin's celebrated argument against Locke's theory of judgment; and this may be taken as a fair exposition of the views now generally entertained upon the subject. But although the other portions of his system would prevent Locke himself from successfully combating the above objections, yet they may easily be met with a complete rejoinder, as the following remarks will tend to show.

When we first acquire that knowledge which is expressed by the judgment, "I exist," it is evident that we are thinking of a particular concrete *me;* this is admitted on all sides. It is likewise evident that, previously to the time of our forming this judgment, we either have the idea of abstract existence, or we have it not; and this, too, is admitted by all. What I undertake to prove, then, is that on either of the last-mentioned suppositions (one of which *must* be the case), when we say, "I—a particular concrete *ego*—exist," we express the recognition of an agreement between two ideas.

In the first place, let it be assumed that, at the time of our acquiring the knowledge of personal existence—*i. e.* when we first say, "I exist"—that at that time we have had no anterior knowledge of abstract existence. I next ask, what are the necessary conditions of conceiving our own concrete individual self? In what manner does consciousness reveal it to us? It cannot be as an *abstract me*—as *ego, per se;* for we are all agreed that it is a *concrete me* which is known. No; it must be as a thinking, percipient *me*—as an *ego* accompanied by some thought or perception. That is to say, we are conscious of something which is *me*, and of something which is *not me*—of an *ego* and of a *non-ego*. But are these two ideas entirely distinct? Can we regard them as disunited, and offering no common quality to consciousness? We cannot. An irresistible law or faculty of the mind compels us towards unity of conception; and, simultaneously with our perception of the *ego* and *non-ego*, we see that they are, in part at least, the same; we reduce the variety to unity. What is this quality, then, in which they agree? It is *existence*. The mind exists, the thought exists; the *ego* exists, the *non-ego* exists; they both exist: *i.e. I*—the concrete formed by *ego* and *non-ego*—exist.

It will thus be seen that the act of knowledge by which we are enabled to say, "I exist," is a duplex perception of the agreement between the idea of the concrete *me* ($= ego + non\text{-}ego$), and that of existence. It should also be noted that the operation, though complex, is simultaneous.

In the second place (although an impossible alternative), let it be assumed that the idea of abstract existence is in the mind previously to our forming the judgment, "I exist." We have then the idea of a something, an $ego + non\text{-}ego$, which we term "I," and which is not conceived as existing, that is, as comprehending the notion of existence, but as a combination of only two elements, the *ego* and the *non-ego*. But we also have the idea of existence; and therefore, in accordance with the imperative dictates of our mental nature, we seek for unity in this variety. We find it; or, in other words, we recognise that both the "I" and "existence" produce a partially similar impression upon our minds. Then, perceiving this, we say, "I exist."

Thus, with or without an anterior knowledge of abstract existence, I have shown that our first idea of *personal* existence is derived from a perception of the agreement between two ideas.

Hence, too, it follows that the doctrine does *not* "set out from abstractions;" and therefore it is obnoxious to neither of the charges brought against it.

Locke, it is true, gives no account which shall serve to throw any light upon the real nature or bearing of his theory concerning judgment; but there is no doubt that he has, upon this subject, formed a more correct opinion than the majority of those who have attacked him. It is merely one phase of the question which has just now been discussed, but in the present place it is impossible to enter upon any more detailed investigation: those, however, who wish for further information upon the subject may be referred to the second series of M. Cousin's *Cours de Philosophie*, and to the *Treatise on Logic, Pure and Applied* (Appendix, articles A, C, and D), in the series to which the present volume belongs.

OF REASON.

1. *Various significations of the word "reason."*—The word "reason," in the English language, has different significations: sometimes it is taken for true and clear principles; sometimes for clear and fair deductions from those principles; and sometimes for the cause, and particularly the final cause. But the consideration I shall have of it here is in a signification different from all these; and that is, as it stands for a faculty in man; that faculty whereby man is supposed to be distinguished from beasts, and wherein it is evident he much surpasses them.

2. *Wherein reasoning consists.*—If general knowledge, as has been shown, consists in a perception of the agreement or disagreement of our own ideas, and the knowledge of the existence of all things without us (except only of a God, whose existence every man may certainly know and demonstrate to himself from his own existence) be had only by our senses; what room then is there for the exercise of any other faculty but outward sense and inward perception? What need is there of reason? Very much; both for the enlargement of our knowledge and regulating our assent: for it has to do both in knowledge and opinion, and is necessary, and assisting to all our other intellectual faculties, and indeed contains two of them, viz. sagacity and illation. By the one it finds out, and by the other it so orders, the intermediate ideas as to discover what connection there is in each link of the chain, whereby the extremes are held together; and thereby, as it were, to draw into view the truth sought for, which is that we call "illation" or "inference," and consists in nothing but the perception of the connection there is between the ideas in each step of the deduction, whereby the mind comes to see either the certain agreement or disagreement of any two ideas, as in demonstration, in which it arrives at knowledge; or their probable connection, on which it gives or withholds its assent, as in opinion. Sense and intuition

reach but a very little way. The greatest part of our knowledge depends upon deductions and intermediate ideas: and in those cases where we are fain to substitute assent instead of knowledge, and take propositions for true without being certain they are so, we have need to find out, examine, and compare the grounds of their probability. In both these cases the faculty which finds out the means, and rightly applies them to discover certainty in the one and probability in the other, is that which we call "reason." For, as reason perceives the necessary and indubitable connection of all the ideas or proofs one to another in each step of any demonstration that produces knowledge, so it likewise perceives the probable connection of all the ideas or proofs one to another, in every step of a discourse to which it will think assent due. This is the lowest degree of that which can be truly called "reason." For, where the mind does not perceive this probable connection, where it does not discern whether there be any such connection or no, there men's opinions are not the product of judgment or the consequence of reason, but the effects of chance and hazard, of a mind floating at all adventures, without choice and without direction.

3. *Its four parts.*—So that we may in reason consider these four degrees: The first and highest is the discovering and finding out of proofs; the second, the regular and methodical disposition of them, and laying them in a clear and fit order to make their connection and force be plainly and easily perceived; the third is the perceiving their connection; and the fourth, a making a right conclusion. These several degrees may be observed in any mathematical demonstration: it being one thing to perceive the connection of each part as the demonstration is made by another; another to perceive the dependence of the conclusion on all the parts; a third, to make out a demonstration clearly and neatly one's self; and something different from all these, to have first found out those intermediate ideas or proofs by which it is made.

4. *Syllogism not the great instrument of reason.*—There is one thing more which I shall desire to be considered concern-

ing reason; and that is, whether syllogism, as is generally thought, be the proper instrument of it, and the usefullest way of exercising this faculty. The causes I have to doubt are these:—

First, Because syllogism serves our reason but in one only of the fore-mentioned parts of it; and that is, to show the connection of the proofs in any one instance and no more: but in this it is of no great use, since the mind can perceive such connection where it really is as easily, nay, perhaps better, without it.

If we will observe the actings of our own minds, we shall find that we reason best and clearest when we only observe the connection of the proof, without reducing our thoughts to any rule of syllogism. And therefore we may take notice that there are many men that reason exceeding clear and rightly, who know not how to make a syllogism. He that will look into many parts of Asia and America, will find men reason there, perhaps, as acutely as himself, who yet never heard of a syllogism, nor can reduce any one argument to those forms: and I believe scarce any one ever makes syllogisms in reasoning within himself. Indeed, syllogism is made use of on occasion to discover a fallacy hid in a rhetorical flourish, or cunningly wrapped up in a smooth period; and stripping an absurdity of the cover of wit and good language, show it in its naked deformity. But the weakness or fallacy of such a loose discourse it shows, by the artificial form it is put into, only to those who have thoroughly studied mode and figure, and have so examined the many ways that three propositions may be put together, as to know which of them does certainly conclude right, and which not, and upon what grounds it is that they do so. All who have so far considered syllogism as to see the reason why, in three propositions laid together in one form, the conclusion will be certainly right, but in another not certainly so, I grant are certain of the conclusions they draw from the premisses in the allowed modes and figures. But they who have not so far looked into those forms are not sure, by virtue of syllogism, that the conclusion certainly follows from the premisses; they only take it to be so by an implicit faith in their teachers, and a confidence in those forms of argumentation: but this is still but believing, not being certain. Now, if of all mankind those who can make syllogisms are extremely few in comparison with those who cannot, and if of those few who have been taught logic there is but a very small number who do any more than believe that syllogisms in the allowed modes and figures do conclude right, without knowing certainly that they do so; if syllogisms must be taken for the only proper instrument of reason and means of knowledge; it will follow that before Aristotle there was not one man that did or could know anything by reason; and that, since the invention of syllogisms, there is not one of ten thousand that doth.

But God has not been so sparing to men to make them barely two-legged creatures, and left it to Aristotle to make them rational; *i.e.*, those few of them that he could get so to examine the grounds of syllogisms as to see that in above threescore ways that three propositions may be laid together, there are but about fourteen wherein one may be sure that the conclusion is right, and upon what ground it is that in these few the conclusion is certain, and in the other not. God has been more bountiful to mankind than so; he has given them a mind that can reason without being instructed in methods of syllogising: the understanding is not taught to reason by these rules; it has a native faculty to perceive the coherence or incoherence of its ideas, and can range them right without any such perplexing repetitions. I say not this any way to lessen Aristotle, whom I look on as one of the greatest men amongst the ancients; whose large views, acuteness and penetration of thought, and strength of judgment, few have equalled; and who, in this very invention of forms of argumentation, wherein the conclusion may be shown to be rightly inferred, did great service against those who were not ashamed to deny anything. And I readily own that all right reasoning may be reduced to his forms of syllogism. But yet I think, without any diminution to him, I may truly say, that they are not the only nor the best way of reasoning, for the leading of those into truth who are willing to find it, and desire to make the best use they may of their reason for the attainment of knowledge. And he himself, it is plain, found out some forms to be conclusive and others not, not by the forms themselves, but by the original way of knowledge, *i.e.*, by the visible agreement of ideas. Tell a country gentlewoman that the wind is south-west, and the weather louring and like to rain, and she will easily understand it is not safe for her to go abroad thin clad in such a day, after a fever: she clearly sees the probable connection of all these, viz., south-west wind, and clouds, rain, wetting, taking cold, relapse, and danger of death, without tying them together in those artificial and cumbersome fetters of several syllogisms that clog and hinder the mind, which proceeds from one part to another quicker and clearer without them: and the probability which she easily perceives in things thus in their native state would be quite lost, if this argument were managed learnedly and proposed in mode and figure. For it very often confounds the connection: and, I think, every one will perceive in mathematical demonstrations, that the knowledge gained thereby comes shortest and clearest without syllogisms.

Inference is looked on as the great act of the rational faculty; and so it is when it is rightly made: but the mind, either very desirous to enlarge its knowledge, or very apt to favour the sentiments it has once imbibed, is very forward to make inferences, and therefore often makes too much haste before it perceives the connection of the ideas that must hold the extremes together.

To infer is nothing but, by virtue of one proposition laid down as true, to draw in another as true; *i. e.*, to see or suppose such a connection of the two ideas of the inferred proposition. *V. g.*, let this be the proposition laid down, "Men shall be punished in another world," and from thence be inferred this other, "Then men can determine themselves." The question now is to know whether the mind has made this inference right or no; if it has made it by finding out the intermediate ideas, and taking a view of the connection of them placed in a due order, it has proceeded rationally, and made a right inference. If it has done it without such a view, it has not so much made an inference that will hold, or an inference of right reason, as shown a willingness to have it be or be taken for such. But in neither case is it syllogism that discovered those ideas, or showed the connection of them; for they must be both found out, and the connection everywhere perceived, before they can rationally be made use of in syllogism: unless it can be said that any idea, without considering what connection it hath with the two other, whose agreement should be shown by it, will do well enough in a syllogism, and may be taken at a venture for the *medius terminus* to prove any conclusion. But this nobody will say, because it is by virtue of the perceived agreement of the intermediate idea with the extremes, that the extremes are concluded to agree, and therefore each intermediate idea must be such as in the whole chain hath a visible connection with those two it is placed between, or else thereby the conclusion cannot be inferred or drawn in; for wherever any link of the chain is loose and without connection, there the whole strength of it is lost, and it hath no force to infer or draw in anything. In the instance above mentioned what is it shows the force of the inference, and consequently the reasonableness of it, but a view of the connection of all the intermediate ideas that draw in the conclusion or proposition inferred? *v. g.*, "Men shall be punished; God the punisher; just punishment; the punished guilty; could have done otherwise; freedom; self-determination;" by which chain of ideas thus visibly linked together in train, *i. e.*, each intermediate idea agreeing on each side with those two it is immediately placed between, the ideas of men and self-determination appear to be connected; *i. e.*, this proposition, "Men can determine themselves," is drawn in or inferred from this, that "they shall be punished in the other world." For here the mind, seeing the connection there is between the idea of men's punishment in the other world and the idea of God punishing, between

God punishing and the justice of the punishment, between justice of punishment and guilt, between guilt and a power to do otherwise, between a power to do otherwise and freedom, and between freedom and self-determination, sees the connection between men and self-determination.

Now, I ask, whether the connection of the extremes be not more clearly seen in this simple and natural disposition than in the perplexed repetitions and jumble of five or six syllogisms? I must beg pardon for calling it "jumble" till somebody shall put these ideas into so many syllogisms, and then say that they are less jumbled, and their connection more visible, when they are transposed and repeated, and spun out to a greater length in artificial forms than in that short, natural, plain order they are laid down in here, wherein every one may see it; and wherein they must be seen before they can be put into a train of syllogisms. For the natural order of the connecting ideas must direct the order of the syllogisms, and a man must see the connection of each intermediate idea with those that it connects, before he can with reason make use of it in a syllogism. And when all those syllogisms are made, neither those that are nor those that are not logicians will see the force of the argumentation, *i.e.*, the connection of the extremes, one jot the better. [For those that are not men of art, not knowing the true forms of syllogism, nor the reasons of them, cannot know whether they are made in right and conclusive modes and figures or no, and so are not at all helped by the forms they are put into, though by them the natural order, wherein the mind could judge of their respective connection, being disturbed, renders the illation much more uncertain than without them.] And as for logicians themselves, they see the connection of each intermediate idea with those it stands between (on which the force of the inference depends) as well before as after the syllogism is made, or else they do not see it at all. For a syllogism neither shows nor strengthens the connection of any two ideas immediately put together, but only by the connection seen in them shows what connection the extremes have one with another. But what connection the intermediate has with either of the extremes in that syllogism, that no syllogism does or can show. *That* the mind only doth or can perceive, as they stand there in that juxtaposition, only by its own view, to which the syllogistical form it happens to be in gives no help or light at all; it only shows that if the intermediate idea agrees with those it is on both sides immediately applied to, then those two remote ones, or, as they are called, "extremes," do certainly agree; and therefore the immediate connection of each idea to that which it is applied to on each side, on which the force of the reasoning depends, is as well seen before as after the syllogism is made, or else he that makes the syllogism could never see it at all. This, as has been already observed, is seen only by the eye, or the perceptive faculty of the mind, taking a view of them laid together in a juxtaposition; which view of any two it has equally whenever they are laid together in any proposition, whether that proposition be placed as a major or a minor, in a syllogism or no.

"Of what use, then, are syllogisms?" I answer, Their chief and main use is in the schools, where men are allowed, without shame, to deny the agreement of ideas that do manifestly agree; or out of the schools, to those who from thence have learned, without shame, to deny the connection of ideas which even to themselves is visible. But to an ingenious searcher after truth, who has no other aim but to find it, there is no need of any such form to force the allowing of the inference; the truth and reasonableness of it is better seen in ranging of the ideas in a simple and plain order. And hence it is that men, in their own inquiries after truth, never use syllogisms to convince themselves, [or, in teaching others, to instruct willing learners,] because, before they can put them into a syllogism, they must see the connection that is between the intermediate idea and the two other ideas it is set between and applied to to show their agreement; and when they see that, they see whether the inference be good or no, and so syllogism comes too late to settle it. For, to make use again of the former instance, I ask, whether the mind, considering the idea of justice placed as an intermediate idea between the punishment of men and the guilt of the punished (and till it does so consider it, the mind cannot make use of it as a *medius terminus*) does not as plainly see the force and strength of the inference as when it is formed into syllogism? To show it in a very plain and easy example: Let *animal* be the intermediate idea, or *medius terminus*, that the mind makes use of to show the connection of *homo* and *vivens;* I ask, whether the mind does not more readily and plainly see that connection in the simple and proper position of the connecting idea in the middle, thus,

Homo——Animal——Vivens,

than in this perplexed one,

Animal——Vivens——Homo——Animal?

which is the position these ideas have in a syllogism, to show the connection between *homo* and *vivens* by the intervention of *animal.*

Indeed, syllogism is thought to be of necessary use, even to the lovers of truth, to show them the fallacies that are often concealed in florid, witty, or involved discourses. But that this is a mistake, will appear, if we consider that the reason why sometimes men who sincerely aim at truth are imposed upon by such loose, and, as they are called, "rhetorical" discourses, is, that their fancies being struck with some lively metaphorical representations, they neglect to observe or do not easily perceive what are the true ideas upon which the inference depends. Now, to show such men the weakness of such an argumentation, there needs no more but to strip it of the superfluous ideas which, blended and confounded with those on which the inference depends, seem to show a connection where there is none, or at least do hinder the discovery of the want of it; and then to lay the naked ideas on which the force of the argumentation depends in their due order: in which position the mind, taking a view of them, ses what connection they have, and so is able to judge of the inference, without any need of a syllogism at all.

I grant that "mode" and "figure" is commonly made use of in such cases, as if the detection of the incoherence of such loose discourses were wholly owing to the syllogistical form; and so I myself formerly thought, till upon a stricter examination I now find, that laying the intermediate ideas naked in their due order shows the incoherence of the argumentation better than syllogism; not only as subjecting each link of the chain to the immediate view of the mind in its proper place, whereby its connection is best observed; but also because syllogism shows the incoherence only to those (who are not one of ten thousand) who perfectly understand "mode" and "figure," and the reason upon which those forms are established: whereas a due and orderly placing of the ideas upon which the inference is made makes every one, whether logician or not logician, who understands the terms, and hath the faculty to perceive the agreement or disagreement of such ideas (without which, in or out of syllogism, he cannot perceive the strength or weakness, coherence or incoherence, of the discourse), see the want of connection in the argumentation, and the absurdity of the inference.

And thus I have known a man unskilful in syllogism, who at first hearing could perceive the weakness and inconclusiveness of a long artificial and plausible discourse, wherewith others better skilled in syllogism have been misled; and I believe there are few of my readers who do not know such. And indeed, if it were not so, the debates of most princes' councils and the business of assemblies would be in danger to be mismanaged, since those who are relied upon, and have usually a great stroke in them, are not always such who have the good luck to be perfectly knowing in the forms of syllogism, or expert in mode and figure. And if syllogism were the only, or so much as the surest way to detect the fallacies of artificial discourses, I do not think that all mankind, even princes in matters that concern their crowns and dignities, are so much in love with falsehood and mistake, that they would everywhere have neglected to bring syllogism into the debates of moment, or thought it ridiculous so much as to offer them in affairs of consequence; a plain evidence to me that men of parts and penetration, who were not idly to dispute at their ease, but were to act according to the result of their debates, and often pay for their mistakes with their heads or fortunes, found those scholastic forms were of little use to discover truth or fallacy, whilst both the one and the other might be shown, and better shown, without them to those who would not refuse to see what was visibly shown them.

Secondly, Another reason that makes me doubt whether syllogism be the only proper instrument of reason in the discovery of truth, is, that of whatever use mode and figure is pretended to be in the laying open of fallacy (which has been above considered), those scholastic forms of discourse are not less liable to fallacies than the plainer ways of argumentation; and for this I appeal to common observation, which has always found these artificial methods of reasoning more adapted to catch and entangle the mind than to instruct and inform the understanding. And hence it is that men, even when they are baffled and silenced in this scholastic way, are seldom or never convinced, and so brought over to the conquering side; they perhaps acknowledge their adversary to be the more skilful disputant, but rest nevertheless persuaded of the truth on their side; and go away, worsted as they are, with the same opinion they brought with them, which they could not do if this way of argumentation carried light and conviction with it, and made men see where the truth lay; and therefore syllogism has been thought more proper for the attaining victory in dispute, than for the discovery or confirmation of truth in fair inquiries: and if it be certain that fallacy can be couched in syllogisms, as it cannot be denied, it must be something else, and not syllogism, that must discover them.

I have had experience how ready some men are, when all the use which they have been wont to ascribe to anything is not allowed, to cry out, that I am for laying it wholly aside. But to prevent such unjust and groundless imputations, I tell them, that I am not for taking away any helps to the understanding in the attainment of knowledge; and if men skilled in and used to syllogisms find them assisting to their reason in the discovery of truth, I think they ought to make use of them. All that I aim at is, that they should not ascribe more to these forms than belongs to them; and think that men have no use, or not so full a use, of their reasoning faculty without them. Some eyes want spectacles to see things clearly and distinctly; but let not those that use them therefore say, nobody can see clearly without them: those who do so will be thought in favour of art (which perhaps they are beholding to) a little too much to depress and discredit nature. Reason, by its own penetration, where it is strong and exercised, usually sees quicker and clearer without syllogism. If use of those spectacles has so dimmed its sight that it cannot without them see consequences or inconsequences in argumentation, I am not so unreasonable as to be against the using them. Every one knows what best fits his own sight; but let him not thence conclude all in the dark who use not just the same helps that he finds a need of.

2. *Helps little in demonstration, less in probability.*—But, however it be in knowledge, I think I may truly say, it is of far less or no use at all in probabilities. For, the assent there being to be determined by the preponderancy, after a due weighing of all the proofs with all circumstances on both sides, nothing is so unfit to assist the mind in that as syllogism; which, running away with one assumed probability, or one topical argument, pursues that till it has led the mind quite out of sight of the thing under consideration, and, forcing it upon some remote difficulty, holds it fast there entangled perhaps, and as it were manacled, in the chain of syllogisms, without allowing it the liberty, much less affording it the helps, requisite to show on which side, all things considered, is the greater probability.

6. *Serves not to increase our knowledge, but fence with it.*— But let it help us (as perhaps may be said) in convincing men of their errors and mistakes; (and yet I would fain see the man that was forced out of his opinion by dint of syllogism;)

yet still it fails our reason in that part which, if not its highest perfection, is yet certainly its hardest task, and that which we most need its help in; and that is, the finding out of proofs, and making new discoveries. The rules of syllogism serve not to furnish the mind with those intermediate ideas that may show the connection of remote ones. This way of reasoning discovers no new proofs, but is the art of marshalling and ranging the old ones we have already. The forty-seventh proposition of the first book of Euclid is very true; but the discovery of it, I think, not owing to any rules of common logic. A man knows first, and then he is able to prove syllogistically: so that syllogism comes after knowledge; and then a man has little or no need of it. But it is chiefly by the finding out those ideas that show the connection of distant ones, that our stock of knowledge is increased, and that useful arts and sciences are advanced. Syllogism, at best, is but the art of fencing with the little knowledge we have, without making any addition to it; and if a man should employ his reason all this way, he will not do much otherwise than he who, having got some iron out of the bowels of the earth, should have it beaten up all into swords, and put it into his servants' hands to fence with and bang one another. Had the king of Spain employed the hands of his people and his Spanish iron so, he had brought to light but little of that treasure that lay so long hid in the dark entrails of America. And I am apt to think, that he who shall employ all the force of his reason only in brandishing of syllogisms, will discover very little of that mass of knowledge which lies yet concealed in the secret recesses of nature; and which I am apt to think, native rustic reason (as it formerly has done) is likelier to open a way to and add to the common stock of mankind, rather than any scholastic proceeding by the strict rules of mode and figure.

7. *Other helps should be sought.*—I doubt not, nevertheless, but there are ways to be found to assist our reason in this most useful part; and this the judicious Hooker encourages me to say, who, in his *Eccl. Pol.*, lib. i. sec. 6, speaks thus: "If there might be added the right helps of true art and

learning (which helps, I must plainly confess, this age of the world, carrying the name of a learned age, doth neither much know nor generally regard), there would undoubtedly be almost as much difference in maturity of judgment between men therewith inured, and that which now men are, as between men that are now and innocents." I do not pretend to have found or discovered here any of those right helps of art this great man of deep thought mentions: but this is plain, that syllogism, and the logic now in use, which were as well known in his days, can be none of those he means. It is sufficient for me, if by a discourse, perhaps something out of the way (I am sure, as to me, wholly new and unborrowed), I shall have given occasion to others to cast about for new discoveries, and to seek in their own thoughts for those right helps of art which will scarce be found, I fear, by those who servilely confine themselves to the rules and dictates of others; for beaten tracks lead these sort of cattle (as an observing Roman calls them), whose thoughts reach only to imitation, *non quo eundum est, sed quo itur*.* But I can be bold to say, that this age is adorned with some men of that strength of judgment and largeness of comprehension, that, if they would employ their thoughts on this subject, could open new and undiscovered ways to the advancement of knowledge.

8. *We reason about particulars.*—Having here had an occasion to speak of syllogism in general, and the use of it in reasoning and the improvement of our knowledge, it is fit, before I leave this subject, to take notice of one manifest mistake in the rules of syllogism; viz., "that no syllogistical reasoning can be right and conclusive but what has, at least, one general proposition in it;" as if we could not reason and have knowledge about particulars: whereas, in truth, the matter rightly considered, the immediate object of all our reasoning and knowledge is nothing but particulars. Every man's reasoning and knowledge is only about the ideas existing in his own mind, which are truly, every one of them,

---

* "Not where the thing sought is to be found, but wherever the road may happen to lead them."—Ed.

particular existences;* and our knowledge and reasoning about other things is only as they correspond with those our particular ideas. So that the perception of the agreement or disagreement of our particular ideas is the w e and utmost of all our knowledge. Universality is but accidental to it, and consists only in this, that the particular ideas about which it is are such as more than one particular thing can correspond with and be represented by. But the perception of the agreement or disagreement of any two ideas, and consequently our knowledge, is equally clear and certain, whether either, or both, or neither of those ideas be capable of representing more real beings than one, or no. One thing more I crave leave to offer about syllogism before I leave it, viz., May one not upon just ground inquire whether the form syllogism now has, is that which in reason it ought to have? For, the *medius terminus* being to join the extremes, *i. e.*, the intermediate ideas by its intervention, to show the agreement or disagreement of the two in question, would not the position of the *medius terminus* be more natural, and show the agreement or disagreement of the extremes clearer and better, if it were placed in the middle between them? which might be easily done by transposing the propositions, and making the *medius terminus* the predicate of the first, and the subject of the second. As thus:

Omnis homo est animal,
Omne animal est vivens;
Ergo omnis homo est vivens.

Omne corpus est extensum et solidum,
Nullum extensum et solidum est pura extensio;
Ergo corpus non est pura extensio.†

---

* As being a *tertium quid*, distinct both from external objects and from mind.—ED.

† " Every man is an animal,
Every animal is living;
Therefore every man is living.

" All body is extended and solid,
Nothing extended and solid is pure extension (*i. e.* space);
Therefore body is not space."

Here Locke has fallen into the common error of supposing that logic insists upon some special arrangement of the premisses in a syllogism.—ED.

I need not trouble my reader with instances in syllogisms whose conclusions are particular. The same reason holds for the same form in them as well as in the general.

9. Reason, though it penetrates into the depths of the sea and earth, elevates our thoughts as high as the stars, and leads us through the vast spaces and large rooms of this mighty fabric, yet it comes far short of the real extent of even corporeal being; and there are many instances wherein it fails us: as,

First, Reason fails us for want of ideas.—First, It perfectly fails us where our ideas fail. It neither does nor can extend itself farther than they do. And therefore, wherever we have no ideas, our reasoning stops, and we are at an end of our reckoning: and if at any time we reason about words which do not stand for any ideas, it is only about those sounds and nothing else.

10. *Secondly, Because of obscure and imperfect ideas.*—Secondly, Our reason is often puzzled and at a loss, because of the obscurity, confusion, or imperfection of the ideas it is employed about; and there we are involved in difficulties and contradictions. Thus, not having any perfect idea of the least extension of matter nor of infinity, we are at a loss about the divisibility of matter; but having perfect, clear, and distinct ideas of number, our reason meets with none of those inextricable difficulties in numbers, nor finds itself involved in any contradictions about them. Thus we, having but imperfect ideas of the operations of our minds, and of the beginning of motion or thought, how the mind produces either of them in us, and much imperfecter yet of the operation of God, run into great difficulties about free created agents, which reason cannot well extricate itself out of.

11. *Thirdly, For want of intermediate ideas.* — Thirdly, Our reason is often at a stand, because it perceives not those ideas which could serve to show the certain or probable agreement or disagreement of any two other ideas: and in this some men's faculties far outgo others. Till algebra, that great instrument and instance of human sagacity, was discovered, men

with amazement looked on several of the demonstrations of ancient mathematicians, and could scarce forbear to think the finding several of those proofs to be something more than human.

12. *Fourthly, Because of wrong principles.*—Fourthly, The mind, by proceeding upon false principles, is often engaged in absurdities and difficulties, brought into straits and contradictions without knowing how to free itself: and in that case it is in vain to implore the help of reason, unless it be to discover the falsehood, and reject the influence of those wrong principles. Reason is so far from clearing the difficulties which the building upon false foundations brings a man into, that, if he will pursue it, it entangles him the more, and engages him deeper in perplexities.

13. *Fifthly, Because of doubtful terms.*—Fifthly, As obscure and imperfect ideas often involve our reason, so, upon the same ground, do dubious words and uncertain signs often, in discourses and arguings, when not warily attended to, puzzle men's reason, and bring them to a nonplus: but these two latter are our fault, and not the fault of reason. But yet the consequences of them are nevertheless obvious; and the perplexities or errors they fill men's minds with are everywhere observable.

14. *Our highest degree of knowledge is intuitive, without reasoning.*—Some of the ideas that are in the mind, are so there that they can be by themselves immediately compared one with another: and in these the mind is able to perceive that they agree or disagree as clearly as that it has them. Thus the mind perceives that an arch of a circle is less than the whole circle, as clearly as it does the idea of a circle: and this therefore, as has been said, I call "intuitive knowledge," which is certain beyond all doubt, and needs no probation,* nor can have any; this being the highest of all human certainty. In this consists the evidence of all those maxims which nobody has any doubt about, but every man (does not, as is said, only assent to, but) knows to be true, as

* *Vide supra*, note on "Intuition."—Ed.

soon as ever they are proposed to his understanding. In the discovery of and assent to these truths, there is no use of the discursive faculty, no need of reasoning, but they are known by a superior and higher degree of evidence. And such, if I may guess at things unknown, I am apt to think that angels have now, and the spirits of just men made perfect shall have in a future state, of thousands of things which now either wholly escape our apprehensions, or which our short-sighted reason has got some faint glimpse of, we in the dark grope after.

15. *The next is demonstration by reasoning.*—But though we have here and there a little of this clear light, some sparks of bright knowledge; yet the greatest part of our ideas are such, that we cannot discern their agreement or disagreement by an immediate comparing them. And in all these we have need of reasoning, and must, by discourse and inference, make our discoveries. Now, of these there are two sorts, which I shall take the liberty to mention here again.

First, Those whose agreement or disagreement, though it cannot be seen by an immediate putting them together, yet may be examined by the intervention of other ideas which can be compared with them. In this case, when the agreement or disagreement of the intermediate idea, on both sides, with those which we would compare, is plainly discerned, there it amounts to demonstration, whereby knowledge is produced; which though it be certain, yet it is not so easy nor altogether so clear as intuitive knowledge; because in that there is barely one simple intuition, wherein there is no room for any the least mistake or doubt; the truth is seen all perfectly at once. In demonstration, it is true, there is intuition too, but not altogether at once: for there must be a remembrance of the intuition of the agreement of the medium or intermediate idea with that we compared it with before, when we compare it with the other; and when there be many mediums, there the danger of the mistake is the greater. For, each agreement or disagreement of the ideas must be observed, and seen in each step of the whole train, and retained in the memory just as it is, and the mind must be sure that no part of what is necessary to make up the demonstration is omitted or overlooked. This makes some demonstrations long and perplexed, and too hard for those who have not strength of parts distinctly to perceive and exactly carry so many particulars orderly in their heads. And even those who are able to master such intricate speculations are fain sometimes to go over them again, and there is need of more than one review before they can arrive at certainty. But yet, where the mind clearly retains the intuition it had of the agreement of any idea with another, and that with a third, and that with a fourth, &c., there the agreement of the first and the fourth is a demonstration, and produces certain knowledge, which may be called "rational knowledge," as the other is "intuitive."

16. *To supply the narrowness of this, we have nothing but judgment upon probable reasoning.*—Secondly, There are other ideas whose agreement or disagreement can no otherwise be judged of, but by the intervention of others which have not a certain agreement with the extremes, but an usual or likely one: and in these it is that the judgment is properly exercised, which is the acquiescing of the mind that any ideas do agree by comparing them with such probable mediums. This, though it never amounts to knowledge, no, not to that which is the lowest degree of it; yet sometimes the intermediate ideas tie the extremes so firmly together, and the probability is so clear and strong, that assent as necessarily follows it as knowledge does demonstration. The great excellency and use of the judgment is to observe right, and take a true estimate of the force and weight of each probability; and then casting them up all right together, choose that side which has the over-balance.

17. *Intuition, demonstration, judgment.*—Intuitive knowledge is the perception of the certain agreement or disagreement of two ideas immediately compared together.

Rational knowledge is the perception of the certain agreement or disagreement of any two ideas by the intervention of one or more other ideas.

Judgment is the thinking or taking two ideas to agree or disagree by the intervention of one or more ideas whose certain agreement or disagreement with them it does not perceive, but hath observed to be frequent and usual.

18. *Consequences of words, and consequences of ideas.* — Though the deducing one proposition from another, or making inferences in words, be a great part of reason, and that which it is usually employed about: yet the principal act of ratiocination is the finding the agreement or disagreement of two ideas one with another by the intervention of a third: as a man by a yard finds two houses to be of the same length, which could not be brought together to measure their equality by juxtaposition. Words have their consequences as the signs of such ideas: and things agree or disagree as really they are; but we observe it only by our ideas.

19. *Four sorts of arguments.*—Before we quit this subject, it may be worth our while a little to reflect on four sorts of arguments that men in their reasonings with others do ordinarily make use of to prevail on their assent; or, at least, so to awe them as to silence their opposition.

First, Ad verecundiam.—First, The first is, to allege the opinions of men whose parts, learning, eminency, power, or some other cause, has gained a name and settled their reputation in the common esteem with some kind of authority. When men are established in any kind of dignity, it is thought a breach of modesty for others to derogate any way from it, and question the authority of men who are in possession of it. This is apt to be censured as carrying with it too much of pride, when a man does not readily yield to the determination of approved authors, which is wont to be received with respect and submission by others: and it is looked upon as insolence for a man to set up and adhere to his own opinion against the current stream of antiquity, or to put it in the balance against that of some learned doctor, or otherwise approved writer. Whoever backs his tenets with such authorities, thinks he ought thereby to carry the cause, and is ready to style it "impudence" in any one who shall stand out against them. This I think may be called *argumentum ad verecundiam*.

20. *Secondly*, Ad ignorantiam.—Secondly, Another way that men ordinarily use to drive others, and force them to submit their judgments and receive the opinion in debate, is to require the adversary to admit what they allege as a proof, or to assign a better. And this I call *argumentum ad ignorantiam*.

21. *Thirdly*, Ad hominem.—Thirdly, A third way is to press a man with consequences drawn from his own principles or concessions. This is already known under the name of *argumentum ad hominem*.

22. *Fourthly*, Ad judicium.—Fourthly, The fourth is the using of proofs drawn from any of the foundations of knowledge or probability. This I call *argumentum ad judicium*. This alone of all the four brings true instruction with it, and advances us in our way to knowledge. For, (1) It argues not another man's opinion to be right, because I, out of respect, or any other consideration but that of conviction, will not contradict him. (2.) It proves not another man to be in the right way, nor that I ought to take the same with him, because I know not a better. (3.) Nor does it follow that another man is in the right way because he has shown me that I am in the wrong. I may be modest, and therefore not oppose another man's persuasion; I may be ignorant, and not be able to produce a better; I may be in an error, and another may show me that I am so. This may dispose me perhaps for the reception of truth, but helps me not to it; that must come from proofs and arguments, and light arising from the nature of things themselves, and not from my shamefacedness, ignorance, or error.

23. *Above, contrary, and according to reason.*—By what has been before said of reason, we may be able to make some guess at the distinction of things, into those that are according to, above, and contrary to reason. (1.) "According to reason" are such propositions whose truth we can discover by examining and tracing those ideas we have from sensation

and reflection, and by natural deduction find to be true or probable. (2.) "Above reason" are such propositions whose truth or probability we cannot by reason derive from those principles. (3.) "Contrary to reason" are such propositions as are inconsistent with or irreconcilable to our clear and distinct ideas. Thus the existence of one God is *according* to reason; the existence of more than one God is *contrary* to reason; the resurrection of the dead *above* reason. Farther: as "above reason" may be taken in a double sense, viz., either as signifying above probability, or above certainty, so in that large sense also, "contrary to reason" is, I suppose, sometimes taken.

24. *Reason and faith not opposite.*—There is another use of the word "reason," wherein it is opposed to faith; which, though it be in itself a very improper way of speaking, yet common use has so authorized it, that it would be folly either to oppose or hope to remedy it. Only I think it may not be amiss to take notice, that, however faith be opposed to reason, faith is nothing but a firm assent of the mind; which, if it be regulated, as is our duty, cannot be afforded to anything but upon good reason, and so cannot be opposite to it. He that believes, without having any reason for believing, may be in love with his own fancies; but neither seeks truth as he ought, nor pays the obedience due to his Maker, who would have him use those discerning faculties He has given him to keep him out of mistake and error. He that does not this to the best of his power, however he sometimes lights on truth, is in the right but by chance; and I know not whether the luckiness of the accident will excuse the irregularity of his proceeding. This at least is certain, that he must be accountable for whatever mistakes he runs into; whereas he that makes use of the light and faculties God has given him, and seeks sincerely to discover truth by those helps and abilities he has, may have this satisfaction in doing his duty as a rational creature, that though he should miss truth, he will not miss the reward of it; for he governs his assent right, and places it as he should, who in any case or matter

whatsoever believes or disbelieves according as reason directs him. He that does otherwise, transgresses against his own light, and misuses those faculties which were given him to no other end but to search and follow the clearer evidence and greater probability. But since reason and faith are by some men opposed, we will so consider them in the following chapter.

NOTE ON THE SYLLOGISM.

An erroneous system, like a mist, is productive of much distortion in the appearance of every fact which it apprehends. It will, therefore, excite no surprise to find that Locke, in the preceding article, is but combating a phantom, or, at best, a very false representation of syllogism as it really exists; and that such is the case may, I think, be proved in the following manner:—

Logic takes cognizance of two things—of the process of thought as existing in the mind; and of the manner in which this process may be verbally expressed. Against this it will possibly be urged that no mental science can be conversant about mere words; but, in reply, I would point out that, as words are the record of thought for all purposes not purely individual, so any science which has thought for its subject-matter must attend to the manner and style, so to speak, of this record. Accordingly, in logic we find two great divisions, thought and words; each of these being subdivided into form and matter. But with regard to these latter heads, matter meets with little more notice than that which is implied in a bare recognition of its existence; while form, on the contrary, is subjected to a complete and exhaustive analysis. Thus, finally, we arrive at a clear notion of logical science; that is to say, we see that it deals with the forms in which all thought must exist, and with the forms in which all record of such thought must be made.

The conclusion from this is easy, nay, irresistible; and, had not Locke been doubly blinded, both by the vices of his own system, and by his complete misapprehension of the scholastic philosophy, he must, indubitably, have perceived it. The fact, then, is, that syllogism has a twofold nature, corresponding to the divisions of logic above mentioned; that it is a form of words indicating a certain arrangement of terms or notions; and that it is, by virtue of its being such an arrangement, a record and expression of a certain form which thought must assume in order to become intelligible and consequential. Locke, however, looked upon it from the former point of view alone; and, not conceiving the existence of any laws of thought, he took it to be a mere *arbitrary* collocation of ideas which had, and could have no universal authority. He was, therefore, merely consistent in his error, when he devoted page after page to a repudiation of all claims on the part of syllogism to any share in the throne of reason. At the same time, his powerful intellect could not fail to obtain some slight and partial glimpses of the truth through the fog of his errant psychology; and, accordingly, we find him in one place (§ 4) saying, "I readily own that *all right reasoning* may be reduced to . . . forms of syllogism." Here was a very near approach to the truth; and, had he not been shackled in his researches, this clue must have led him to an opinion in accordance with the facts of the case.

It is by no means necessary to enter into a detailed refutation of Locke's arguments against syllogism, since they all hinge upon the radical misconception which has been here pointed out.

OF FAITH AND REASON, AND THEIR DISTINCT PROVINCES.

1. *Necessary to know their boundaries.*—It has been above shown, (1) That we are of necessity ignorant, and want knowledge of all sorts where we want ideas. (2.) That we are ignorant, and want rational knowledge where we want proofs. (3.) That we want general knowledge and certainty as far as we want clear and determined specific ideas. (4.) That we want probability to direct our assent in matters where we have neither knowledge of our own nor testimony of other men to bottom our reason upon.

From these things thus premised, I think we may come to lay down the measures and boundaries between faith and reason; the want whereof may possibly have been the cause, if not of great disorders, yet at least of great disputes, and perhaps mistakes, in the world: for till it be resolved how far we are to be guided by reason, and how far by faith, we shall in vain dispute and endeavour to convince one another in matters of religion.

2. *Faith and reason what, as contradistinguished.*—I find every sect, as far as reason will help them, make use of it gladly;

and, where it fails them, they cry out, "It is matter of faith, and above reason." And I do not see how they can argue with any one, or ever convince a gainsayer, who makes use of the same plea, without setting down strict boundaries between faith and reason, which ought to be the first point established in all questions where faith has anything to do.

Reason therefore here, as contradistinguished to faith, I take to be the discovery of the certainty or probability of such propositions or truths which the mind arrives at by deduction made from such ideas which it has got by the use of its natural faculties, viz., by sensation or reflection.

Faith, on the other side, is the assent to any proposition, not thus made out by the deductions of reason, but upon the credit of the proposer, as coming from God in some extraordinary way of communication. This way of discovering truths to men we call "revelation."

3. *No new simple idea can be conveyed by traditional revelation.*—First, then, I say, that no man inspired by God can, by any revelation, communicate to others any new simple ideas which they had not before from sensation or reflection: for, whatsoever impressions he himself may have from the immediate hand of God, this revelation, if it be of new simple ideas, cannot be conveyed to another, either by words or any other signs; because words, by their immediate operation on us, cause no other ideas but of their natural sounds; and it is by the custom of using them for signs that they excite and revive in our minds latent ideas, but yet only such ideas as were there before. For, words seen or heard recall to our thoughts those ideas only which to us they have been wont to be signs of; but cannot introduce any perfectly new and formerly unknown simple ideas. The same holds in all other signs, which cannot signify to us things of which we have before never had any idea at all.

Thus, whatever things were discovered to St. Paul when he was rapt up into the third heaven, whatever new ideas his mind there received, all the description he can make to others of that place is only this, that there are such things as "eye hath not seen, nor ear heard, nor hath it entered into the heart of man to conceive." And supposing God should discover to any one, supernaturally, a species of creatures inhabiting, for example, Jupiter or Saturn (for that it is possible there may be such, nobody can deny), which had six senses, and imprint on his mind the ideas conveyed to theirs by that sixth sense, he could no more by words produce in the minds of other men those ideas imprinted by that sixth sense, than one of us could convey the idea of any colour by the sounds of words into a man who, having the other four senses perfect, had always totally wanted the fifth of seeing. For our simple ideas, then, which are the foundation and sole matter of all our notions and knowledge, we must depend wholly on our reason, I mean, our natural faculties, and can by no means receive them, or any of them, from traditional revelation; I say, "traditional revelation," in distinction to original revelation. By the one I mean that first impression which is made immediately by God on the mind of any man, to which we cannot set any bounds; and by the other, those impressions delivered over to others in words, and the ordinary ways of conveying our conceptions one to another.

4. *Traditional revelation may make us know propositions knowable also by reason, but not with the same certainty that reason doth.*—Secondly, I say, that the same truths may be discovered and conveyed down from revelation, which are discoverable to us by reason and by those ideas we naturally may have. So God might, by revelation, discover the truth of any proposition in Euclid; as well as men, by the natural use of their faculties, come to make the discovery themselves. In all things of this kind there is little need or use of revelation, God having furnished us with natural and surer means to arrive at the knowledge of them. For, whatsoever truth we come to the clear discovery of, from the knowledge and contemplation of our own ideas, will always be certainer to us than those which are conveyed to us by traditional revelation: for the knowledge we have that this revelation came at first from God, can never be so sure as the knowledge we have from the clear and distinct perception of the agreement or disagreement of our own ideas: *v. g.*, if it were revealed some ages since, that

the three angles of a triangle were equal to two right ones, I might assent to the truth of that proposition upon the credit of the tradition that it was revealed: but that would never amount to so great a certainty as the knowledge of it upon the comparing and measuring my own ideas of two right angles, and the three angles of a triangle. The like holds in matter-of-fact, knowable by our senses: *v. g.*, the history of the deluge is conveyed to us by writings which had their original from revelation; and yet nobody, I think, will say he has as certain and clear a knowledge of the flood as Noah, that saw it, or that he himself would have had, had he then been alive and seen it. For he has no greater an assurance than that of his senses, that it is writ in the book supposed writ by Moses inspired; but he has not so great an assurance that Moses writ that book as if he had seen Moses write it. So that the assurance of its being a revelation is less still than the assurance of his senses.

5. *Revelation cannot be admitted against the clear evidence of reason.*—In propositions, then, whose certainty is built upon the clear perception of the agreement or disagreement of our ideas, attained either by immediate intuition, as in self-evident propositions, or by evident deductions of reason in demonstrations, we need not the assistance of revelation as necessary to gain our assent and introduce them into our minds; because the natural ways of knowledge could settle them there, or had done it already, which is the greatest assurance we can possibly have of anything, unless where God immediately reveals it to us; and there too our assurance can be no greater than our knowledge is, that it is a revelation from God. But yet nothing, I think, can under that title shake or overrule plain knowledge, or rationally prevail with any man to admit it for true, in a direct contradiction to the clear evidence of his own understanding: for, since no evidence of our faculties by which we receive such revelations can exceed, if equal, the certainty of our intuitive knowledge, we can never receive for a truth anything that is directly contrary to our clear and distinct knowledge: *v. g.*, the ideas of one body and one place do so clearly agree, and the mind has so evident a perception of

their agreement, that we can never assent to a proposition that affirms the same body to be in two distant places at once, however it should pretend to the authority of a Divine revelation: since the evidence, first, that we deceive not ourselves in ascribing it to God, secondly, that we understand it right, can never be so great as the evidence of our own intuitive knowledge, whereby we discern it impossible for the same body to be in two places at once. And therefore no proposition can be received for Divine revelation, or obtain the assent due to all such, if it be contradictory to our clear intuitive knowledge, because this would be to subvert the principles and foundations of all knowledge, evidence, and assent whatsoever: and there would be left no difference between truth and falsehood, no measures of credible and incredible in the world, if doubtful propositions shall take place before self-evident, and what we certainly know give way to what we may possibly be mistaken in. In propositions, therefore, contrary to the clear perception of the agreement or disagreement of any of our ideas, it will be in vain to urge them as matters of faith. They cannot move our assent under that or any other title whatsoever: for faith can never convince us of anything that contradicts our knowledge, because, though faith be founded on the testimony of God (who cannot lie) revealing any proposition to us, yet we cannot have an assurance of the truth of its being a Divine revelation greater than our own knowledge; since the whole strength of the certainty depends upon our knowledge that God revealed it, which, in this case, where the proposition supposed revealed contradicts our knowledge or reason, will always have this objection hanging to it, viz., that we cannot tell how to conceive that to come from God, the bountiful Author of our being, which, if received for true, must overturn all the principles and foundations of knowledge He has given us; render all our faculties useless; wholly destroy the most excellent part of His workmanship, our understandings; and put a man in a condition wherein he will have less light, less conduct, than the beast that perisheth. For if the mind of man can never have a clearer, and perhaps not so clear, evidence of anything to be a Divine revelation as it has of the principles of its own reason, it can never have a ground to quit the clear evidence of its reason, to give place to a proposition whose revelation has not a greater evidence than those principles have.

6. *Traditional revelation much less.*—Thus far a man has use of reason, and ought to hearken to it, even in immediate and original revelation, where it is supposed to be made to himself: but to all those who pretend not to immediate revelation, but are required to pay obedience, and to receive the truths revealed to others, which, by the tradition of writings or word of mouth, are conveyed down to them, reason has a great deal more to do, and is that only which can induce us to receive them. For, matter of faith being only Divine revelation and nothing else, faith (as we use the word, called commonly "divine faith") has to do with no propositions but those which are supposed to be divinely revealed. So that I do not see how those who make revelation alone the sole object of faith can say that it is a matter of faith, and not of reason, to believe that such or such a proposition, to be found in such or such a book, is of Divine inspiration; unless it be revealed that that proposition, or all in that book, was communicated by Divine inspiration. Without such a revelation, the believing or not believing that proposition or book to be of Divine authority can never be matter of faith, but matter of reason; and such as I must come to an assent to only by the use of my reason, which can never require or enable me to believe that which is contrary to itself: it being impossible for reason ever to procure any assent to that which to itself appears unreasonable.

In all things, therefore, where we have clear evidence from our ideas, and those principles of knowledge I have above mentioned, reason is the proper judge; and revelation, though it may, in consenting with it, confirm its dictates, yet cannot in such cases invalidate its decrees: nor can we be obliged, where we have the clear and evident sentence of reason, to quit it for the contrary opinion, under a pretence that it is matter of faith; which can have no authority against the plain and clear dictates of reason.

7. *Things above reason.*—But, Thirdly, there being many

things wherein we have very imperfect notions, or none at all; and other things, of whose past, present, or future existence, by the natural use of our faculties, we can have no knowledge at all: these as being beyond the discovery of our natural faculties and above reason, are, when revealed, the proper matter of faith. Thus, that part of the angels rebelled against God, and thereby lost their first happy state: and that the dead shall rise, and live again: these, and the like, being beyond the discovery of reason, are purely matters of faith, with which reason has, directly, nothing to do.

8. *Or not contrary to reason, if revealed, are matter of faith.*—But since God, in giving us the light of reason, has not thereby tied up His own hands from affording us, when he thinks fit, the light of revelation in any of those matters wherein our natural faculties are able to give a probable determination, revelation, where God has been pleased to give it, must carry it against the probable conjectures of reason; because the mind, not being certain of the truth of that it does not evidently know, but only yielding to the probability that appears in it, is bound to give up its assent to such a testimony, which, it is satisfied, comes from One who cannot err, and will not deceive. But yet it still belongs to reason to judge of the truth of its being a revelation, and of the signification of the words wherein it is delivered. Indeed, if anything shall be thought revelation which is contrary to the plain principles of reason and the evident knowledge the mind has of its own clear and distinct ideas, there reason must be hearkened to as to a matter within its province: since a man can never have so certain a knowledge that a proposition, which contradicts the clear principles and evidence of his own knowledge, was divinely revealed, or that he understands the words rightly wherein it is delivered, as he has that the contrary is true; and so is bound to consider and judge of it as a matter of reason, and not swallow it, without examination, as a matter of faith.

9. *Revelation, in matters where reason cannot judge, or but probably, ought to be hearkened to.*—First, Whatever proposition is revealed, of whose truth our mind, by its natural

faculties and notions, cannot judge, that is purely matter of faith, and above reason.

Secondly, All propositions whereof the mind, by the use of its natural faculties, can come to determine and judge, from naturally acquired ideas, are matter of reason; with this difference still, that in those concerning which it has but an uncertain evidence, and so is persuaded of their truth only upon probable grounds, which still admit a possibility of the contrary to be true, without doing violence to the certain evidence of its own knowledge, and overturning the principles of all reason; in such probable propositions, I say, an evident revelation ought to determine our assent even against probability. For where the principles of reason have not evidenced a proposition to be certainly true or false, there clear revelation, as another principle of truth and ground of assent, may determine; and so it may be matter of faith, and be also above reason, because reason, in that particular matter, being able to reach no higher than probability, faith gave the determination where reason came short, and revelation discovered on which side the truth lay.

10. *In matters where reason can afford certain knowledge, that is to be hearkened to.*—Thus far the dominion of faith reaches, and that without any violence or hinderance to reason; which is not injured or disturbed, but assisted and improved, by new discoveries of truth, coming from the eternal Fountain of all knowledge. Whatever God hath revealed is certainly true: no doubt can be made of it. This is the proper object of faith: but whether it be a Divine revelation or no, reason must judge; which can never permit the mind to reject a greater evidence to embrace what is less evident, nor allow it to entertain probability in opposition to knowledge and certainty. There can be no evidence that any traditional revelation is of Divine original, in the words we receive it, and in the sense we understand it, so clear and so certain as that of the principles of reason: and therefore nothing that is contrary to, and inconsistent with, the clear and self-evident dictates of reason has a right to be urged or

assented to as a matter of faith, wherein reason hath nothing to do. Whatsoever is Divine revelation ought to overrule all our opinions, prejudices, and interests, and hath a right to be received with full assent: such a submission as this of our reason to faith takes not away the landmarks of knowledge; this shakes not the foundations of reason, but leaves us that use of our faculties for which they were given us.

11. *If the boundaries be not set between faith and reason, no enthusiasm or extravagancy in religion can be contradicted.*—If the provinces of faith and reason are not kept distinct by these boundaries, there will, in matter of religion, be no room for reason at all; and those extravagant opinions and ceremonies that are to be found in the several religions of the world will not deserve to be blamed; for to this crying up of faith in opposition to reason, we may, I think, in good measure, ascribe those absurdities that fill almost all the religions which possess and divide mankind. For men having been principled with an opinion that they must not consult reason in the things of religion, however apparently contradictory to common sense and the very principles of all their knowledge, have let loose their fancies and natural superstition; and have been by them led into so strange opinions and extravagant practices in religion, that a considerate man cannot but stand amazed at their follies, and judge them so far from being acceptable to the great and wise God, that he cannot avoid thinking them ridiculous and offensive to a sober, good man. So that, in effect, religion, which should most distinguish us from beasts, and ought most peculiarly to elevate us as rational creatures above brutes, is that wherein men often appear most irrational, and more senseless than beasts themselves. *Credo quia impossibile est,* "I believe because it is impossible," might, in a good man, pass for a sally of zeal, but would prove a very ill rule for men to choose their opinions or religion by.

INDEX.

Absolutists, 66.
Actions, cannot be the same in different times or places, 71.
Adequate ideas, none of species of substances, 177.
Arguments, ad verecundiam, 206; ad ignorantiam, 207; ad hominem, 207; ad judicium, 207.
Aristotle, 64.
Arithmetic, use of cyphers in, 171.
Assent to maxims, 10, 15; a mark of self-evidence, 17; but not of innate, 39.
Atheism, 30.
Atom, what, 71.

Belief, when without reason is against our duty, 208.
Berkeley, 65.
Best, in our opinion, not a rule of God's actions, 34.
Buffier, 92.
Butler, 92.

Certainty, depends on intuition, 151.
Chronological view of philosophical systems, 64.
Common-sense philosophy, 4.
Condillac, 4.
Consciousness, makes the same person, 77, 83; probably annexed to the same individual immaterial substance, 88; necessary to thinking, 52, 53, 59; what, 59.
Cosmothetic idealists, 66.
Cousin, 5, 92, 150.

Democritus, 64.
Demonstration, what, 153, 204; not so clear as intuition, 153, 154; intuitive knowledge necessary in each step of, 154.
Descartes, 65; his doctrine of innate ideas, 46.
Disputes, are they merely verbal? 150; their multiplicity owing to the abuse of words, 125; are most about the signification of words, 137.
Disputing, art of, prejudicial to knowledge, 114; destroys the use of language, 116.
Diversity and identity, 69.
Dreaming, 55; seldom in some men, 56.
Dreams, for the most part irrational, 57; contain no ideas but of sensation or reflection, 58.

Epicurus, 64.

Faith and reason, 210; not opposite to reason, 208; as contradistinguished from reason, 210; cannot convince us in opposition to reason, 213; its matter can only be Divine revelation, 217; and is only that which is above reason, 217.
Fichte, 4.

Gassendi, 3.
God, the idea of, not innate, 29; His existence obvious to reason, 31; the notion of, likeliest to spread and continue, 32; the idea of, late and imperfect, 35—37; best notions of, got by thought and application, 36; His Being certain, 37, 43.

Hume, 4, 65.
Hypotheses, are to be built on matter of fact, 53.

Idealists, 66.
Ideas, in general, 59; their original in children, 27, 35, 61; none innate, 38, 39; are what the mind is employed about in thinking, 47; all from sensation or reflection, 48, 62; the way of getting them observable in children, 50; of reflection got late and negligently, 51; that we are incapable of, 174; that we cannot attain, 175, 176; particular, are first in the mind, 99; different in different men, 102.
Identity, of a plant, 72; of animals, 73; of a man, 73, 74; and diversity, 69; personal, Locke's theory of, discussed, 92; not always made by unity of substance, 74; depends on same consciousness, 77; is made by continued existence, 91.
Ignorance, our, infinitely exceeds our knowledge, 173; causes of, 173, 175, 181.
Illation, what, 187.
Imperfection, of words, 95.
Impossibility, not an innate idea, 27.
Impression, on the mind, what, 7.
Incompatibility, how far knowable, 166.
Individuationis principium, is existence, 71.
Innate ideas, Cartesian doctrine of, 46.
Innate notions, 6.
Innate principles, the doctrine of, has ill consequences, 45.
Innate truths, the first known, 23.
Intuition, 182.
Intuitive knowledge, 151; our highest certainty, 203.

Jouffroy, 5.

Kant, 4, 66.
Knowledge, Locke's theory concerning, 183; Cousin's argument against, 184·

Cousin's argument against, rejoinder to, 185; has great connection with words, 127; depends mainly on our senses, 146; its beginning and progress, 13, 14; to be got only by the employment of our own mind, 44; human, extent of, 158; certain and universal, where to be had, 180.

Language, its imperfections, 95; double use of, 95; ends of, 126; its imperfections, remedies of, 134.

Laws of thought, 25; dispute between Locke and Leibnitz concerning, 25.

Learning, its ill state at present, 95; of the schools, 114.

Leibnitz, 4, 65.

Locke, his essay, analysis of, 1; his essay, its style, 3; his system, résumé of arguments by which it has been assailed, 66; his system, considered historically and critically, 63; his system, its character and position, 3; his system, statement of, 63; his misconception of the Cartesian doctrines, 46; his notion of Logic, 152.

Logic, has introduced obscurity into language, 114; has hindered knowledge, 115.

Malebranche, 65.

Man, the same, what, 86, 91; the same, may be in different persons, 85.

Materialists, 66.

Matter, what, 104; whether it may think is not to be known, 160.

Maxims, when first known, 10, 14; how they gain assent, 18; not in the understanding before they are actually known, 19.

Mind, is it always consciously active? 68.

Morality, capable of demonstration, 142, 169; discourses in, if not clear, the fault of the speaker, 142.

Names, of mixed modes doubtful, 97; of substances doubtful, 101; of simple ideas least doubtful, 107.

Natural philosophy, not capable of science, 177.

Nihilism, 4.

Nihilists, 66.

Obscurity, unavoidable in ancient authors, 100.

Parrot, mentioned by Sir W. Temple as holding a rational discourse, 75.

Person, what, 77; a forensic term, 89.

Personal identity, 92; Locke's theory of, discussed, 92.

Plato, 64.

Principles, none innate, 6.

Proofs, 152.

Qualities, secondary, 164; of substances, 165; of spirits, 168.

Rationalism, 4.
Rationalists, 66.
Realists, 66.
Reason, its various significations, 187; in four parts, 188; where it fails us, 202, as contradistinguished from faith, 210.
Reflection, 49.
Reid, 4, 65, 92.
Remembrance, what, 39.
Revelation, traditional, cannot convey new simple ideas, 211; not so sure as our reason or senses, 212; cannot overrule our clear knowledge, 217; should overrule probabilities of reason, 216.
Rhetoric, an art of deceiving, 130.
Royer-Collard, 5.

Sagacity, 153.
Same, 91.
Scepticism, 4.
Schelling, 66.
Schoolmen, the, 131; their system, 64.
Schools, wherein faulty, 114.
Science, none of natural bodies, 177.
Scripture, interpretation of, 110.
Self, what makes it, 85, 87.
Sensation, 48.
Sensitive knowledge,
Sensualism, 4.
Sensualists, 66.
Serjeant, 3, 92.
Soul, thinks not always, 52; its immateriality we know not, 161.
Species, 123.
Spirits, their operation on bodies not conceivable, 179; what knowledge they have of bodies, 174; how far we are ignorant of them, 178.
Substance, the idea of, 38; three sorts of, 70.
Subtilty, what, 115.
Syllogism, no help to reasoning, 189; its use and inconveniences, 189; helps not to new discoveries, 198; Locke's misapprehension of, shown, 209.

Thinking, an operation of the soul, 52; without memory, useless, 56.
Transcendentalism, 4.

Understanding, passive in the reception of simple ideas, 62.

Voltaire, 4.

Whole and part, not innate ideas, 29.
Wolf, 4, 65.
Words, abuse of, 111; imperfection of, 95; coined by the schools, 111; rendered obscure by the schools, 114; their uses, 126; their civil and philosophical use, 95; should be constantly employed in the same sense, 149.
Worship, not an innate idea, 29.
Writings ancient, why hardly to be precisely understood, 100.

PRINTED BY VIRTUE AND CO., LIMITED, CITY ROAD, LONDON.

www.ingramcontent.com/pod-product-compliance
Lightning Source LLC
Chambersburg PA
CBHW021836230426
43669CB00008B/984